THE HISTORY *of* FUNDAMENTALISM

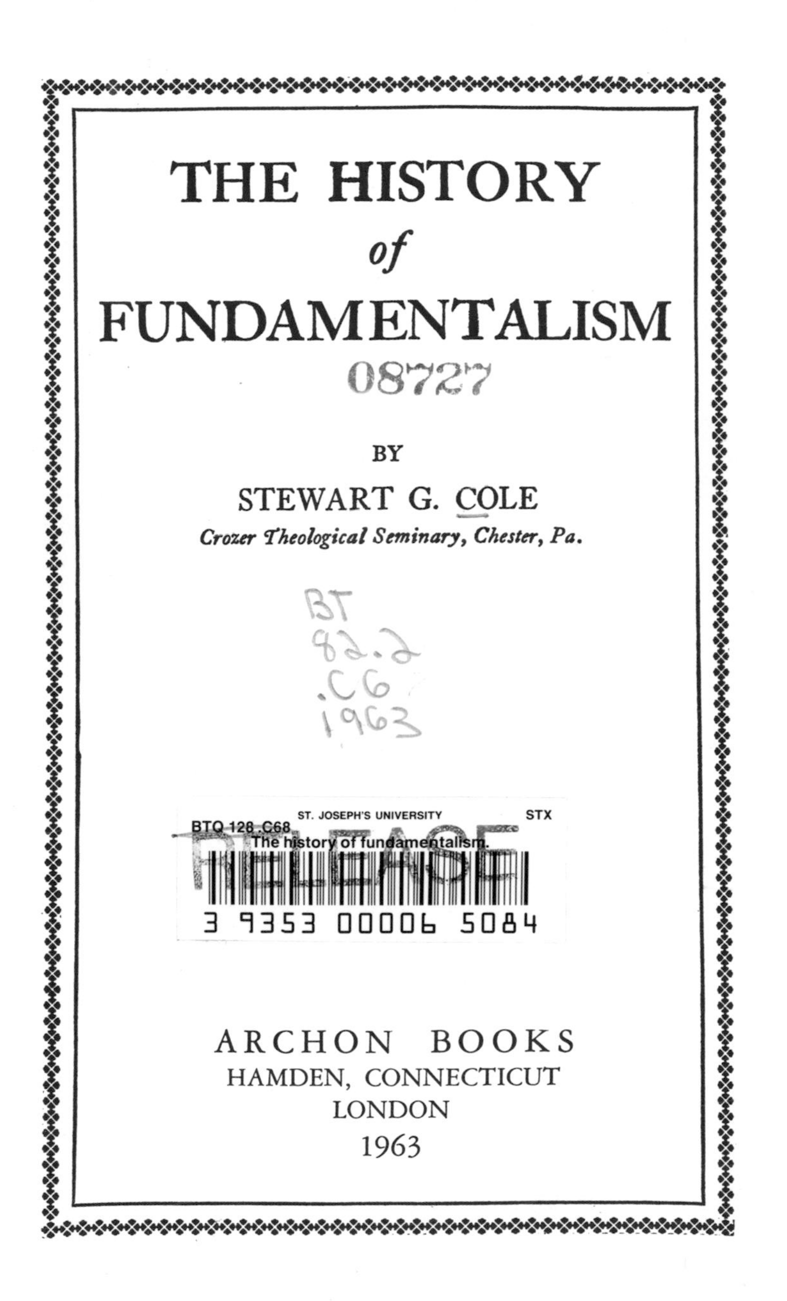

THE HISTORY *of* FUNDAMENTALISM

BY

STEWART G. COLE

Crozer Theological Seminary, Chester, Pa.

ARCHON BOOKS
HAMDEN, CONNECTICUT
LONDON
1963

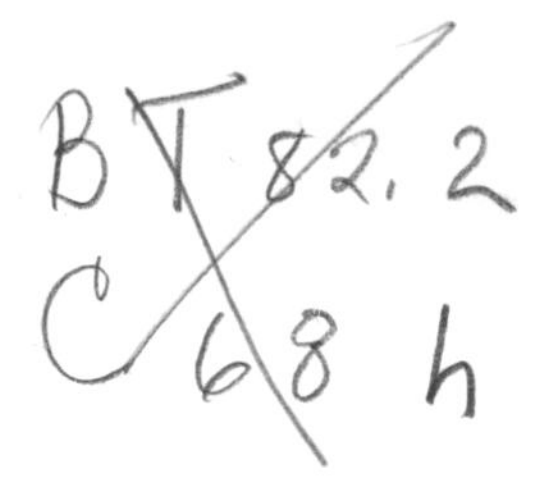

LIBRARY OF CONGRESS CATALOG NO.: 63-13761
PRINTED IN THE UNITED STATES OF AMERICA

TO MY FATHER

WHO EXEMPLIFIED THE SPIRIT OF
SOCIAL CHARITY AND RELIGIOUS QUEST.

TABLE OF CONTENTS

PART ONE

THE BACKGROUND OF CURRENT CHRISTIAN CONFLICT

PART TWO

CURRENT CONFLICT WITHIN THE CHURCH

PART THREE

CURRENT CONFLICT BEYOND THE CHURCH

PART FOUR

CONCLUSION

INTRODUCTION

How different the structure of American society is today from what it was two generations ago is obvious to every student. In the course of its development western civilization has shifted from a colonial naïveté of the frontier to the far-reaching machinations of nationalism and from an agrarian pattern of occupation to the industrial one, with a consequent revolution in human desire, ideal and behavior. Owing to its loss of cultural orientation in the new America, Christianity has reached a critical state. Besides, scientific thought has penetrated religious circles, discrediting many of its cherished convictions. For a half century the church has suffered a conflict of social forces about and within it that accounts for the present babel of witnesses to Christian truth and purpose. Only the most painstaking psychological study of interplaying inherited and contemporary types of culture can account for the precarious condition of Protestantism, and point the way forward. In the pages that follow, the writer has attempted to trace the outline of this conflict, especially as it has involved the loyalties of divergent groups of Christian people. To the task of interpreting the clash of secularism and Christianity, with the consequent change of prophetic function thrust upon the latter, he is committing himself in a companion study. With this division of the writer's interest, the reader will not find a complete portrait of either liberal or conservative Christian in the present volume.

That current Christianity should have become extremely polymorphous is natural in an inchoate period of "fumble and success" experimentation. That discordant voices and acerbity of language should have characterized the occasion is likewise to be expected. The writer could scarcely have touched themes concerning which there is such a wide diversity of convictions. Even so, he has sought with singleness of mind to clarify objectively this near-at-hand and searching controversy that has strained church morale for the past few decades. He invites those who shall judge adversely his view of religious change to entertain towards the problems involved the charitable disposition that he has made every effort to practise.

Although such an empirical investigation may not be as popular as reflections upon idealistic Christianity, it is truer to fact and essential to fit churchmanship. Men must learn to think understandingly of each other upon what they conceive to constitute the verities of religion. To try, as many liberals have tried, to patch up fundamental differences in Christian viewpoints or to engage in platitudinous exchange of theological opinions as a pretense to ecclesiastical harmony, is folly. It is advisable to recognize that the primary values of present-day Christianity are pluralistic in quality as in definition, and to welcome the principle of a comprehensive church fellowship. On the other hand, to close eyes to such pathological conditions as prevail in the religious cause is fatal. However painful and humiliating for all concerned the clinical investigation of the church is, it must be carried forward. There is no substitute for an intelligent loyalty to changing faith. Ecclesiastical leadership rests with those who observe what has happened to American religion and—

> "To whom in vision clear
> The aspiring heads of future things appear,
> Like mountain-tops whose mists have rolled away."

The reader who desires to inquire further into the documentary evidence that supports the theme of this study should refer to the accompanying bibliography. However disappointing it was to be obliged to omit additional source materials from the main body of the study that would have reinforced his viewpoint, the author found it necessary to do so in order to keep the manuscript within reasonable bounds. Unfortunately for later students who will engage in research in this field, not a little of the literature apropos to the subject perished almost as soon as it was circulated.

Words are feeble instruments to express my sense of indebtedness to those who have cooperated with me in the supply of information and in an advisory capacity, without whose aid this contribution to an understanding of contemporary Christianity would have been impossible. To my former teacher and counsellor, the late Gerald Birney Smith, who first suggested to me the subject of investigation; to Dean Shailer Mathews of the Divinity School, University of Chicago, Dr. Wm. B. Pugh, legal (ecclesiastical) advisor to the General Assembly of the Presbyterian Church, Professor W. E. Garrison of the Disciple Divinity House, and to Professor A. W. Nagler of Garrett Biblical Institute, who gave me the benefit of their criticism of chapters five, six, seven and eight, respectively; to my colleague, Professor R. E. E. Harkness who read the manuscript; to my wife, Nina Bremner Cole, whose counsel was sought frequently; and to librarians, editors, correspondents and interviewees, in North and South and from coast to coast who responded to my request for materials, I offer my deep and abiding gratitude. Although shared suggestion was acted upon repeatedly, the author alone is responsible for the position that he has taken.

Crozer Campus,
Feburary, 1931.

STEWART G. COLE

PART ONE

The Background of Current Christian Conflict

CHAPTER ONE

THE SOCIAL PATTERN OF INHERITED CHRISTIANITY

[1.] Colonial Foundations of Religion

The early makers of America were a devoutly religious people. They were determined to escape the Christian despotism in Europe and to establish their own ideals in a new world. One of their first public exercises upon reaching the Atlantic seaboard, having thanked God for their safe arrival, was to construct a frame "meeting-place" in which to honor His name. Every colony cherished its church. Whether in theocratic New England, in the middle colonies composed of sectarian groupings, or in Virginia where the Church of England was dominant, this social institution, with its sacred ministrations of worship and salvation, served as the main support of the people's morale. It was an aggressive fellowship that spread the principles of Protestantism throughout American life.

The Christianity these people sustained was strictly evangelical, a vital product of the Protestant reformation in seventeenth-century Europe. It is true that it took different structure in Anglican, Pilgrim, Quaker, Baptist and other groups, but withal it was undergirded with a compelling gospel of redeeming grace. The growing settlements of the American wilderness were formative factors leavening a new order of Protestantism. The warm pietistic fervor of Lutheranism, the strict disciplinary vigor of Calvinism, the passionate regard for ordinate living of the Puritan, practised in closely-knit frontier communities, blended to constitute an evangelizing faith of colonial Christianity.[1] Later, Methodism was imported, contributing its revivalistic zeal. The absorbing interest of Christians was engaged in spreading the good news of salvation, while the principle of voluntariness allowed them to express their saving faith in sectarian organizations. The open Bible was the source of men's hopes for eternity and the adequate ground of social control for this life.

Revivals were seasonal phenomena in America. The Great Awakening shook every New England community to its foundations. The effect of the movement was felt throughout the populated country. Scores of churches were erected giving men opportunity to embody their neighborhood loyalties. When families migrated across the Ohio River their Christian attachments usually remained an integral part of their shifting situation. When a whole community turned westward the people took their minister with them and thus carried forward their unbroken fellowship. Preaching stations were constructed on the plains as rapidly as circumstances permitted. Itinerant clergy served the far-flung settlements of homesteaders. The Methodist circuit-riders occupied a signal place in the pioneer mid-west. Camp meetings

[1] This process of blending is what Peter G. Mode calls "an Americanizing of Christianity." *Frontier Spirit in American Christianity* (New York, 1923), p. 11.

became regular district agencies of redemptive propaganda. By the universal stress upon congregational religion in the new world, people found God and His redeeming grace.

Early in the nineteenth century denominational trunk-lines of organization spread across the continent to gather up the loosely scattered congregations into more strictly sectarian movements. During this stage of Protestant accommodation competing sects exhibited tense feelings. They were jealous for their own rights. Polemic preaching was not infrequent. Doctrinal homilies and debates were common. Most self-respecting individuals belonged to one of the religious communions. Surrender to God and indoctrination into the Christian cult were paramount to good breeding, as well as imperative to personal redemption. The weekly sermon and the parish school session reiterated appeals to young and old to obey the holy will of God. The Second Awakening in 1800 intensified the loyalty of Christians in East and South, and aroused missionary enthusiasm. They adopted their own frontier in the West as a field for evangelistic endeavor. Within a few decades the gospel had been carried into the most remote sections of the great plains. Sectarian churches were built and manned. The American people were enlisted in moral support of the tenets of evangelical Christianity.

[2.] The Religious Control of Education

The maintenance of an adequate Christian leadership became one of the most perplexing problems facing the church in America. In early colonial times the needs were met by migratory clergy from Great Britain and the Continent. As the population increased throughout the colonies colleges were built to provide a trained ministry. William and Mary, Harvard, Yale, Brown and the "Log College" were sponsored by Christian enterprisers, and mainly for ministerial purposes.

As the settlements of the mid-west became rooted the clergy followed their parishioners to the new territory. Lack of leadership became more apparent in both East and West. So acute was the demand for ministers that the frontiersmen themselves took means to recruit their churchmen by establishing denominational colleges. During the first one hundred years of Methodism in America this denomination founded nearly three hundred schools and colleges. While Indiana and Ohio were little more than a wilderness, DePauw University (founded as Indiana Asbury University in 1847) was organized by this church; and two years after the discovery of gold and eighteen years before the establishment of the State University, it instituted the College of the Pacific (founded as the University of the Pacific in 1851). In 1850 there were six thousand academies in America under church auspices. In 1860 of the two hundred and forty-seven colleges in the land only seventeen were state institutions. The development of higher schools of learning was one of the most significant means of cultivating the cause of religion during the nineteenth century.

The testimony of church-founded colleges had significant bearing upon historic American culture. Though the institution's aim was educational, its class-room emphasis was qualified by strong religious influences. Its president was usually a member of the senior clergy.

Classical languages occupied a primary place in the curriculum. These disciplines helped students to understand the ancient scriptural documents, a training considered necessary for the most thorough appreciation of God's revelation to man. Much attention was given to moral science and deductive philosophy in order to inspire high ideals. The "Evidences of Christianity" were set forth in a course in apologetics which was, as a rule, a prescribed course for seniors. Youth were prepared to "give a reason for the faith that was within them" and to fortify themselves to meet the arguments of unbelievers.[2]

College administrators not only made a place for Christian traditions in their curriculum, but they promoted evangelical activities. Bible study was customary and often obligatory. Prayer meetings were regular events, and periodic revivalistic efforts were accepted as a matter of course. It was one of the cherished ambitions of every college faculty to see its student body converted to Christ before the day of granting diplomas. Repeated appeals were made and financial inducements offered to men to enter the sacred calling of the Christian ministry. The atmosphere of the small college was permeated with the gospel motif. Every student, whether in preparation for the ministry or in training for secular pursuits, was faced with the absolute necessity of conversion from sin, the redemptive appeal of God in Jesus Christ, and the primacy of the local church in American community life. Church and college united in fostering a religious view of life.

[2] Washington Gladden has illustrated this procedure in Williams College, *Recollections* (New York, 1909), pp. 71–73.

[3.] Toward a Christian Civilization

The rise of the church to cultural domination in America was no imperialistic policy of priest or statesman. It rose normally to take social supremacy.[3] Christian standards were of such a nature that men met congregationally to enjoy approved fellowship. Besides, they participated in supernatural grace through a preaching medium. And the environment in which colonists sought to build a new world made the local church a welcome rallying center through which they could reinforce their democratic ideals.

To the Roman Catholic mind God chose the holy church as it embodied itself in hierarchy and sacrament to convey redemption to man. The Protestant conceived the sacred Scriptures as the vehicle through which God revealed His salvation and this Book authorized men to congregate in the church in order to experience inwardly the benefits of the gospel. Theologically the church occupied a vastly different place in Protestantism than in Catholicism; psychologically it served the human need similarly. Whether as a formal theocracy in New England or as an independent agent elsewhere, it acted as the structural and authoritative embodiment of the deepest spiritual needs of the people. Since it conveyed redemption to men, it became socially indispensable, focal in thought, sacred among the people. Men respected its mission and claimed its rewards. It

[3] This position is abundantly illustrated in Wm. B. Sprague's *Annals of the American Pulpit* (New York, 1857); and in the introductory essay, "The Influence of the Preacher," by Edward A. Park, in Henry C. Fish's *Pulpit Eloquence in the Nineteenth Century* (New York, 1857).

provided the Christian with a sense of supermundane security and with happiness, while he lived out his short span on a bleak seaboard or an open prairie.

Evangelicalism also tended to promote a church-centered civilization. Most citizens grew up under the shadow of a nearby "house of God." Every week this agency, representing the highest aspirations of men, gave direction to their civil consciousness. As late as 1844 the progenitors of the Republican party, meeting in Buffalo to nominate a candidate for president, conceived of a platform in Christian terms. By informal social contact men learned to look upon the church as the voice of conscience in all human activities. The Puritans maintained that only professing Christians were fit to officiate in public affairs. The remarks of Daniel Webster expressed the sentiment of his contemporaries, "The religion of the New Testament—that religion which was founded in the teachings of Jesus Christ and His apostles—is as sure a guide to duty in politics and legislation as in any concern in life."

This conception of Christianity required of believers a rather strenuous program. Fear of the Almighty was a strong provocative force in conduct. Churchmen were to pray fervently for the salvation of the lost. Strict censure was in vogue to prohibit such worldly behavior as dancing, card playing and extravagant dress. America became in large measure an evangelically-disciplined social order. What Ernst Troeltsch called "a civilization of church authority in the fullest sense" did not misrepresent the occidental experiment.[4] It re-

[4] *Protestantism and Progress.* Translated by W. Montgomery (New York, 1912), pp. 11–12.

produced the mediaeval culture to a considerable degree, though it brought it about by a more strictly democratic approval.

[4.] The Basic Appeal of Biblicism

In such a culture the highest premium was placed upon a knowledge of the Scriptures. Since the Bible brought God's revealed will to man, it behooved every individual to familiarize himself with it. This position was fundamental in the viewpoint of American Christianity. Men knew their Bible. They used it in family devotions and in public oration. Its wisdom on all subjects was irrefutable.

At church the Scriptures were expounded weekly in long and minute exegesis. The only strict requirement put upon the clergy was that they have a professional acquaintance with the Book. This text gave them their gospel. The homily overshadowed all else in the program of worship. The *General Instructions* given to the clergy by the American Home Missionary Society (May, 1830) specified that "the preaching of the Gospel holds the first and highest place in the vows and responsibilities of the ministerial office." [5]

Closely akin to familiarity with the Scriptures, evangelicals associated right doctrinal beliefs. It was essential that good Christians know *the* truth, for that only would preserve their faith.[6] "Thus saith the Lord!"

[5] Quoted by Peter G. Mode, *Source Book of American Church History* (Menasha, Wis., 1921), p. 423.

[6] The "knowledge" theory of participation in Christianity prevailed universally until recent times. John Miley presented the major premise of the position when he insisted that "clearly a knowledge of the central truths of Christianity conditions Christian consciousness and must be first in order." *Systematic Theology* (New York, 1893), vol. 1, p. 21.

was the greatest purchase that a man could take upon his own or any other soul. All Christians were free to possess such an assurance through the teaching and preaching ministry of the local church. The catechetical class introduced the novitiate to revealed truth. Preaching and evangelism popularized the doctrines, and testimony meetings afforded men an opportunity to express them lucidly. The story of the fall of man, his hopelessness in sin, God's free grace in Christ, the universal need of salvation, the rules of the righteous life, means of sanctification, the second coming, final judgment, rewards and punishments, all became common subjects of knowledge and necessary to a valid evangelicalism.

Such strict regard to make people biblically conversant was not solely the aim of the church. The public school and the sectarian college inspired their programs with a similar ideal. In the elementary school system scriptural materials constituted a major subject of study for the first hundred and fifty years of American history.[7] In a monograph, *Colleges Essential to the Church of God; Plain Letters Addressed to a Parishioner,* John Todd interpreted the scholastic attitude of the church. To the question, "Why must our churches be called upon to endow and raise up colleges in which to educate physicians and lawyers?", he answered,

"There can be no doubt but we must have lawyers and physicians; and they must be educated by somebody. Which is wisdom—to have them brought under the power of an education strictly Christian, which will exert a silent influ-

[7] E. P. Cubberley, *Public Education in the United States* (New York, 1919), pp. 15–25.

ence upon them for life—imbued with the philosophy of the church—trained by her intellectual principles, breathing in her atmosphere, or to have them cast off to be educated under the influence of infidelity, or even by teachers who live for this world alone? What an inconceivable difference it would make in this nation if all who studied law or medicine or became teachers had been educated in schools not controlled by the piety of the Church of God? . . . This is precisely the principle on which she acts when she rears a college to educate her ministers and yet makes provision so amply that all the mind which is educated in the land may be trained under the most decided Christian influence."

The personal test of Christianity was two-fold—right belief and proper conduct. Norms of behavior grew out of Puritan experience, and principles of doctrine sprang from strict devotion to the Bible and its associated evangelical scheme. As a matter of fact, owing to the church's chief emphasis upon the exposition of God's Word in sermon and testimony, the test tended to become a way of discourse rather than a standard of living. Proper knowledge was prerequisite to personal salvation. A Christian faith centered in the Bible and a community life presided over by the church, constituted the supreme religious values in American civilization.

[5.] Ideals of Church and Society

This traditional idealism was so different from that with which men are familiar today that it will bear further analysis.[8] To simply affirm that people were dominated by churchism in their whole range of human interest may not indicate clearly the manner in which

[8] The contrast will become clear in chap. II, part five.

Christian character developed. What was the personal structure of this society? The prevailing this-worldly concern of men was agricultural.[9] Whether living in country or town (there were no cities in the present-day sense), persons came together in simple, face-to-face associations in order to produce and exchange the goods of the soil. The neighborhood was a vital factor in life and represented an intimate interplay of personalities. Friendship or enmity relations between individuals were powerful forces. Some emotional urge was regnant in every social enlistment of the individual. Indeed, the human contacts of a community were like those of the old-fashioned family.

Difficulties constantly burdened the minds of these pioneering souls. In the face of the stubborn forces of nature, bravely they tried to wrest a secure settlement. Deeply concerned to have their sins blotted out, they sought safety in God's economy of grace. Before anxieties natural and spiritual, men turned to the local church as a sufficient haven of refuge. This institution's assurance of pardon from guilt and of participation in a perfect world to come fell like manna from heaven upon the toilers for food and the seekers for salvation. It was not strange therefore that the church of the evangel towered over other forces in community influence. It was little wonder that the people looked up to it as Almighty God's servant at work among them. The personal significance of this religious appeal and

[9] In 1800 four per cent. of the population lived in towns of over eight thousand inhabitants; in 1850, twelve per cent. Even in 1880 forty-four per cent of the people still engaged in agriculture; by 1920 the proportion had dropped to twenty-six per cent. Charles H. Sears, *Church City Planning* (Philadelphia, 1928), pp. 1, 49–50.

the social rating it received can scarcely be overestimated.[10]

Within such a culture ideals became rigid and absolute. The intimate basis upon which society was organized required their fixedness. Folkways and traditions determined social standards. There were no two "rights." Virtues and vices took on the form of finalities. Local sentiment and criticism supervised private conduct. Taboos were definitely and strictly enforced. Idiosyncrasies of personality were not weighed on merit; social treatment was extended without objective diagnosis. The status of a person was set by neighbors who knew him well. Temperamental motives fixed community punishments and rewards for the individual. All life was governed by emotional and compulsive principles.

To observe the Christian church in this type of situation is to recognize a regulative agent of the first magnitude. It did play the role of a mediaeval martinet or that of a humanitarian saviour, as occasion demanded. Its ideals were as fixed as those of its milieu: either an individual accepted salvation and became a Christian, or he wilfully neglected divine forgiveness and was informed of the sufferings he would experience in the next world; either a man sought and shared the fellowship of the saints, or he divorced himself from the church and endured the role of the religiously disclaimed. When conversion occurred the highly emotional experience insured reality to the so-called new birth. In suppliant

[10] Descriptions of this type of community life are to be found in such books as Washington Gladden's *Recollections* (New York, 1909), and William Lawrence's *Fifty Years* (New York, 1923).

prayer for pardon and peace, undoubtedly the sinner was helped to reform his character. Thus, a full and abiding salvation was guaranteed to any person who obeyed the evangelical rule. That immeasurable blessing claimed, the Christian took as his daily master the voice of the church which spoke in the disciplinarian terms of prevailing culture. When, therefore, the historian describes traditional civilization as evangelically dominated, he has in mind the quality of individual and corporate community life that has been treated above. On the background of this American heritage certain important events have transpired in church and society.

CHAPTER TWO

THE IMPACT OF SECULARISM UPON CHRISTIANITY

THE Civil War introduced a new era in America that has since revolutionized social culture. Following the Revolutionary War New England adopted the factory system of its divorced motherland. But for a hundred years community reorganization was limited to relatively few centers; and even in such, social ideals never lost their pronouncedly religious form. The old culture broke down on a continental scale during the last seventy-five years. It happened when trade and industrial expansion opened up new channels of economic development. Agrarian life-interests ceased to measure the desires of men as the great city became a reckoning power. Suburban communities multiplied rapidly and old settlements were repeatedly reborn.

Not only the face of society but the idealism of men was transformed. The forces working this change include industry, applied science, popular education and the World War. The church participated in the cultural evolution by virtue of the fact that it was involved in the structural process.[1] This chapter suggests how

[1] The following books estimate degrees of religious change: Shailer Mathews, *The Church and the Changing Order* (New York, 1907); Gerald Birney Smith, *Social Idealism and the Changing Theology* (New York, 1913); William Lawrence, *Fifty Years* (New York, 1923); and W. J. Tucker, *My Generation* (New York, 1919).

secular change affected the church in its ministry to human life.

[1.] The Industrialization of Society

Probably no other institution in America has modified the habits of men more than big industry. Like a mushroom growth this business skill covered the North.[2] Inventive genius drove men to tap resources of soil, forest, mine and waterfall, and to experiment until they could manufacture an endless variety of human commodities. This wholesale utilization of nature's materials necessitated thorough-going changes in the lives of men. The small self-sufficient community gave way to the cosmopolitan area interdependent with a national chain of other such trade areas. People were massed in large armies to furnish "hands" for factories. European and Negro immigration was accelerated. Problems of adequate housing, unemployment, markets, profits and lawlessness accompanied this industrial expansion. The modern city emerged as a new phenomenon consonant with the machine age.

This industrial society developed without regard for the well-being of Christianity. Material goods began to rival spiritual values in human lives. Although business turned romantic for some men, giving opportunity for risk and adventure, the rank and file of workers exercised most concern to maintain a full dinner pail. Sunday as a rest day was almost lost in the shuffle for power. Pleasure attractions abounded to intoxicate social impulses. Many standards of action were

[2] Note the statistics indicative of the rapidity of industrial expansion, Symposium, *American Journal of Sociology,* July, 1928, p. 140 f.

wrenched from private control and delegated to impersonal institutions. Conduct was thrust more and more upon an experimental basis. As a result industrial peoples were slowly weaned away from the old feeling of dependence upon the church for salvation, and became engaged in aggressive enterprising or grim endeavor in the work-a-day world.

Unfitted to meet the community needs of working youth, the church witnessed the rise of the Young Men's and Women's Christian Associations and kindred organizations. Strangely enough, slavery contributed to the weakening of church-controlled culture, for anti-slavery reform led to contradictory Christian testimonies and divided certain denominational bodies. The Civil War lowered public morals and hence enfeebled the civic influence of ecclesiasticism.[3] A noticeable decline in church attendance was apparent toward the end of the century. Many congregations furnished "'attractions', often in keen competition with rivals" in an effort to continue unabated their historic appeal. Howard A. Bridgeman, one of the editors of *The Congregationalist,* recognized "a changed conception of religion" among men and dared to claim that a person might be "a Christian man without allying himself with the church."[4]

Some Christians learned how to express their religious

[3] For an illustrative statement of the slavery issue in one church, consult, "Dr. Durbin and the General Conference of 1844," A. E. Ballard, *Christian Advocate,* April 6, 1916, p. 452; Washington Gladden has described moral conditions following the Civil War, *Applied Christianity* (New York, 1886), pp. 295–99.

[4] "Men and the Churches," *The Independent,* Nov. 3, 1898, p. 1253; note also "The Problem of Church Attendance," as discussed by Professor B. W. Bacon in the same journal, Nov. 10, 1895, p. 1329.

ideals in non-ecclesiastical service. Neighborhood houses were built to answer needs which the denominations neglected. Hull House, Chicago, stands out as a brilliant illustration. A prohibition party was organized in national politics in 1869. The Student Volunteer and Laymen's Missionary movements, arising independently of church boards, succeeded in converting them to more appropriate methods of evangelical effort. Independent biblical scholars made claims for the application of the teachings of Jesus to distressing industrial conditions.[5]

The church contained members who entertained both friendly and unfriendly attitudes toward shifting morals. One element assumed a rational approach to determine the nature of Christian duty. Such names as Horace Bushnell, Washington Gladden, and Walter Rauschenbusch suggest a succession of social prophets who worked upon the gospel of applied Christianity. Experimental clergy built so-called institutional churches to minister to every phase of human need. In some instances they secured the appointment of denominational commissions to investigate the liquor traffic and the well-being of the labor class and dependent orphans. These liberal churchmen incorporated into their conception of Christianity the best ideals of the rising secular culture.

Another church leadership insisted upon a more exacting maintenance of the traditional ministries of Protestantism in order to correct prevailing difficulties. In the late seventies they disapproved of the Young Men's Christian Association because it added amusement

[5] One of the earliest scholars to attempt this was Shailer Matthews; note his book, *The Social Teachings of Jesus* (New York, 1897).

rooms to its equipment, and two decades later they criticized the institutional church for the same reason. In 1872 this type of men forced the Methodist Episcopal Church, North, to add laws to its Book of Discipline prohibiting members from dancing, card playing and theater going.[6] This Christian element within the denominations treated all human interests that took their rise outside the church as "worldly," and as forces to be made comfortable to the sovereign faith of historic orthodoxy.

[2.] Appeals of Modern Science

The expansion of a scientific worldview kept abreast of industrial developments in America. Men learned to employ mechanical instruments that divulged infinitely large and correspondingly small systems of reality. Phenomena that were considered for centuries as due to supernatural interventions in this world, became known as the working of freshly discovered natural laws. Students learned that the universe behaved in a dependable manner. The principle of evolution became a working hypothesis in cosmic, biological and social thought, so that its influence in scholarly circles for fifty years can scarcely be measured.

The people discovered how to use nature for pleasure and profit. The naïve fear toward the universe, that historic Christianity had nurtured, lost its power over the tutored layman. Men did not feel it necessary to suffer for their sins by the sweat of the brow, in so far as they could relieve burdens by employing scientific

[6] Note quotations in "Our Mistaken Legislation on Amusements," by Edwin H. Hughes, *Methodist Review*, Sept., 1923, pp. 719–729.

inventions. Christians knew that the service of a skilled physician was as imperative in illness as were the prayers of the faithful, and that play activity proved complementary rather than detrimental to piety. So effective did applied science become in lifting human fears and fatigues that it challenged the historic testimony of the Christian faith.

A protracted conflict of theology with science ensued. When Professor Agassiz lectured at Harvard in 1873 upon the subject of the age of the world and said, "Gentlemen, the world is older than we have been taught to think. Its age is as if one were gently to rub a silk handkerchief across Plymouth Rock once a year until it was reduced to a pebble," he shocked most Christians seriously; for they still believed that the world was made in six days in the year 4004 B.C. The significance of Darwin's *Origin of Species* began to reach the clergy in the last quarter of the nineteenth century. While a minority tried to reconcile its views and the book of Genesis, most leaders repudiated the man-made theory in favor of the doctrine of revelation. Such courageous souls as Washington Gladden advanced the science of human welfare,[7] and Henry Van Dyke the gospel for an age of doubt,[8] to mediate faith in troublous times. Though the doctrine of the Inerrancy of the Scriptures received its fatal blow in the seventies, higher critics were thrust out of churches and educational chairs even within the twentieth century.

Divergent types of religious loyalty grew up in the church. One party looked to prescientific theology for

[7] *Applied Christianity* (New York, 1886), chap. VII.
[8] Yale Lectures on Preaching, 1896.

its content of Christianity and defended the same in order to carry forward a genuine piety. Appeal was made to an aristocratic authority in the form of biblical literalism. Another group trusted in the method of experimental religion and discovered Christian truth as they would any other form of knowledge. These men rested their case upon the grounds of democratic scholarship. The idealisms of science and Christianity provoked a conflict within the church that has continued in some quarters until this day.

[3.] The Universal Challenge of State Education

Public school education in America bore its religious impress until the second quarter of the last century. More than any other person, Horace Mann freed the school from the teachings of the church and led it in constructing a modern curriculum.[9] Materials bearing on science and civics crowded into the background Christian subject-matter. The colonial teaching institution gave way to independent state and church school systems: religious education took form in the rapidly maturing Sunday school movement; secular education prepared youth for membership in the industrial and democratic state.

State education spread independent thinking, which took the place of the omniscient church in community circles. People became increasingly at home in *this* world and chose to work out their own intellectual salvation. Youth learned to question everything, including the most sacred realities of life. Overlooking the tradi-

[9] E. P. Cubberley, *Public Education in the United States* (New York, 1919), pp. 56, 327.

tions of the church, educators charted their course of training and made it the common property of every American child.

This action made it difficult for evangelicalism to continue its testimony unimpaired. Many churchmen discountenanced the state's policy fifty years ago and advocated the general principle, "better be untaught than ill-taught." They claimed that non-religious education fostered a "spirit of rationalism" which was hostile to the Christian faith. An editorial that appeared in the *Methodist Review* (November, 1899) took the viewpoint: "Christian churches . . . have no more urgent duty than to see to it that (secular) education shall be made positively and powerfully Christian. . . . If Christianity has not vindicated its supreme and singular authority to the academic mind by this time, then it is time that we threw the so-called academic mind overboard . . . "

Theological schools availed themselves of the benefits of modern education in the form of the historical method of Bible study. Teachers examined the Scriptures to know first of all what messages the writers meant to convey to their fellow-countrymen. The more liberal ones also applied the principles of social science to the canons of the church in an effort to appreciate the cycles of faith through which Christianity had advanced. Religious psychologists taught the view of the positive worth of children in the Kingdom of God.

These revaluations of Protestantism called forth the severest reprimands from old-fashioned Christians. Typical of their attitude was that expressed by William H. Burns when he criticised the position of the editor of his church's Sunday school publications: "It never was the theory of the church that the child does not need conversion . . . that these teachings are contradictory to our church doctrines will be clearly seen, by comparing them with our standards."[10] The state university, completely free from churchism, was frequently labelled "godless" by similar religious minds, because it encouraged the spirit of free inquiry in adult education. The rapid progress of secular training did not make it easy for certain Christians to redefine their precious heritage.

[4.] World-War Forces

The paganizing grip of the World War affected the church deeply. This tragic event caught up the American populace in a passionate desire to crush a European people. War agents presented enemy atrocities in lurid form in order to incite morale for the devastating cause, while the state carried out punitive threats against the "disloyal." A tremendous drive of mob-motives juggled the people into the ways of military expediency. It became popular to hate Germans and to instil prejudice against anything that was German-made. The fighting instinct of primitive human nature was marshalled to win for the stars and stripes.

The churches throughout the land joined the militaristic crusade.[11] No persons spent more energy for the cause than did Christians. Lay people labored for the increase of war efficiency and the clergy stimulated social

[10] *Crises in Methodism* (1909), p. 19.

[11] The story is told briefly by Henry K. Rowe, *The History of Religion in the United States* (New York, 1924), chap. IX.

action by begging men to find their ethical ideals in the world conflict. Some churchmen lost faith in the possibility of allied success and resorted to Messianic prophecy to arrest their political pessimism. They concluded that God would intervene soon and redeem the faithful from a cursed world.[12] More optimistic idealists predicted with the late President Woodrow Wilson that the allies would defeat Germany because the Almighty was with them in "a war to end war." Thus they were permitted to give unqualified moral support to the service.

When hostilities ceased in Europe the abnormal emotional set of American minds was not easily curbed. Especially was this true with illiterate people. Exploiters of the masses soon set themselves to sublimate war hates into organized bursts of social unrest, class passion and religious prejudice.[13] The Ku Klux Klan, the anti-World Court crusade, "one hundred per cent Americanism," tirades against labor and bolshevism, sabbatarianism, fundamentalism, suggest the new cults. Not a few people were in a humor to prefer grievance to goodwill.

[12] Shirley Jackson Case, *The Millennial Hope: A Phase of War-Time Thinking* (Chicago, 1918).

[13] Consider the sentiment of R. A. Torrey in an address, "That Blessed Hope," published in the conference volume, *Christ and Glory* (New York, 1918), pp. 21–22: "We are hearing a great deal in these days of how men are dreaming, and planning, and speaking of a league of nations and the permanent peace that is to follow. Such hopes are delusive; they will end in disappointment and dismay. There may be a league of nations, but no peace will come from such a league except a temporary peace, and then the most awful universal war that this old world has ever seen will follow."

For other phases of social reactionism, consult John M. Mecklin, *The Ku Klux Klan* (New York, 1924); and contributed article, "Is It Right to Hate the Hun?", *The Presbyterian,* Jan. 23, 1919, pp. 9–10.

Milton's claim for the anti-social leader, "Better to rule in hell than serve in heaven," had many sympathizers. The spirit of disaffection entered the church in the claim advanced by certain orthodox Christians that the new thought penetrating religious circles was German-made. Therefore liberal theologians should be considered enemies of the Kingdom and deserving of personal attack. Suspicion and ill-will were focused upon them with the same zeal that manifested itself during the World War. Much of the intolerance absorbed in Protestantism in recent years was due directly to the technique and spirit of wartime carried over into the days of social reconstruction.

[5.] Changing Ideals of Church and Society [14]

The writer has defined a few secular movements that have compelled signal changes in American civilization. The colonial-conceived culture, described in chapter one, has almost collapsed; a relatively new structure of society has emerged. The self-perpetuating family, neighborhood and local church are surrendering in favor of the complicated interdependency of social institutions. Whereas pre-industrial life was simple and homogeneous, recent times have given rise to a social order that is "highly differentiated and stratified on the basis of specialized interests and activities." To the majority of people, how men live in society has become an unsolved conundrum.

Two geographical areas did withstand the forces of change with a measure of success: the South and the

[14] Cp. chap. I, part five.

rural North.[15] The clergy in these areas have been the outstanding figures in community life by virtue of their superior education and the historic prestige accorded their profession. Because the religious training of these men has been bookish, doctrinal, orthodox, they have attempted to suppress liberal thinking and to stabilize traditional Christianity. It will be observed later that not a few of the clergy in the North who did most to propagate the fundamentalist faith received their formative training in character and in church administration in the South. Though they have frequently served urban churches, they represent the pre-industrial type of conventional culture.

But generally speaking, the church was actively involved in this cultural shakeup. Although it attempted to preserve the principles of historic Protestantism, it contained a leavening influence that worked otherwise. The church embraced a liberalizing outlook through its emphasis on free men's faith and congregational government. Particularly strong in Baptist, Congregationalist and Quaker traditions, it was shared by every denomination. The historian may hold churchmen responsible for the survival of the authoritarian regulation of believers, but he must also give it credit for its contribution to this experimental age. Roger Williams and kindred spirits kept the prophetic element focal in the spread of evangelical religion; Puritans who attempted to make of the Bible a legalistic and syllogistic set of doctrinal rules of living, represent the priestly features of Protestantism.

[15] Note the claims of B. J. Kendrick, *Life and Letters of Walter H. Page* (New York, 1925), chap. I; Ralph A. Felton, *Our Templed Hills* (New York, 1926), chap. I.

Within the shifting conditions of the urban-patterned society (the old society assumed an agricultural pattern), citizens and Christians forged ideals out of unique experience. Standards of living became flexible and relative to immediate ends as people accommodated their conduct to institutional demands and novel life-situations. Where formerly the judgment of friends determined largely a person's status in the community, more recently public opinion tended to standardize social breeding. Professional principles were substituted for simple folkways and family sentiments in shaping the life-work of youth. The old community was a rather fixed entity necessitating inclusive human relations; people have since learned to move freely from place to place forming more cursory personal ties. Influences emanating from industry, popular education, and the war weakened the ex cathedra appeal of religion and its priests. The passing of the saint marked an important event in Protestantism as well as in Catholicism. Healthy-minded Christians surrendered faith as a means of rescue out of this world and substituted a stirring confidence in the possibility of social progress. The church has been forced from the center of community culture toward the circumference, so that its leadership has been compelled to rediscover its purpose amid confusing circumstances.

[6.] A Conflict of Christian Cultures [16]

Christianity had no cultural rival in America for two hundred years. Men embraced it confidently as the

[16] Cp. John Dewey, *Individualism Old and New* (New York, 1930), chap. VII, "The Crisis in Culture."

sufficient servant of the supernatural. In the Bible Christians discovered the basis for their social idealism, and through the preaching medium they gave their values to the world. Society was conceived to be morally sound as it became a church-saved order. During the latter part of the last century this type of Protestantism came under critical inquiry. It was questioned by men of a scientific and industrial age. Thousands of good people disregarded the historic domination of the church in civic affairs. These individuals found non-ecclesiastical methods of self-enrichment and of community goodwill. Nor did they think that they had lost their souls in the readjusted program. Secularism was developing its own standards of culture.

Adventurous Christians attempted to maintain a working acquaintance with the ideals of the new social order. As they assimilated the viewpoint of the urban civilization they realized that the church could not continue its aristocratic policy. Rather, Christianity must become one of many salutory forces with which men needed to reckon in order to live well. These men set themselves the dutiful task of reinterpreting the religious witness in the face of secularism. They became the liberals of the church.

On the contrary, many Christians failed to live apace with the current revolutionary movements. From their point of view, society was in the throes of demonic possession; classical orthodoxy only was the test of true cultural allegiance. To allow any other agent to share honors with the church in determining ideals, or to suggest the advisability of reconsidering the function of religion, was to compromise with "the world." Christianity should remain the nucleating center around which civilization must order itself. Such advocates became the conservatives of the church.

Two Christian cultures have conflicted in recent decades of American life. Conservatives and liberals chose divergent methods of attempting to correct what had developed into a most distressing ecclesiastical situation. In the earliest efforts of churchmen to harmonize testimonies, certain orthodox reactions arose.

CHAPTER THREE

CONSERVATIVE REACTIONS TO LIBERAL CHRISTIANITY

During the half century antedating the World War conservative Christians defined their ecclesiastical task in two-fold terms. They sought to evangelize sinners who instinctively followed worldly manners of living, and they undertook to discipline such churchmen as fraternized with secular idealism. They defended the authoritativeness of the traditional faith in an increasingly inhospitable society, for they candidly believed that their religion was the only divinely acceptable one. In the prosecution of this purpose the Bible and prophetic conference movement, professional evangelism, Bible schools, tractarian propaganda, and polemic preaching were instituted.

[1.] Bible and Prophetic Conferences

Bible conferences joined orthodox evangelicals of all denominations to deepen class fellowship and to contend for the soundness of their testimony. These men assumed the role of God's favored interpreters and discovered their apologetical teachings in the prophetic materials of the Scriptures.

The first Bible conference was held at Swampscott,

Massachusetts, in the centennial year of America. No report of the proceedings was published, though it has been claimed that this meeting was the herald of the later notable Niagara Bible Conference. The New England meeting was introduced to the churches by a strong aggregation of clergy whose reputation for the old-time religion was known nationally.

In 1877 an important Prophetic Conference was called by a committee of eight men [1] in the Church of the Holy Trinity, New York City. It was concerned almost exclusively with the promotion of extreme adventism and the rebuke of postmillennial theologians. The editor of the proceedings advertised the addresses as "a very encyclopaedia of pre-millenniarianism by the ablest expositors." The far-reaching influence of this convention may be gathered from the following words published eight years later in the report of the next conference:

> "The addresses delivered on our Lord's personal and premillennial return to this earth were then eagerly heard by the hundreds of ministers, and thousands of intelligent Christian people who were then and there assembled. The New York *Tribune* published an edition of 50,000 copies, giving in full these essays. . . . Such was the influence of the movement that for more than two years following the Conference important and valuable discussions on prophetic themes occupied the pages of not a few of our religious newspapers, journals, and magazines, and a new impetus for Bible study was given to multitudes whose attention had so long been turned away from the great and almost entirely neglected fields of divine prophecy.

[1] A complete report of the conference is found in *Premillennial Essays* (Chicago, 1879). Edited by Nathaniel West. Its promoters included J. H. Brookes, A. J. Gordon, Geo. C. Needham and Stephen H. Tyng, Jr.

. . . . The doctrine of our Lord's expected advent has gained ground among spiritual believers of all churches, as the revival of no other truth in modern times has done." [2]

This next convocation of premillennialists met in Farwell Hall, Chicago. The *Inter Ocean*, one of the city's leading newspapers, printed the proceedings of every session in detail. Concerning the first day of the conference this journal announced:

"There were present ministers of all denominations from all parts of the United States and Canada. Nearly all the city clergy were present, and hundreds of earnest Christians of every shade of belief from every Church, charitable institution, and missionary institution in the city."

Quite explicitly the conference was conceived to solidify the forces of conservative Protestantism. Their sectional interests were strengthened by the intimate fellowship engendered through fervent singing and personal testimony. These evangelicals exploited the postmillennial beliefs of liberal churchmen and pictured the poverty of a lost world-order.[3] The church at large had put its trust in the ideals of secular culture. Leaders, fearing the influence of reason in religion, asked men to subordinate science and philosophy to revelation, to reinstate the Bible as supreme authority in the church, and thus be saved from confusion. The enthusiasm of the conference was heightened by extended greetings from several outstanding adventists in Europe.[4]

[2] Geo. C. Needham, *Prophetic Studies* (Chicago, 1886), pp. 1–2.

[3] Note the six-fold purpose of the conference, as presented by Geo. C. Needham, op. cit., pp. 215–16.

[4] Among them were Professor Koch of Bardenwisch, Oldenburg; Professor Valch of the University of Dorpat, Russia; Dr. Frank Delitzsch of the University of Leipzig, Germany; Rev. A. G. Brown of the East London Tabernacle, and Andrew A. Bonar of Glasgow.

No annual retreat did more to reinforce old-fashioned Protestantism than the Niagara Bible Conference.[5] For a quarter of a century, beginning in 1876, men used this medium to condemn the findings of biblical scholarship and to maintain a sheltered security in a shaken classical orthodoxy. In 1895 the Niagara group put forth the famous Five-Points statement of doctrine, in which they insisted upon universal Christian acceptance of the Inerrancy of the Scriptures, the Deity of Christ, his Virgin birth, the Substitutionary Atonement of Christ, and his physical Resurrection and coming bodily Return to earth. In conjunction with this assembly the North American Branch of the China Inland Mission[6] (a reactionary enterprise founded by J. Hudson Taylor in 1865) was organized and promoted. Such Niagara leaders as A. J. Gordon, A. T. Pierson, C. I. Scofield, and James M. Gray frequently accused Dwight L. Moody of misrepresenting Christianity when he invited such liberals as Henry Drummond, W. R. Harper and John A. Broadus, to share in his celebrated Northfield conference. The Niagara fellowship became known as the heresy-hunting agent of Moody's time.

The Winona[7] and Rocky Mountain[8] (Denver) Bible Conferences were the rallying centers for mid-west and far-west conservatives, respectively. The evangelist, J. W. Chapman, was the director of the former institution and succeeded in building up a noteworthy

[5] "The Niagara Bible Conference," L. W. Munhall, Moody Bible Institute *Bulletin*, XXII, 1921–22, pp. 1104–05; also, editorial, *The Christian Workers' Magazine*, Dec., 1913.

[6] Article, *China's Millions*, Dec., 1914, p. 159.

[7] *The Institute Tie*, IV, 1903–04, p. 20.

[8] Reported by John C. Page in *The Coming and Kingdom of Christ* (James M. Gray, editor) (Chicago, 1914), pp. 144–45.

annual assembly. Addison Blanchard and Joshua Gravett assumed control of the movement in the Denver region. Many other loci of orthodoxy produced their prophetic retreats. They were particularly popular in the agrarian sections of the middle West. William Pettingill instituted several in the environs of the Philadelphia School of the Bible. It was not difficult to draw a following, for the intimate loyalties awakened in gospel song, intercessory prayer and informal fraternal intercourse, made the occasions refreshingly welcome amid the distraught conditions of church and society.

The Bible conference movement (continued later in this study when it joined with fundamentalism) represented fifty years of conservatives' effort to maintain their Christian witness in a cultural situation that was slipping from their control. In degree as churches accepted the ideals of biblical criticism and the social gospel, conference promoters stressed the doctrines of the old gospel. Culturally perplexed, they fell back upon the Protestant Book to assure them of the reality of the Christian Messiah who would soon come to succor saints and destroy the faithless human order. When these men entered periods of social calm, their adventist dogma lost its pronounced religious value and sank down to the level of a secondary philosophy. When premillennialism was neglected at a Bible conference, another issue was brought forward; for this fellowship was an "issue" movement, in which the biblical resources of literalism were constantly being pressed against the new cultural standards of the day. A misunderstood social revolution with its miscellaneous problems and values constituted for these people the sins of the age.

[2.] THE PROMOTION OF PROFESSIONAL EVANGELISM

Revivals supplied the landmarks in American Christianity until urban society developed. The last of the great evangelists was Dwight L. Moody. His notable campaigns in the early seventies marked a dividing line in methods of religious propaganda. The immense crowds drawn to the protracted meetings of itinerant Methodism and the universal moral persuasion attending the efforts of Edwards, Whitfield and Finney had waned. Moody's work suffered a handicap unknown to former zealous gospelers. The collapse of simple, pre-industrial community life meant also the disintegration of those human ties incident to successful large scale evangelism.[9] The better understanding of the development of religious experience helped to break the naive appeal of the revivalist; while the multiple challenges of downtown institutions satisfied desires for personal security, social recognition and genuine pleasure, hitherto the special contributions of the redemption cult. Revivalism naturally retired in the face of the growth of urban community interests and parish evangelism.

Notwithstanding the church's introduction of less spectacular and more reasonable appeal to the unchristian, there have been many old-time revivalists since Moody. Hundreds of evangelists felt called to deliver the good news to the lost world. One has only to mention such names as Needham, Pierson, Munhall, Torrey,

[9] The conservative recognized this change, but he accounted for it as the baneful influence of higher criticism. Note especially W. E. B., *Jesus is Coming*. Third Edition (New York, 1904), p. 232; also, editorial, "'Christian' Rationalism," *Methodist Review*, May, 1896, pp. 445–50.

Alexander, Chapman, Smith and Sunday, to suggest the large catalogue of itinerant preachers. These men, when their work is judged by that of earlier national figures, have proved decidedly less convincing leaders. The times were against them. Their theological message became more and more foreign to the empirical thinking of ordinary citizens.

The persistency of the profession can be accounted for only as one examines the biographies of these revivalists and learns their misplaced reasons for attempting to project traditional tabernacle preaching into the modern structure of society. The majority have been unschooled individuals who trace their call to preach to some ecstatic experience of conversion overtaking them in mature life. They assume that the street preaching or mission efforts that led to their redemption are the methods required to reach the world, which they think necessarily suffers from the same ethical fall that characterized them. Other leaders have been recruited from the faculty and graduates of Bible schools; the conditions that produce them are considered later.

The following indictment of changing civilization is typical of the point of view of the last two generations of evangelists. A. T. Pierson has described the world to which the gospel must be conveyed:

"What is the real character of our present civilization? We may as well face the facts. It is gigantic in invention, discovery, enterprise, achievements, but it is gigantically worldly; sometimes and somewhere monstrously God-denying and God-defying. This 'Christian civilization' has produced giants in these days, men of renown, but they often use their intellect, knowledge and fame only to break down, as with the iron flail of Talus, all Christian faith. Philosophy now blooms into a refined pantheism, or a gross, blank materialism or a subtle rationalism or an absurd agnosticism. Science constructs its systems of evolution but leaves out a personal God; spontaneous generation becomes the only creator, natural law the only determining Providence. . . . Civilization is turned into a stronghold of unbelief; its imaginations and inventions are high towers that exalt themselves against the knowledge of God and the thoughts of our great thinkers have not been brought into captivity to the obedience of Christ. We have the ripest form of worldly civilization but ripeness borders on rottenness."[10]

No words could portray better the outlook of these men. They had become aware of the scientific interests of modern society, and they observed that emancipated students flouted revealed Christianity by ignoring religion, or substituted for orthodoxy an optimistic faith in the development of a Christian world order. The evangelist whose only estimation of man was biblical and whose only vernacular of interpretation was orthodox, naturally repudiated both "worldly religion" and "Christian civilization." In the name of the Lord he was called to correct what he conceived were paganism and pantheism. For years men have promoted such a recrudescence of revivalism in a futile effort to check social change.

There were two groups of Americans among whom revivalism has flourished somewhat in late decades: rural-minded communities and the discontented masses in large cosmopolitan regions. Many agricultural areas were still characterized by the social viewpoint of frontier civilization. Unmoved by the thrilling sense appeals which daily challenged their urban neighbors,

[10] Geo. C. Needham, *Prophetic Studies* (Chicago, 1886), p. 33.

they responded gladly to the call of the evangelist to adventure into the Kingdom of grace by means of familiar song and conversion testimony.

The restless people who milled about in downtown tenement areas answered to this same appeal. During the rapid development of industry, with its consequent revolution in home and leisure-hour habits of men, sick souls multiplied in every large city. They suffered from want of self-respect, social recognition, moral victory. The old-fashioned gospel afforded such men a glorious opportunity for cultural readjustment. There was One who loved them and invited their affection. He waited to blot out sinners' transgressions, and to guarantee them salvation in this hard world and a crown of life in eternity. The goodwill aroused in the tabernacle itself lent compensation to discouraged souls. The preacher's "either—or" philosophy (either accept God's pardon without money or price and receive eternal life, or neglect this supernatural gift and suffer His disfavor forever) appealed to these men. Having put on Christ in conversion, the defeated men became respectable members in the Christian group. They had full status in an ecclesiastical fellowship and were superior persons in God's company of the redeemed.

The revivalist's service to rural and downtown people was a mixed blessing. Many otherwise lost through denominational neglect found a haven in an unkind world. On the other hand, the pessimistic attitude of the evangelist towards society always met with a responsive chord in inferior classes and intensified their human fatalism. That practically all revivalists were ardent premillennialists has not been a matter of chance.[11] They had suffered cultural loss in the scholastic realm as the prodigal had in the moral sphere. These leaders made life a cross to be borne rather than a challenge to be enriched. Moreover, the doubt which the gospeler cast upon the validity of churchism did not make for a united Protestantism. Rather, it intensified suspicions already active in prodigals and made them disbelievers in organic Christianity. Again, the theology which formed the framework of sermons was so ultra-conservative that it encouraged cultural lag in its inherents, and in some cases provoked dissension with the better forces of the community. There is evidence that for decades professional evangelists were sowing seeds of doctrinal divisiveness and exclusive sectarianism, which later reaped a full harvest of reactionism against progressive religious culture.

[3.] The Genesis of Orthodox Schools

The increase of scientific materials in the public schools pressed religious studies more and more into the background, until finally the Sunday school became responsible for the Christian education of youth. Most denominational colleges adopted the educational standards of secular learning and neglected the dogmatics of Protestantism. Although these shifts of emphasis troubled many conservatives, they were more alarmed by the popularization of methods of scholastic inquiry and truth-testing which discounted tenets of the old faith. The changes did impose heavy responsibilities

[11] Note the philosophical position taken by Ernest B. Gordon in *Adoniram Judson Gordon: A Biography* (New York, 1896).

upon schoolmen and led to frequent conflict between teachers and preachers.

A few illustrations of this situation will indicate the trend. The professor of geology at Vanderbilt University, Alexander Winchell, in the year 1875 conveyed to his students the information that the human race descended from preadamitic stock. He was dismissed by the university board with the explanation that "this is an age in which scientific atheism, having divested itself of the habiliments that most adorn and dignify humanity, walks abroad in shameless denudation . . . we will have no more of this."[12] Vanderbilt, like so many other colleges with church background, later became free from strict denominational supervision and taught science and religion in adjoining classrooms without permitting either to exercise dominion over the other.

Theological institutions did not fare more happily than the colleges. The Andover Seminary controversy was a case in point. In a series of editorials which appeared in the *Andover Review* in 1885, progressive views were announced which left the institution open to criticism.[13] When the liberal, Egbert C. Smith, was appointed to the Chair of Theology, the matter of its denominational support came to a climax. *The Congregationalist*, representing the traditionalists, sought to control the seminary. When the faculty were invited to subscribe to a creed two members resigned. The

[12] John M. Mecklin, *Survival Value of Christianity* (New York, 1926), p. 180.

[13] W. J. Tucker, *My Generation* (New York, 1919), chap. VII; "The Tragic Fate of a Famous Seminary," John A. Faulkner, *Bibliotheca Sacra*, 1923, pp. 449–64.

Andover Case was on trial for six years. Tucker, an instructor, touched the matter of greatest moment when he wrote, "The controversy was incidental to the movement, though a large and necessary incident it proved to be. It was to become in time a fight for theological freedom." Union Theological Seminary in New York City [14] and the Divinity School in Chicago [15] passed through similar periods of controversy. Practically all well-known seminaries in the North (except Princeton) experienced a liberalizing conversion, in spite of the effort of orthodox leaders to keep them in accord with their historic testimony.

The increasing emancipation of denominational colleges and seminaries was only one phase of this collegiate movement. In certain cases conservative policy prevailed. Some schools refused to accept the principles of the new learning and chose to hold securely to the precepts of revealed religion. Wheaton College in Illinois trained youth consistently in such materials of the arts and sciences as could be accommodated to the ideals of classical theology. Such institutions looked upon liberal colleges as dangerous and used their influence to undermine the faith of the public in them. The University of Chicago has been a special target from its beginning; church people were begged to avoid this so-called hot-bed of heresy.[16]

Ultraconservatives founded Bible schools to correct the views of liberal seminaries. The history of Moody

[14] Pamphlet, *The Defense of Professor Briggs Before the Presbytery of New York, Dec. 13, 14, 15,* 19, 1892.

[15] *Christian Work and Evangelist,* July 3, 1909, p. 5.

[16] For a typical iconoclastic editorial see *Sunday School Times,* Mar. 7, 1925.

Bible Institute, established in 1886, typified the intent of this educational movement. Dwight L. Moody, its founder, specified that its purpose was "to raise up men and women who will be willing to lay their lives along side the laboring class and the poor, and to bring the gospel to bear upon their lives." It should be observed that Moody's desire did not remain its dominant purpose.[17] Less than a decade after its organization R. A. Torrey, the first superintendent, added another mission, "to increase the spirituality of the church." This was necessary owing to "the advancing apostasy predicted in the Bible."[18] Thus he intimated slyly that his school was fitted to provide ministers with more spirituality than were seminaries. The Chicago school felt increasingly its self-importance to Providence and avowed openly that it had "come to the Kingdom for such an apostate time as this."

In Bible schools scholastic requirements for matriculation, promotion and graduation, were not exacted as in theological seminaries. Revivalistic and missionary zeal was stressed. Students were called upon to "attempt great things for God." Out of appreciation of rich and unmerited grace extended to sinners they were urged to convey the good tidings to "the heathen." "Faith" movements emanated from their halls. Excessive devotion to religious projects developed in students a sense of social superiority over less spectacular ministers of the church. Thousands of youth who desired

[17] Note the correspondence that passed between Elmer W. Powell, Henry P. Crowell (chairman of the Institute's Board of trustees), and Paul D. Moody (the founder's son), through the columns of *Christian Work*, Apr. 19, July 12, Oct. 4, 1924.

[18] Moody Bible Institute *Bulletin*, IV, June, 1924, p. 6.

to achieve Christian leadership at small cost and in secure keeping frequented such training institutions.

An examination of the Moody school catalogue for 1925 gives the reader a sample program of studies. The Scriptures were examined from such points of view as Synthesis, Analysis (synthetic study precedes analytic, because "the Bible must be mastered before it can be studied"), Chapter Summary, Dispensational Study, and Biblical Criticism. In the Analysis course special attention was given to such books as Leviticus and Deuteronomy to show how the Mosaic sacrificial system was typical of the redemption of Christ. The course, Chapter Summary, had "the merit of simplicity." In Dispensational Study premillennialism was stressed. When Biblical Criticism was considered, "specialized scholarship" pointed out the prevailing "rationalistic and destructive" attitudes toward it, "against which the students are put on their guard." A course in biblical psychology was offered, "since in the Bible only is to be found the truth concerning man's origin and nature." In brief, the entire program was a system of precepts supported by biblical proof-texts in order to combat popularly conceived enemies of God's Word and to make the Scriptures simple formula for parish evangelism.

Such is sufficient evidence of the defense character of these institutes. Invariably the Bible schools sought to check the progress of secular culture and to oppose participation in a liberal Christianity.[19] The graduates of these institutions allied themselves with faith missions, sectarian groups preaching primitive church

[19] Recent manifestations of this cause are presented in chap. XI, part one.

views, or rural parishes of the larger denominations. Wherever they settled, they undertook to substitute the orthodox tradition for the position of forward-looking Christians.

[4.] Programs of Tractarian Propaganda

The printed page has been a strong ally to traditional Protestantism. Before secular literature became abundant and when good religious reading was still at a premium, agents of orthodoxy published considerable material on behalf of their cause. Besides magazines and books, newspaper publicity was secured whenever possible. The men who advocated the supremacy of biblicism and related themes took themselves, their purpose and their literary productions, seriously.

No Christian leaders were better known in the late seventies and eighties than J. H. Brookes and A. J. Gordon. They had enjoyed popularity as evangelists and organizers of prophetic conferences. The former edited a paper known as *The Truth,* and the latter *The Watchword* (later merged and published as *The Watchword and Truth* in Boston), periodicals that kept focal the promise of the approaching advent of the Lord. Fifty thousand copies of the proceedings of the 1878 Bible Conference, *Premillennial Essays* [20] were circulated among the churches. *The Christian Herald* (M. Bantes, editor), dedicated to the promotion of the old faith, was a widely consulted weekly journal. A small brochure, *Jesus is Coming* (written by "W. E. B."), won a generous reception and was reprinted several times. It

[20] Of a similar nature were *Prophetic Studies* (Chicago, 1886), Geo. C. Needham, editor; *Forty Coming Wonders* (author unknown).

contained a proof-text presentation of the tenets of adventist dogma.

The conservative press was not without able theologians to support its viewpoint. Writers assailed the productions of liberals, not always quoting them discreetly, in the campaign against higher criticism. Perhaps no man wrote more voluminously or with greater philosophical skill than the late James Orr. Augustus H. Strong of Rochester Seminary set forth the reasonableness of the historic faith in three large volumes, *Systematic Theology*. Robert Dick Wilson of Princeton made spirited claims for the authenticity of Old Testament documents, and E. Y. Mullins of Louisville maintained the supremacy of the supernatural in religious thinking. The *Princeton Theological Review* was a custodian of Simon-pure Calvinistic doctrines and the *Bibliotheca Sacra,* the oldest theological quarterly in America, editorially represented a checkered career.[21] Of less scholarly equipment but constantly writing for the defense of the faith were such Bible school men as R. A. Torrey, James M. Gray, W. H. Griffith-Thomas and C. I. Scofield. The *Bible Champion* and similar periodicals popularized the militant campaign among the clergy, while publishers circularized the laity with countless small tracts.

The background of the *Bible Champion* is significant. In 1894 a group of churchmen issued "a providential call to a great awakening in the churches and in

[21] Soon after its inception (1844), it was adopted by the faculty of Andover Theological Seminary; forty years later when this school became too liberal, its Board transferred the quarterly to the Oberlin faculty. In due time this school of religion advocated the principles of modern scholarship, and the journal was turned over to the faculty of Xenia Theological Seminary. George B. McCready has become editor-in-chief.

Christendom." Eighty thousand clergy were appealed to for sympathy, and a gospel campaign committee was appointed to inspire what they considered to be an "old-time reverence" for the Bible. The American Bible League was effected and *The Bible Student and Teacher,* as official organ, published. The journal opened a "Council of War" department (later, "The Arena") to defend "the evangelical Christian faith against the assaults of its infidel adversaries (within the church)." Later and under new leadership the cause revived its energy by changing its personnel, its name to "The Bible League of North America," and that of its periodical to the *Bible Champion.* The journal continues; the League has been inactive since the World War.

A conflict of ecclesiastical minds was inevitable. Liberal writers gave primacy to reliable method in scholarship and submitted their principles to the test of personal experience or historical evidence; apologists were primarily concerned for sound content and supported their doctrines by appeal to the super-rational standards of revelation and intuition. The one group availed themselves of the academic tools of progressive education; the other reproduced the mediaeval authority of supernaturalism.[22]

[5.] The Recrudescence of Polemical Preaching

Divisive issues that had engaged the denominations a century ago were settled finally by resort to compromise. But soon another conflict arose to repeat the spirit if not the problems of former days. The neces-

[22] This subject was treated carefully in Gerald Birney Smith's *Social Idealism and the Changing Theology* (New York, 1913), chap. IV.

sity for philanthropic work following the Civil War led Christian prophets to socialize religion in order to meet changing conditions. During the same period German methods of Bible investigation claimed eager disciples among American students. Men went abroad to pursue graduate work and returned to occupy theological chairs in seminaries and to command pulpits of influence. They used the Scriptures historically and advocated inductive theological thinking. Orthodox leaders singled out the social gospel and higher criticism as the two corruptives of Christendom.[23]

The social gospel attempted to orient Protestantism amid the new industrial forces that shaped human character.[24] There were grievous wrongs incident to congested urban quarters that required correction. Spokesmen felt burdened for the salvaging of victims of the liquor traffic. They knew from sad experience that simply waiting upon God would not relieve the national menace, but that public opinion inducing legislative action was necessary. These reformers preached temperance and organized anti-saloon leagues to demand constitutional reparation. Conservative church leaders often called down anathemas upon their brethren.[25] The faultfinders insisted that the social practitioners put the mundane welfare of man before the will of God. No

[23] Francis L. Patton predicted a theological "war" over the biblical question at the funeral of his colleague, Caspar W. Hodge, in 1891: *The Presbyterian,* Feb. 4, 1926, p. 4; "'Yellow' Theologies—Their German Genesis," *The Bible Student and Teacher,* June, 1909, p. 384 f.

[24] For a review of how one denomination developed a social program in terms of the increasing needs of the industrial order, see *Christian Advocate,* Pt. II, Sept. 9, 1926, pp. 1208–36.

[25] See the "Department of Biblical Evangelism" in the *Bible Student and Teacher* during the early years of this century.

better compliment was paid the ethical crusaders of the church than that intended to be a bitter condemnation of them:[26]

"The social gospel lays enormous stress on a man's physical and material well-being. Religion is held to be nothing more than a plan of social well-being. Christianity is considered a scheme of social improvement. It is reduced to humanitarianism. . . . Education and sanitation take the place of personal regeneration and the Holy Spirit."

That liberals denied the potential spiritual experience of the new birth in their regard for human rights was contrary to fact. But this was the impression given Christians by opposing clergy. Prompted by well-meaning motive, they attempted to malign the motives and defeat the end of the social gospelers, for had not Providence called them to save Christianity from humanitarism? Their theological viewpoint prevented them from seeing the real forces that were transforming the destiny of the nation. But more seriously, this professional attitude tended to introduce shortcoming in personal conduct. For, defense of evangelical orthodoxy in a socially creative age was conducive to ethical orthodoxy in conduct. Lecky, the historian, has characterized the situation thus,[27]

"When theologians during a long period have inculcated habits of credulity, rather than habits of inquiry; when they have persuaded men that it is better to cherish prejudice than to analyze it; better to stifle every doubt of what they have been taught than honestly to investigate its value, they will at last succeed in forming habits of mind that will instinc-

[26] John Horsch, *Modern Religious Liberalism* (Scottdale, Pa., 1921), p. 134.
[27] *History of European Morals* (New York, 1897), vol. I, p. 101.

tively and habitually recoil from all impartiality and intellectual honesty. If men continue to violate a duty they may at last cease to feel its obligation."

Biblical criticism also was responsible for reshaping the viewpoint of the preacher. The scriptural records were seen to be the creatures of real men in an ancient civilization. Whether the Bible "was" or "contained" the Word of God became an open question for the clergy.[28] Liberals began to preach about the human side of Jesus' life, and the national development of Hebrew ideals was indicated. The ethical values of the Cross took precedence over the substitutionary theory of the atonement in evangelistic appeal. Toward the end of the century certain ministers began to cast discredit upon the dogma of the Virgin birth. They appealed to the "experience" of Christ as their basis of religious authority. The theory of evolution gained in recognition, so that a reasonable gospel was displacing a miraculous one.

On the contrary, a strong party insisted upon re-emphasizing the absolute authenticity of the Word of God. They cast suspicion upon the new findings, and not infrequently discounted the sincerity of their sponsors. Thinking through the implications of the biblical science was difficult; accusation won the support of the uneducated and orthodoxy was a source of genuine comfort in troublous times: [29]

"If we have any bias, it must be against a teaching which unsteadies heart and unsettles faith. Even at the expense

[28] "The Significance of Current Religious Unrest," S. O. Barnes, *Methodist Review,* May, 1899, pp. 461–64; W. N. Clarke, *The Use of the Scriptures in Theology* (New York, 1901), chap. III.

[29] Dyson Hague, "The History of Higher Criticism," *The Fundamentals* (Chicago, 1910), vol. I, pp. 41–42.

of being thought behind the times, we prefer to stand with our Lord and Saviour Jesus Christ in receiving the Scriptures as the Word of God."

The loyal literalists reasoned that the "whole" Bible had been the corner-stone of their inherited evangelicalism; Puritans and Pilgrims alike rested their salvation upon it; the founders of the United States of America had trusted it implicitly; what was good enough for their God-fearing forefathers was good enough for the generation hard-pressed by the new learning. Episodes were told and retold to show forth the great miracles which the Scriptures had accomplished. Enemies of the Book were challenged to destroy it. How could a natural man, however learned, shatter the work of the supernatural! How puerile human reason when raised against divine revelation! One can imagine the social impact that a man, gifted with eloquence and fine physique, would make upon a convention, when [30]

"Clasping to his heart a great Bible and lifting one hand on high, Dr. Munhall, in a voice that thrilled with emotion, cried aloud: 'Go on thy way, thou message from the skies; dispel earth's gloom and save from Satan's power the sons and daughters of men. God pity any man who seeks to criticize thee!'"

Little wonder that people arose spontaneously and sang,

"How firm a foundation, ye saints of the Lord,
Is laid for your faith in His excellent Word!"

Orthodoxy was vindicated. In the midst of a confused social and religious era, the historic Bible-centered culture of America was re-established for them.

[30] Pamphlet, L. W. Munhall, *The Book of Books,* p. 3.

CHAPTER FOUR

THE RISE OF FUNDAMENTALISM

[1.] *The Fundamentals,* A Reactionary Protest

The preceding pages give evidence that old-fashioned evangelicals labored strenuously to reinstate their cult in the changing milieu. Two movements militated against them—secularism, and a liberal religion which attempted to incorporate secular values into the Christian structure. Conservatives witnessed sanctions of conduct, hitherto dominated by ecclesiastical motive, taking on increasing mundane quality. More disturbing was the rude shock to their sense of divinely-appointed leadership: people paid less and less regard to their priestly office, and they observed that a different type of men were taking positions of denominational trust. The forces of a democratic, industrial and scientific age were substituting for the regulations of a mediaeval Christianity in church and society.

The traditionalists had failed to accomplish their full purpose. A profound religious restlessness possessed them; the commanding role that liberals chose annoyed them. As a supreme gesture to re-establish their treasured faith and to insure the permanence of their official primacy in America, a group of earnest believers organized a reactionary protest in 1909. In twelve volumes of *The Fundamentals* they delivered their orthodox manifesto as a test of Christian loyalty and as a corrective to the position of liberals. This event gave the party an aggressive policy and a consciousness of social solidarity in an urgent cause.

In this action the historian finds the clear emergence of fundamentalism. Fundamentalism was the organized determination of conservative churchmen to continue the imperialistic culture of historic Protestantism within an inhospitable civilization dominated by secular interests and a progressive Christian idealism. The fundamentalist was opposed to social change, particularly such change as threatened the standards of his faith and his status in ecclesiastical circles. As a Christian, he insisted upon the preservation of such evangelical values as at one time had been accepted universally, but in recent years were widely abandoned for more meaningful ideals. Those churchmen who attempted the task of re-defining Christianity to meet the conditions of shifting culture became known as modernists.[1]

[2.] The Stewarts' Project

The generosity of two wealthy laymen in California made possible the publication of the twelve indoctrinational volumes. Lyman and Milton Stewart felt called providentially to invest large funds in the defense of the old-time gospel. They founded the Los Angeles

[1] Consider the descriptions of fundamentalism as others have conceived it: John Horsch, *Modern Religious Liberalism* (Scottdale, Pa., 1921), p. 16; F. M. Goodchild, "What is Fundamentalism?", *Watchman-Examiner,* March 2, 1922; editorial, "What is a Fundamentalist?", *The Presbyterian,* Jan. 24, 1924, p. 4; Joseph A. Leighton, "The Problem of Religion and Culture," *The Churchman,* Jan. 26, 1924; Shailer Mathews, "Orthodoxy Estimated," *Christian Century,* Dec. 1, 1921; Gerald Birney Smith, *Current Christian Thinking* (Chicago, 1928), chap. V.

Bible Institute and established the Stewart Evangelistic Fund with which to spread the tenets of orthodoxy throughout the world. Robert Dick Wilson was sent to the Orient to encourage missionaries to retain their theological moorings; later, W. H. Griffith-Thomas followed and organized fundamentalists in China into a divisive Bible Union, paving the way for considerable trouble within the American denominations. The Stewarts directed the reprinting of the manual, *Jesus is Coming* (by "W. E. B."), and its presentation to every minister in the United States and Canada. To illustrate how productive this text was in making premillennial crusaders, consider such appreciative words (in the Presentation Edition, 1908) as:

"Our Lord's coming . . . was merely a theological conception until I read the book, *Jesus is Coming*. It was this that first brought me to definite convictions and made the doctrine not only clear, but very precious." R. A. Torrey. "This book completely revolutionized my thinking, gave me a new conception of Christ. . . ." J. Wilbur Chapman. "To the Christian just awakening to the truth of Christ's second coming, I always recommend the book. . . ." James M. Gray. "*Jesus is Coming* has done an immense good in arresting the attention of Christians, and compelling them to the study of prophecy." W. J. Erdman.

These quotations express the sentiment of the book:

"Ever since the sin of Adam and Eve this world has been a dark place, a moral 'night.' " "The professing church itself will lose its saltness (in this present age), becoming nominal and lukewarm, fit only to be spued out of the Master's mouth." "This wicked world is so radically opposed to God, and under the present control of His arch enemy, is not growing better. On the contrary, judgment, fire and perdition are before it. Perilous times are coming."

In 1909 the Stewart brothers selected an editorial committee headed by A. C. Dixon to supervise the publication of *The Fundamentals*. The chairman organized the Testimony Publishing Company in Chicago (later of Los Angeles) to disseminate ultra-conservative literature. It published the twelve volumes; Dixon was editor-in-chief of the first five; Louis Meyer, the second five; R. A. Torrey, the last two. The two laymen deposited a trust fund of three hundred thousand dollars with Ziles Kellogg and J. S. McGlashan of Los Angeles and Chicago respectively, who acted as trustees of the fund. Thomas E. Stephens, editor of the *Moody Church Herald,* became the business manager of the enterprise.

In "A statement by the Two Laymen," a preface to the last volume, they announced

> "that over 2,500,000 copies of the twelve volumes have been published and circulated, and that the call for back volumes has been so insistent as to make necessary the reprinting of over a quarter of a million additional copies of the earlier issues, thus bringing the total output to nearly 3,000,000 copies. Approximately one-third of those 3,000,000 copies have gone to countries outside of the United States. About one-half of the latter have been sent to various parts of Great Britain, and the rest to other foreign countries. The great majority of Protestant missionary workers of the world have received them."

[3.] The Editorial Committee's Policy

By the will of the editorial committee "pastors, evangelists, missionaries, theological professors, theological students, Y. M. C. A. secretaries, Y. W. C. A. secretaries, college professors, Sunday school superintendents, and religious editors in the English-speaking world," received the publications. The forewords to the twelve volumes provide a key to the policy of the Stewart-Dixon party. The first volume bore the imprimatur of the "two intelligent, consecrated Christian laymen" who were willing to bear the expense of the venture "because they believed that the time had come when a new statement of the fundamentals of Christianity should be made."

When the third volume was ready for the press the editors had received "10,000 letters of appreciation, which have come from all parts of the world." They reported that "the adverse criticisms have been almost equally encouraging, because they indicate that the books have been read by some who need the truth they contain, and their criticism will attract the attention of others." Introducing the fourth number, the committee informed the public that other thousands of letters of appreciation had come, though fewer adverse criticisms were registered. Those who believed "in the God who answers prayer" were begged to pray daily that "the truth may 'run and be glorified.'" In the last volume under Dixon's direct supervision, he commented how "very gratifying" it was that "opposition bordering sometimes on bitterness" was provoked by these tracts. This opposition emanated "from the religious people who have really ceased to be Christian in their faith, while, for some reason, they desire to retain the label of Christianity." The orthodox were requested to exercise faith that "the unbelief, which in pulpit and pew has been paralyzing the Church of Christ, may be overcome."

Under Louis Meyer's direction the sixth volume was released. He claimed for the series a three-fold purpose: "the strengthening of the saints . . . the defense of the truth against the insidious attacks of the present day, and . . . the conversion of sinners." Friends of the movement had organized a cycle of prayer to uphold the testimony. The forewords to the next two numbers called the sympathetic to prayer for "enemies and unfriendly critics" that their goodwill might be gained. The articles in the ninth volume were "carefully and prayerfully selected . . . (for) . . . the re-establishment in the truth of those who are wavering in the faith." The remaining volumes assured conservatives that the books continued to win moral support, though they were sent to considerably fewer people. In the last number of the series the Stewarts informed their friends that the witness of orthodoxy would be carried forward through the medium of *The King's Business,* the official organ of the Bible Institute of Los Angeles. This decision insured that men of like mind would have a permanent agent through which to rally their strength for the defense of the gospel.

[4.] THE APPEAL OF *The Fundamentals*

The articles appearing in the *The Fundamentals* were written by men who were renowned for being sound in the faith. The contributors included representatives from England, Germany, Scotland, Ireland and Canada, as well as from the United States. The names of a few theological professors are found in the list, and those of such laymen as Philip Mauro, C. G. Trumbull, Howard A. Kelly and Robert E. Speer. Evangelists who had been active in the Bible school and prophetic conference movements provided a fair share of materials. R. A. Torrey contributed three articles to the symposium, James Orr four, and A. T. Pierson five.

The following words illustrate the approach to religious truth in the composite work: [2]

> "Perhaps the most wonderful change which was manifest to my consciousness, when my mind began to resume its normal activity (after a sudden conversion in a gospel tabernacle) and to inquire into what had happened, was this, that all my doubts, questionings, skepticism and criticism concerning God the Father, Son and Holy Spirit, concerning the full inspiration, accuracy and authority of the Holy Scriptures as the incorruptible word of God, concerning . . . were swept away completely. From that day to this I have never been troubled by doubts of God and His Word . . . my doubts and difficulties . . . were simply removed when I believed on the Crucified One."

Similarly Sir Robert Anderson testified, "Unhesitating faith is our right attitude in the presence of divine revelation, but where Scripture is silent let us keep silence." [3] In classical words James Orr presented the ground of orthodoxy: "The Bible is a record of revelation. Christianity is a supernatural system. Miracle in the sense of a direct entrance of God in word and deed into human history for gracious ends, is of the essence of it." [4] A few authors saw the menace of "scientific evolutionism . . . (and) the rising tide of social demo-

[2] IV, pp. 111–12.
[3] VI, p. 49.
[4] I, p. 336.

cratic ideals. . . . Great is the mischief already accomplished by these mighty agencies of evil, and we are as yet but at the beginning of their destructive career." [5] The same writer affirmed that "to establish and to make universal the principles of pure democracy is the object, whether consciously or unconsciously, of the great thought movements of our era; and the essence and marrow of democracy is the supreme authority of Man. Hence the conflict with the Bible." [6] The historian's method of biblical criticism was interpreted in this manner: [7]

> "The 'assured results' of the higher criticism have been gained, after all, not by inductive study of the biblical books to ascertain if they present a great variety of styles and vocabularies and religious points of view. They have been attained by assuming that the hypothesis of evolution is true, and that the religion of Israel must have unfolded itself by a process of natural evolution. They have been attained by an interesting cross-examination of the biblical books to constrain them to admit the hypothesis of evolution. The imagination has played a large part in the process."

The central figure in the writings of the twelve volumes was the person of the Christ. With rare exceptions He occupied the preeminent place in every article contributed, regardless of the nature of the subject treated. His authoritative lordship in Christianity was to be conserved at any price. That Christ was the revelation from God was evidenced by his Incarnation, Virgin birth, Miracles and Resurrection. "He is heaven come to earth. . . . He speaks of Himself as God's

[5] II, p. 97.
[6] V, p. 7.
[7] I, p. 61.

Other,"[8] claimed B. B. Warfield; and in like manner G. Campbell Morgan, "the whole teaching of Holy Scripture places the Incarnation at the center of the methods of God with a sinning race."[9] Howard A. Kelly, medical professor at Johns Hopkins University, offered the following defense of the Christian Saviour,[10]

"I believe Jesus Christ to be the Son of God, without human father, conceived by the Holy Ghost, born of the Virgin Mary . . . I believe he who thus receives Jesus Christ as his Saviour is born again spiritually, has new privileges, appetites and affections; that he is one body with Christ the Head and will live with Him forever."

Philip Mauro states the contributors' attitude towards higher education in America thus,[11]

"The great universities of England and America which were founded for the purpose of maintaining the doctrines of Scriptures, and spreading knowledge of them as the revelations of the living God, and as the foundations of all true learning, have been despoiled of all that made them useful for the nurture of young minds, and that made them valuable to the communities wherein they have flourished; and this momentous change has been accomplished through the agency of philosophy and vain deceit . . . and not according to Christ."

Because the familiar tenets of historic evangelicalism occupied the attention of the editorial committee, such doctrines as the following were expounded: the authenticity of the biblical records, the assured supernatural character of the same, and their absolute sufficiency for man's redemption; the saviourhood of

[8] I, p. 25.
[9] I, p. 29.
[10] I, p. 124.
[11] II, p. 93.

the virgin-born, vicariously dying, miraculously resurrected, and second coming Christ; disavowal of the scholarship and method in schools of religion, and of the arts and the sciences in free colleges; repudiation of the trustworthiness of such churchmen as directed the policies and preachments of the leading evangelical denominations; and exaltation of themselves as the divinely-appointed priests of God to call back wayward civilization and a heterodox church to repentance and conformity in "the faith once for all delivered to the saints."

[5.] Trends of the Fundamentalist Movement

The far-reaching influence of *The Fundamentals* can scarcely be measured. The books were welcomed by tens of thousands of churchmen. The language in which the themes were delivered stirred in sympathetic readers, first, anxiety for the well-being of Christianity, then fear for the preservation of the historic faith, and then spirited defense of the old gospel. Correspondence, caucus, revival, multiplied to promote the aims of the critical cause. During the five or six years these publications were in process of dissemination, frequent Bible and prophetic conferences were interspersed throughout the country to fan the flame of religious discontent into open reactionism. Factious periodicals intensified fears and suspicions. The World War did not so much initiate controversy as it accentuated divisive forces that had been nurtured for years. *The Fundamentals* having accomplished their leavening work, and the war psychology having concentrated religious militancy, conservatives *became* the fundamentalist movement.

The fundamentalist method of appeal was two-fold: conservatives directed their energies to gain control of evangelicalism for the purpose of reinstating Christian orthodoxy; they also undertook reformative measures beyond the church with a view to checking the standards of secular culture and substituting the principles of the historic faith.

PART TWO

Current Conflict Within the Church

PART TWO

CURRENT CONFLICT WITHIN THE CHURCH

FUNDAMENTALISM involved every evangelical denomination in America in a conflict of ideals. The problems were not identical in each church, but the social attitudes awakened were the same. Advocates of the older religious order exhibited supreme loyalty to historic Christian values; but, when they reacted against change in ritual, creed or polity they met the situation in an uncompromising and reformative manner. Protestantism faced in its constituted bodies "the great divide": whether it should make the past authoritative over the present, or should set present and future free to reorganize religion in response to living needs. Conservatives attempted to perpetuate *as such* the distinctive tenets that their several denominations had stressed in former years. Two cultures clashed within the Christian church.

CHAPTER FIVE

ORTHODOXY WITHIN THE NORTHERN BAPTIST CONVENTION

The faith of Baptists has been marked with its own religious distinctions. The Bible, particularly its Christo-centric documents, was the only and sufficient seat of authority for this people. In the New Testament they claimed to discover proper conditions of church membership: spiritual regeneration and baptism by immersion; the soul liberty of the individual before God and the administrative independence of the local congregation of believers, which became their principles of social organization; and the great commission as the missionary obligation to a lost world. To carry forward such appointments, Baptists sponsored a policy of leadership training in denominational schools. These five traits have given individuality to Northern Baptists and formed the foci of controversy in the recent conflict of ideals. Another trait, the principle of separation of church and state, did not gain recognition in the controversy, for the reason that no situation arose to change the application of the doctrine.

[1.] The Principle of Biblical Authority

As early dissenters the Baptists discovered the ground of their Christian faith in the infallible Word of God as preserved in the New Testament. This doctrine was unquestioned until biblical criticism became a method of clerical study. As men discovered the historical soil out of which the Book grew, they applied the principle of relativism to the scriptural pattern of the Christian life and proceeded to restate the question of religious authority.

Augustus H. Strong, president emeritus of Rochester Theological Seminary, voiced orthodox sentiments on the subject in 1917. He had just completed a tour of Baptist missions,[1] and observed that the historical approach to the Bible had led certain missionaries to distrust the sufficiency of scriptural revelation. These individuals, he believed, were disseminating doubts, losing the passion for souls, and imperiling the cause of Christ. "We Baptists must reform or die," was the burden of his warning. He begged his denomination and its theological schools to return to the authority of the supernatural Book and thus preserve the harmony of its people.

The *Watchman-Examiner,* an unofficial Baptist journal published in New York City, carried forward this criticism of the seminaries as the source of disregard for Bible authority. A member of the Colgate faculty met the restless spirit abroad in the churches by suggesting that if Baptists thought their schools were "tearing the Bible to tatters," they should investigate them.[2] In May, 1920, one hundred and fifty leaders in Northern Baptist churches issued a call to their brethren to meet

[1] His comments published in *A Tour of the Missions* (Boston, 1918). Earlier reactionary movements within the denomination were cited by Henry C. Vedder, in an article, "Fifty Years of Baptist History," *Bibliotheca Sacra,* Oct., 1900, pp. 660–79.

[2] Letter, *Watchman-Examiner,* Nov. 14, 1918.

in a Pre-Convention Conference on Fundamentals of Our Faith, in the introduction to which they gave notice of "an immediate and urgent duty to restate, reaffirm and reemphasize the fundamentals of our New Testament faith."[3] For this orthodox group the question of proper loyalty to the Bible involved a right interpretation, which necessitated in turn the defense of certain doctrines.

The pre-convention party paid full allegiance to a divinely inspired Bible. They concluded that should their schools forsake critical methods of investigation and adopt the simple attitude of faith in its final authority, all phases of denominational friction would cease. At the regular Convention J. C. Massee, spokesman for this party, moved that Baptist schools be investigated with "special attention to the question of whether these schools and individual teachers are still loyal to the great fundamental Baptist truths as held by the denomination in the past, with particular reference to the inspiration of the Word of God, the deity of Christ. . . ." The motion was carried, and a committee of nine began its study.

Meanwhile denominational journals were occupied with controversial subjects. Church members became aware of conflicting ideals between orthodox and liberal leaders, and it was believed widely that the seminaries were responsible for the unhappy conditions. The New York weekly coined the term "fundamentalists" to represent those "who mean to do battle royal for the fundamentals."[5] When the second annual conference

[3] Introduction, *Baptist Fundamentals.* (Philadelphia, 1920).
[4] *Annual* of the Northern Baptist Convention, 1920, p. 48.
[5] *Watchman-Examiner,* editorial, July 1, 1920.

(pre-convention) was called in Des Moines in June, 1921, the party decided to make binding a doctrinal test of fellowship upon Northern Baptists. Massee, as chairman, declared that the Convention must "agree definitely on the fundamentals or divide; there is no alternative." The substance of the historic Philadelphia and New Hampshire Confessions of Faith was presented to the conference by F. M. Goodchild, and adopted as their norm of orthodoxy. For some reason the fundamentalists did not believe it opportune to ask the Convention to accept the creed when it assembled. The commission investigating the schools reported, but confirmed no heresy charges such as had been laid against them; it did extend to them its moral support.

Notwithstanding the Convention's vote of confidence in its schools in accepting the commission's report, the conservatives' committee [6] directed a letter to churchmen declaring that "Baptist seminaries should expel from their faculty every teacher who has in any wise departed from the historic Baptist faith. Baptists cannot tolerate a scientific attitude toward the Bible." This action was so unfair that Cornelius Woelfkin circularized the ministry in an effort to mediate a more reasonable attitude on the part of Baptists toward their Bible instructors.[7] However, the committee forwarded another letter to the churches urging them to adopt the Des Moines Confession of Faith, maintaining that if the denomination would only approve "a uniform statement

[6] Members included J. C. Massee, J. M. Dean, Floyd Adams, F. M. Goodchild, and C. L. Laws.

[7] Pamphlet, *A Communication to the Pastors Within the Territory of the Northern Baptist Convention,* signed by Woelfkin and four other liberals.

of faith . . . (it would) hinder the departure from the faith so deplorably in evidence in certain directions." At the next pre-convention conference William J. Bryan, spoke on the subject "Tampering with the Mainspring," *i.e.*, revelation. The orator insisted that theological professors had tried to destroy the very heart of Christianity by their confidence in scientific principles. The delegates were told that the controversy hinged between faith in a supernatural Book and confidence in naturalism as seminary teachers presented it in what he termed the expurgated Bible.

On the day following, the disturbed party presented the New Hampshire Confession of Faith to the regular Convention. Woelfkin moved a counter-resolution: "The Northern Baptist Convention affirms that the New Testament is the all-sufficient ground of our faith and practice, and we need no other statement."[8] After a spirited debate, in which it became evident that some conservatives (the William B. Riley group) chose a more reactionary attitude than others (the J. C. Massee group) in defending the creedal test, the house adopted the liberal principle of authority by a large majority. This official decision defeated the fundamentalist effort to impose a doctrinal basis of authority upon Baptists, and reaffirmed the denomination's loyalty to one of its historic distinctives.

Extreme fundamentalists suffered a grievance by this action. To them it was evidence of modernist control of the church. Their patience was exhausted when Harry Emerson Fosdick preached in the First Presbyterian Church, New York City, May 21, 1922, on the subject,

[8] *Annual* of the Northern Baptist Convention, 1923, p. 133.

"Shall the Fundamentalists Win?" Fosdick had just returned from China where he had conferred with missionaries and discovered that representatives of orthodoxy in America had visited the foreign field and sown seeds of dissension, leading to the formation of the divisive Bible Union of China. This condition, together with his observance upon return to America that reactionary Protestantism was increasing at home, led him to preach the sermon.

The sermon was published in *The Baptist*.[9] Because Fosdick was a Baptist and had mentioned this church's dilemma, his delivery was accepted by Baptist fundamentalists as a challenge to battle for the control of their denomination.[10] As a matter of fact, the preacher made a plea for tolerance within the churches, in which great ideals were at stake. He disclaimed the dogma of biblical inerrancy and regretted the stress which was laid upon such doctrines as the Virgin birth and the Second Coming. Were there not more fitting themes in the church's business with a sinful world! Fosdick's closing words were tense:

> "And now in the presence of such colossal problems in Christ's name and for Christ's sake the fundamentalists propose to drive out from the Christian churches all the consecrated souls who do not agree with their theory of inspiration. What immeasurable folly!"

As a protest against this view and conditions generally, radical fundamentalists organized an independent

[9] June 10, 1922. A group of sympathetic laymen circulated it throughout the country, using the tract-title, "The New Knowledge and the Christian Faith."

[10] Note the series of "Defamatory Statements "which liberals were supposed to have made against orthodoxy, as mentioned editorially in autumn numbers of the *Watchman-Examiner*.

fellowship, The Baptist Bible Union of North America.[11] The Union planned to make the literal Word of God binding upon the conscience of all Baptists. Its executive was engaged so strictly in advancing a universal reformative program in 1923 that it overlooked the regular Convention in Atlantic City. The more moderate fundamentalists approached the sessions in a conciliatory mood. A year later when the president read his annual address to the Convention, he recommended that the "Message" put forth by the late Baptist World Alliance (held at Stockholm, Sweden) be accepted as the official attitude of Northern Baptists. The Massee group acquiesced but the Riley faction presented a substitute, the so-called Milwaukee Declaration of Faith. After a prolonged controversy, the Convention chose the ideals embodied in the "Message" rather than the non-Baptistic standard of militant orthodoxy.

The conservatives had made two unsuccessful attempts to change the ground of Baptist authority from that of freedom of individual interpretation of the Scriptures. The one proposed to control schools for biblical orthodoxy; the other, the Northern Baptist Convention. When John R. Straton made a motion at Milwaukee that the missionary forces be investigated for conditions of heterodoxy he made trial of a third theological test. It was voted. The following May the commission's findings and recommendations were published in *The Baptist* in advance of the Seattle Convention. Six or eight men were singled out of several hundred as unfit for Baptist service because they would not affirm their belief in certain popular doctrines. The report urged that only those individuals who accepted "the Gospel"

[11] A history of this pan-American union is traced in chap. XIII.

be retained as missionaries of the Convention. A rider to the report defined "the Gospel" as:

"The good news of the free forgiveness of sin and eternal life (beginning now and going on forever) through a vital union with the crucified and risen Christ, which brings men into union and fellowship with God. This salvation is graciously offered on the sole condition of repentance and faith in Christ, and has in it the divine power of regeneration and sanctification through the Spirit. The only reason we have for accepting this Gospel is our belief in the deity of Christ in whom we see the Father, a faith founded on the trustworthiness of the Scriptures and the fact that we have experienced this salvation in our own hearts."

Bible Unionists accepted the report unanimously but recommended that the theological statement incorporated in this gospel be strictly applied to every workman under the jurisdiction of the Foreign Mission Board. W. B. Hinson made such a motion. This involved an inquisitive supervision of missionary and Board members. Only fine parliamentary procedure saved the Convention from approving the resolution, for the Riley-Hinson forces were very strong on the Pacific coast. It was commonly reported that the Bible Union had packed the Convention. This group was so routed by the official decision that they withdrew full missionary support of their affiliated churches from the Convention's treasury and set up an independent orthodox department of missions.

The fourth attempt that fundamentalists made to impose a binding authority upon the Northern Convention took the form of an ecclesiastical regulation.[12] When

[12] Shailer Mathews, "Shall We Have a General Assembly?", *The Baptist*, Apr. 17, 1926, p. 324.

delegates from the Park Avenue Church, New York City, applied for seats in the Seattle meeting, their rights were challenged. Orthodox leaders insisted that since the congregation waived baptism by immersion as a condition of church membership, it was unbaptistic. Unsuccessful in their immediate intent, these men asked for an amendment to the by-laws of the Convention defining a Baptist church as one "composed only of baptized believers."[13] The overture was accepted and final action upon it deferred until the following year.

A group of fifty-eight liberal churchmen convened at Wallace Lodge, N. Y., in December to plan a steering campaign on the subject of defining a Baptist church. They concluded that they would consider one without reference to baptism. This decision was in keeping with the growth of open-membership ideals. This policy did not commend itself to conservatives nor to *The Baptist*, on account of the ex parte nature of the Lodge group. Whereupon, J. Whitcomb Brougher called a company of fundamentalists and liberals to Chicago to express their sentiment on the question. They recommended the following overture for consideration in Washington:[14]

> "The Northern Baptist Convention recognizes its constituency as consisting of those Baptist churches in which immersion of believers is recognized as the only scriptural baptism; and The Convention hereby declares that only immersed members will be recognized as delegates to the Convention."

This resolution was presented at the next Convention. W. B. Riley moved that Northern Baptists should not only "recognize" immersion as scriptural, but "practise . . . (it) as a prerequisite to membership." In the

[13] *Annual* of the Northern Baptist Convention, 1925, p. 245.
[14] "A Chicago Conference," *Watchman-Examiner*, Apr. 22, 1926.

debate which ensued, his earlier colleagues in the fundamentalist movement, in the persons of Brougher, Massee and others, were now the leaders in opposing him and his Bible Union associates.

The Chicago resolution was adopted. An analysis of this by-law reveals the principle that, while Northern Baptists recognized that the Bible teaches baptism of believers by immersion only, they were free to treat the injunction as they pleased in the local church. The compromise section did not refer to "believers" but required that delegates to the Convention be "immersed members." This decision was a clear vindication of historic Baptist policy, in that the Bible rather than an official interpretation, remained the spiritual authority.

Since the Washington Convention in 1926, this denomination has faced no issue involving a redefinition of the basis of religious control. In the four cases that arose during ten years of fundamentalist controversy, each problem was retired without changing the progressive purpose of the denomination. The missionary work did suffer somewhat owing to compromise methods of relieving tension. However, officially Northern Baptists have remained free in the use and interpretation of the Bible, to which they continue to pay genuine loyalty.

[2.] The Democratic Government of the Churches

The situation which gave rise to the organization of the Northern Baptist Convention, stirred many conservatives to criticize the proposed change in policy.[15] For several years liberal leaders had been agitating for a closer correlation of missionary societies. Their service

[15] Note the editorials in Baptist weekly papers during April-May, 1907.

work within the churches had become unwieldy. At the annual assembly in Washington (1907) a previously appointed committee recommended that the delegates proceed at once to form the Northern Baptist Convention.

The advocates of change claimed that the new plan would permit the denomination's cause to develop more expeditiously, while it would preserve to Baptists their democratic rights. An executive of the American Baptist Publication Society defended an official class within the society who feared that the change meant a loss of their prerogatives. They disliked to surrender their ecclesiastical control. The forward-looking leaders gained their objective, however, and the genius of Baptist polity was conserved in the by-laws of the Convention. They provided for "the independence of the local church," "the advisory and representative nature of the local and state associations," and the purpose of the Convention "to give expression to the sentiment of its constituency upon matters of denominational importance." [16]

Within a decade the church's program had advanced markedly in bulk and in efficiency of supervision. Some strong men who were unable to appreciate spiritual gain accused officials of exploiting their positions. Henry C. Mabie claimed that nominally the Northern Convention was "a delegated ecclesiastical control," but actually it had become "a pure oligarchical autocracy." Baptists had forsaken their basis of organization as determined in the New Testament.[17] The *Watchman-Examiner* supported this criticism. The *Standard* denied the jus-

[16] "Constitution," *Standard,* May 25, 1907, p. 1185 f.

[17] *From Romance to Reality* (Boston, 1917), pp. 248–51.

tice of Mabie's accusation and claimed that there were other scriptural passages to underwrite the policy of the Convention.

Following the World War Northern Baptists enlarged their ministry in terms of a five-year "New World Movement" program. In May, 1919, the Denver Convention instituted a General Board of Promotion to reconstruct its service agencies. To finance the new plan required one hundred million dollars. Since the *Watchman-Examiner* had not been kindly disposed to progressivism, the Convention voted to publish its own paper, *The Baptist,* to help inspire its ideals. Definite opposition to the Board developed immediately after the Denver meeting. The New York paper announced that "with the new paper we shall maintain a friendly rivalry." It discouraged the participation of local churches in the Inter-Church World Movement, an action the Convention had ratified, and it began to discredit liberal Baptists. The "Call" to the first pre-convention conference on fundamentals announced the firm conviction that though "the vast majority of our Baptist people are as loyal as were our fathers . . . this loyalty will not long continue unless something is done to stay the rising tide of liberalism." The delegates chose a permanent committee on conferences on Baptist fundamentals to safeguard the ideals of conservatism.

The committee's purpose was introduced in the Buffalo Convention when Massee moved that *The Baptist* be sold to the highest bidder. This led the liberals to organize a steering committee under the direction of C. Wallace Petty to care for the broader interests of the Convention. The former party contended that they had no adequate representation of their views in the weekly paper. The motion was lost. As a second effort to withhold progressivism, it was moved and carried to investigate the fitness of Baptist schools to perpetuate denominational ideals. The 1921 reports of the inquiry showed clearly how unbaptistic administrative regulation of its schools would be. It read in part: [18]

> "The purposes of the Convention are practical, not controversial or judicial. Nor has the Convention any right of control over our Baptist schools . . . the real power of control over our schools is in the Baptist constituency in the general locality where the school stands . . . we must leave the matter of dealing with false teachers to the local body of Baptists who are clothed with ample authority to dispose of practically every case. . . ."

Notwithstanding the fact that the report on schools assured the church of their integrity, fundamentalists remained critical. Their executive circulated letters among schools and churches threatening to stop financial support to the New World Movement unless restitution to their wishes was made. Modernists were accused of exercising discrimination against them in committee appointment, and of forcing Baptists into affiliation with the Federal Council of Churches of Christ in America. Churches were urged to send "a crowd of independent Baptists" to Indianapolis to see that "every officer of the Convention this year should be distinctly and pronouncedly a conservative man." Such ultra-conservatives, as John R. Straton and William B. Riley called themselves, were even more severe in their cen-

[18] *Annual* of the Northern Baptist Convention, 1921, p. 92.

sure. When the Indianapolis Convention met, they could not agree with the more moderate viewpoint of the Goodchild-Massee group. Consequently, they helped organize the Baptist Bible Union of America to express their sectional aims. At its initial meeting it declared war on modernism, and resolved:

> "Whereas it is now the policy of modernists, and of ecclesiastical machines controlled by them, to undermine, and if possible to force the resignation of fundamentalist ministers, We the Executive Committee of the Baptist Bible Union urge our loyal pastors to refuse to flee position and duty at the behest of a few critics, from within or without the church; . . . and we pledge our cooperation with all orthodox churches that desire our counsel or aid in securing and retaining as pastors men of God's appointment."

Henceforth there were three organized agencies working among Northern Baptists, each one of which sought to govern denominational policy: the progressives, the committee on fundamentals within the Convention, and the divisive Union. The absence of the Riley organization from the Atlantic City Convention, for reasons already ascribed, permitted a more peaceful procedure. The *Watchman-Examiner* remarked that a new dignity graced the occasion.

The breach between the Bible Unionists and the committee on fundamentals within the Convention had become so evident that F. M. Goodchild felt it necessary to clarify the situation in the eyes of the church at large. In a contributed article,[19] he insisted that the Bible Unionists were not fundamentalists, and certainly the fundamentalists did not care to be classed

[19] *Watchman-Examiner,* April 19, 1923. Six differences were given.

with the Unionists. His party had been accused by the latter of betraying trusts. On the contrary, fundamentalists had exhibited more courage than their accusers, for they had kept up reformative efforts within the Convention rather than seceding from it. Yet, as if to warn progressives who in large measure controlled the situation, he pointed out how easy it would be for his colleagues to become Unionists in case their grievances were not met.

The two conservative parties functioned independently at the Milwaukee Convention. The more moderate group moved nearer a possible basis of administrative harmony within the denomination, while the Union withdrew further. The reactionaries had cut in upon the loyalty of local churches and made it clear that the Convention could not reach the objectives of the New World Movement.[20] Straton had accomplished his desire to have the foreign missionary enterprise investigated. He warned his supporters that, "the great danger of the present hour is that true believers will stop to parley with the foe, who come in the name of friendship and helpfulness. . . ." He wanted to witness the complete capitulation of modernists before the Bible Union would discontinue its work. Liberal churchmen used every means to pacify the moderates in the interests of goodwill. *The Baptist* published a series of articles in which the pastoral efficiency of conservatives was commended. The same organ introduced a sequence of editorials on subjects of harmonistic and constructive character.

[20] Note the report of the committee on finance in the 1924 *Annual* of the Northern Baptist Convention.

The moderate conservatives functioned in a very halting manner at the Seattle Convention. Massee having signed the mission report as a member of the investigating body, was bound to support its findings. He did not attend the Convention. This double disappointment to fundamentalists led them to doubt the advisability of his leadership in their party organization. Soon after, Massee resigned as chairman of the committee on fundamentals, and F. M. Goodchild succeeded him. This shift proved a disintegrating force, for such other leaders as Melborne P. Boynton and J. Whitcomb Brougher discontinued an aggressive partisanship.

During the next year Brougher was employed by the Board of Promotion to visit churches with a view to re-establishing confidence in the denomination's work. Genial and sportsmanlike, he traveled widely delivering his "Play Ball" oration. He succeeded in getting together a representative group of liberals and conservatives at Chicago to define a Baptist church.[21] In appreciation of his service, Northern Baptists elected him their president in Washington the next summer. He, Massee and Boynton spoke for the Convention and against the Riley-Goodchild viewpoint. Massee, pleading for a controversial armistice for six months during which time all churches should engage in concentrated evangelistic effort, was hailed by delegates as a peerless preacher. His challenge had a sobering effect and delegates agreed to accept the suggestion. This decision crushed the spirit of fundamentalism as nothing had done in previous conventions, and it introduced a peaceful procedure in denominational work.

At the caucus meeting of Unionists, Riley and Straton

[21] See page 73.

confessed in sorrow the spiritual collapse of their erstwhile colleague, Massee. Disapproving his recommendation for a truce, Riley explained, "This is not a battle. It is a war from which there is no discharge." Massee was considered an apostate and classified with Fosdick. The Union renewed its pledges to the tenets of militant orthodoxy.[22] Although the moderate fundamentalists continued as an organization, they have occasioned no Convention problem since the Washington meeting. Four influences contributed to a return of harmony among Northern Baptists at Chicago in 1927: the tolerant attitude of the president, J. Whitcomb Brougher; the devotional talks of George W. Truett of Dallas; the absence of Bible Union leaders; and the official recognition of conservative men. Massee preached the Convention sermon and Goodchild was elected to the Board of Education.

[3.] The Christian Life and Church Membership

Historically, Baptists considered that there were two necessary prerequisites to membership of an individual in a New Testament Church: the new birth and baptism by immersion. The necessity of the first gave Baptists their evangelistic gospel, and the ordinance of believer's baptism opened the way for a scriptural fellowship within the church.

A generation ago, The Baptist Congress[23] and the Brotherhood of the Kingdom[24] had made independent efforts to rethink the denomination's preface to the

[22] For later events in the history of the Union, see chap. XIII.

[23] A. H. Newman, *A Century of Baptist Achievement.* (Philadelphia, 1901), pp. 289–93.

[24] *Report* of the third annual conference of the Brotherhood, 1895, p. 2.

Christian life. The former became a popular annual medium for the discussion of current questions. The Brotherhood, under the guidance of a few men such as Walter Rauschenbusch and W. N. Clarke, enjoined that "every member shall lay special stress on the social aims of Christianity, and shall endeavor to make Christ's teachings concerning wealth operative in the church." Although these movements helped to broaden views of Christian ideals, they also accentuated orthodox tendencies in Baptist circles.

There has always been a large conservative constituency among Northern Baptists. By reason of low standards of ordination, men anxious to preach the good news may resort to short-cut courses of training in Bible schools, and enter the ministry to spread their sectional gospel. Many fundamentalist leaders, born and disciplined in the atmosphere of southern Christian orthodoxy, moved North and brought their inherited viewpoint.[25] Others, graduates of seminaries when theological training was universally traditional, had failed to live abreast of modern social and religious changes, and became defenders of classical orthodoxy.

A. H. Strong and Henry C. Mabie appealed favorably to this type of churchmen in 1917 when they expressed grave doubt for the validity of the gospel which missionaries were preaching. Due to liberal scholarship in seminaries, it was feared that their graduates were substituting the message of social service for justification by faith. The demands for an investigation of schools in

[25] It should be noted that most of the fundamentalist leaders in the Northern Baptist Convention were born and reared in the conservative South.

1920, and of missionary work in 1924, were inspired in part by this feeling.

Somewhat typical of the perverted attitude of fundamentalists towards social Christianity, is the following sentiment of a writer in the *Watchman-Examiner:*

"The doctrine of social service is very plausible and attractive . . . but it is a dangerous misinterpretation of the teachings of Jesus to assert that civilization and environment are Christianity. . . .

"What, then, is the social ideal in its final analysis? It is briefly this; surround the individual or community with a good environment and salvation will result. No greater or more insidious heresy ever issued from hell than this. . . .

"Out of this fallacy I think has sprung the greatest present peril of Christianity. That peril is the gradual forsaking of the doctrine that faith in, and acceptance of, Jesus Christ is the only essential to salvation from sin. When we abandon Jesus Christ as Saviour and Redeemer we abandon all. . . ."

The Northern Baptist Convention has made an effort to meet this criticism during the last few years by giving prominence to evangelistic conferences at each annual meeting. Outstanding conservatives have been invited to contribute to the programs. At such times the new birth has been emphasized as the one and sufficient prerequisite to candidacy for Christian fellowship, and ministers are urged to make this conviction central in their preaching.

Though Baptists historically have claimed the necessity of regenerate church membership, it is doubtful if this evangelical principle has been as significant a source of misunderstanding within the Northern Convention as has the baptismal rite. Traditionally, this sect became strict immersionists, while in recent times certain congregations have changed their by-laws to permit of open-membership privileges. The orthodox considered this as a departure from the New Testament regulation and a mark of infidelity to the Saviour. Liberals, on the other hand, believed their allegiance to Christ was not measured by conformity to a physical act, but by adhering to an inner and spiritual ideal.

The announcement of Cornelius Woelfkin, minister of the well-known Park Avenue Church, New York, that he was in favor of a Baptist plan of open-membership, was the occasion for widespread unrest. Two years later when Fosdick was called to be his successor and when he made a similar affirmation, the subject of baptismal policy became a denominational issue. At the Seattle Convention it was moved to change its constitution to define a Baptist church in the orthodox manner.

During the year preceding official action on the subject, fundamentalists made a strenuous effort to convert local churches to the literal acceptance of New Testament baptismal teachings. The names of Fosdick and Rockefeller (of the Park Avenue Church), were drawn in to lend zealous suspicion to the issue. It was claimed that influential men were attempting to dictate a method contrary to Christ's teaching. "Are we a lot of idiots?", asked F. M. Goodchild, editor of the fundamentalist page in the *Watchman-Examiner,* "three hundred years of Baptist history and do not know a Baptist church . . . a Baptist church today is not essentially different from what a Baptist church was in New Testament times!" This writer, like the Bible Unionists, took the subject seriously and became a militant campaigner.

While doctrinally the decision registered at Washington[26] brought satisfaction to a majority of liberals, legally it had no power whatever. Since the Northern Convention functions in an administrative manner only, churches were free to disagree with the official standard. Many reaffirmed their faith in the dogma that baptism by immersion was an essential of membership in a Baptist church. The Philadelphia Association of Churches in October, 1926, decided that "We are Baptists and nothing else!" A few months later the Chicago Association narrowly avoided taking a similar stand.

Local Baptists continue to register differences of opinion on the baptism question. But there is every indication that the controversial subject has passed out of the jurisdiction of the Convention for the present. Progressive churchmen have perpetuated democratic government, permitting congregations to choose their own alternative on conditions of the Christian life and church membership.

[4.] A Question of Missionary Policy

Although conservatives began to question the orthodoxy of Baptist missionaries before the World War, other reforms of primary concern engaged them until 1922. In that year Massee interrogated the Foreign Mission Board concerning its right to send ministers of modernist training to those he regarded as unregenerate men. O. W. Van Osdel of Grand Rapids called the attention

[26] See pp. 73–74.

of the churches to the fact that only twenty-three cents out of every dollar contributed to the New World Movement was spent to convert "the heathen," while the remainder was used "for civilization, Americanization, and social service."[27] A stenographer of the American Baptist Foreign Missionary Society, who had access to the correspondence files of the Society, believed she detected modernism in the letters of certain missionaries. She informed her friend, John R. Straton, who exploited the stenographer and her reports in his parish paper in June, 1922. Disaffection grew rather rapidly.

From the floor of the 1924 Convention Riley accused a certain missionary of holding heretical views in theology. James H. Franklin, secretary of the Foreign Missionary Society, arose immediately and refuted the remarks, at the same time reading a letter from the one involved to support his contention. This rebuff was a severe check to the cause of extremists at Milwaukee. Notwithstanding, Straton moved for an investigation, naming on the personnel of the committee himself and Riley. The convention laughed heartily. The moderate fundamentalists presented a counter-resolution that a committee be named by the president of the Convention "with power and authority to investigate and report at the next meeting of the Northern Baptist Convention the conduct, policies and practices of the Board of Managers of the American Baptist Foreign Missionary Society and of its secretaries in the selection of missionaries in the foreign field. . . ."[28] A leading liberal seconded the motion. This tact confused the Bible Union leaders

[27] *Baptist Temple News,* Oct. 23, 1920.

[28] *Annual* of the Northern Baptist Convention, 1924, p. 41.

and saved the assembly from prolonged debate. The motion passed by such a small margin that a division of the house was taken. *The Baptist* (December 12, 1925) pointed out that the commission was approved by liberals "in order to placate belligerents, calm the fears of the suspicious, and promote unity."

This weekly sought to inspire the churches with confidence in their cause by advocating an inclusive policy on mission fields. It maintained that the Convention did not stand for doctrinal uniformity but that it laid first emphasis upon moral integrity. There should be room, therefore, for liberal and conservative representatives abroad. The *Watchman-Examiner* believed that such a confession allowed "some Unitarians, who have an exceptionally high average character" but lack right beliefs, to work under the banner of Baptists. The same journal claimed the doctrinal unfitness of many missionaries, as if to pre-judge the commission's findings. The editor argued for an exclusive policy, sound theology marking the dividing line.

As previously mentioned, the committee's report criticized only a few men who dissented from certain essentials of "the Gospel."[29] At this 1925 Convention the Baptist Bible Union made a supreme effort to apply these essentials rigidly to every worker under the Mission Board's auspices. A counter-resolution urged upon the Board "such action, in the light of the facts reported by the Commission, as seems to them will best conserve our denominational interests and best advance the Kingdom of Christ." [30] The testing vote of confidence

[29] See pp. 71–72.
[30] *Annual* of the Northern Baptist Convention, 1925, p. 174.

in the Board numbered seven hundred and forty-two in its favor and five hundred and seventy-four in opposition.

The committee on fundamentals within the Northern Convention chose new leadership following the Seattle meetings.[31] Though this party tried to maintain a distinctive position, there was no ground between the official action of the Convention and that of the Bible Union. On the fundamentalist page of the *Watchman-Examiner*, F. M. Goodchild as the new leader made a statement (innocuous as far as missionary procedure was concerned) to the effect that his party would insist on more strictly orthodox pledges *within* the Convention.

The majority of moderate fundamentalists followed the lead of Massee and gave their moral support to regular missions. Occasionally some designated their gifts to objects which they could approve conscientiously, but their funds passed into the official channels of the church. The Bible Unionists organized their own missionary department at a meeting in Paul Rader's Tabernacle, Chicago, November 1, 1925. T. T. Shields, their president, informed Baptists:[32]

> "The Baptist Bible Union has received hundreds of letters asking for advice respecting contributions to Foreign Missions. We can now answer in a sentence: Do not give one solitary cent for any purpose into hands of the Foreign Mission Board of the Northern Baptist Convention. After the exhibition made at this Convention, we would as soon trust Judas Iscariot. . . ."

The Foreign Mission Board dropped a few liberals from its service during the ensuing year. Still dissatis-

[31] For reasons, see p. 80.

[32] *The Searchlight,* Frank Norris, editor, July 10, 1925.

fied, the irreconcilable group made one more effort to shift the denomination's policy. In an effort to unseat Secretary James H. Franklin of the Board, at the Washington Convention, the Union selected their own official slate to run against the ballot of the regular nominating committee. The poll showed that four hundred and eighty-one had signed the Union ticket, seventeen hundred and eight the committee ballot, and two hundred and eighty-four had scattered their votes. Thus, a series of signal defeats closed the fundamentalist campaign to direct the business of foreign missions within the Northern Baptist Convention.

[5.] The Independence of Denominational Schools

Northern Baptists built a considerable number of institutions of learning during the nineteenth century. These schools entertained a common religious purpose until the spread of scientific learning. Then administrators elected such a policy as expressed their evaluation of science.

The first charge that theological schools were disqualified for Christian work was announced by A. J. Gordon in 1889 when he organized the Boston Missionary Training School. A British friend of his had canvassed seminaries for recruits for his faith mission on the Congo, but with slight response. The *Examiner* accounted for his lack of appeal on the ground that he was a Plymouth Brother, but Gordon complained that the seminaries had surrendered their evangelical passion. Contrary to the will of regular Baptists, he established the New England School. It advocated extreme Calvinistic doctrine, premillennialism, and a short-course preparation for the ministry. The disapproving publicity which the *Examiner* brought against it and the numerous missionary and prophetic conferences which Gordon conducted in its favor, won for the school a generous following.[33] Upon the death of its founder, the institution became known as the Gordon Bible College.

The founding of the University of Chicago in the early nineties strained loyalties within the denomination. The type of scriptural scholarship which its founder and his associates employed was unwelcome to many congregations, unprepared for the ministry of modernly trained men. Professor George B. Foster was disfellowshipped from the Chicago Baptist Ministers' Conference because it was alleged that he had repudiated the Bible plan of salvation in a book, *The Finality of the Christian Religion.*[34] The Divinity School of the University likewise failed to win universal approval among Baptists. Its instructors were criticized constantly for advancing dangerous doctrinal views.

In 1913 the Northern Baptist Theological Seminary was founded in the same city as an antidote to progressive theological education. J. M. Dean, its first president, chose a faculty which pledged themselves to be "loyal to the Word of God," and to teach "the positive, changeless and glorious doctrines of grace as opposed to the negations of the new rationalism." The curriculum's aim was to incorporate "the best features of the Bible institutes of the country."[35] Its student body

[33] Ernest B. Gordon, *Adoniram Judson Gordon: A Biography* (New York, 1896), chap. XX.

[34] *Christian Work and Evangelist,* July 3, 1909, p. 5.

[35] *First Annual,* 1914–15, pp. 8–14.

and denominational approval increased rapidly from year to year. In the autumn of 1919 the Illinois Baptist Convention voted to recognize the seminary as an official school and to commend it to the churches for financial and moral support. Thus the school became a standard institution representing conservative sentiment within the Northern Baptist Convention.

By the time that A. H. Strong had discredited new methods of Bible study, the faith of many Baptists in their schools was shaken. Shailer Mathews sent forth a tract during the World War suggesting that the output of premillennial literature might be an occasion for government inquiry to learn whether it had been aided by enemy sympathizers. He spiritualized the reality of Christ's second advent and discounted the genuineness of scholarship in Bible schools. This warning increased the skepticism of conservatives toward their progressive schools.[36] Professor E. D. Burton's large part in conceiving and instituting the Board of Promotion in connection with the New World Movement, gave a basis for the suspicion that modernist teachers were trying to control the church.

Early in 1919 the *Watchman-Examiner* published a series of editorials on "The Old and New Theologies" and raised a question of alarm, "What have we a right to expect of our seminaries?" Correspondents asked their presidents to inform Baptists what their attitudes were toward such doctrines as the inspiration and authority of the Scriptures, the Virgin birth, the Second Coming, and so on. The answers of Colgate, Newton,

[36] Tract by I. M. Haldeman, *Professor Shailer Mathews' Burlesque on the Second Coming of our Lord Jesus Christ.*

and the Kansas City schools (the other institutions remaining silent) were too elusive to satisfy William B. Riley. He issued a demand that all theological seminaries publish their statements of faith, intimating that these would reveal that some had departed absolutely from Baptist doctrine and that they should have to take the consequences.

At the first pre-convention conference on fundamentals held in Buffalo, J. C. Massee informed delegates that the teachings of many Baptist colleges and seminaries were disastrous to the faith of church youth. Riley preferred specific charges of heresy against school and teacher alike. At the urgent request of these agitators, the regular Convention appointed a committee to investigate the theological teaching of the schools. Meanwhile, the leader of the fundamentalist committee characterized the modernism in these institutions as a new tyrant, in the face of which he could give neither financial nor moral support to the denominational program. Pamphlets were circulated quoting from such authors as W. N. Clarke, Walter Rauschenbusch, Shailer Mathews, Henry C. Vedder, Gerald B. Smith and Shirley J. Case to illustrate how skeptical Baptist seminaries were.

The inquiring committee reported to the next Convention that "here and there doubtless is a teacher who has departed from the Baptist faith or has lost the Saviour's spirit," but that on the whole the schools were accomplishing a most commendable task. (The committee's recommendation, strictly Baptistic, has already been mentioned.) The effect of this serious study upon fundamentalists may be judged by the following excerpts from a letter which their executive sent to the trustees of Baptist schools:[37]

"We are sure that you are aware with us that the report has not allayed the suspicion against the schools in the minds of the great masses of our people. From every direction protests against the continuance of the present educational policy reach us. From every direction pastors and churches indicate that they will not contribute further to the support of our schools or even of our Board of Promotion as long as this policy continues. It is not too serious a statement to make that the very solidarity of our denominational life is put in jeopardy by the present situation in the schools. . . .

"We write therefore, as your brethren, to advise you: (1) That the agitation for correction in our schools will be continued; (2) To ask that you personally and your Board will cooperate with us in an effort to remove occasion for complaint and in safeguarding the essential faith and interests of our beloved denomination."

Although fundamentalists continued propaganda to shift theological education from its progressive trend to classical orthodoxy, the Buffalo-Des Moines incidents closed their efforts to accomplish a wholesale delivery through the medium of the Northern Baptist Convention. The democratic organization of Baptist work forbade corporate control of local institutions of learning. Therefore conservatives turned their reform interests to individual schools.

Soon a critical situation arose in fundamentalist loyalty to the Northern Baptist Theological Seminary.[38] Doctrinal changes of a less rigidly orthodox kind introduced

[37] Copy of the letter on the author's files.
[38] *Baptist Beacon,* April, 1925, pp. 12–14.

disharmony between the Bible Unionists and the more moderate conservatives. When the seminary gained full status in the Convention in 1919 it dropped the names of Riley and Straton from its Advisory Board and erased other marks of ultra-orthodoxy from its policy. At a Baptist Bible Union meeting in Moody Institute, the school was declared to be untrue to its charter. Seminary students arose and defended their alma mater's honor. During the debate that was provoked, it became clear that members of the faculty had been kindly disposed to the Divinity School of the University of Chicago. According to the Unionists, this fact alone proved the heresy of the school and merited its future distrust. Simultaneously, *The Baptist* was featuring Northern Seminary as a providentially-inspired institution meeting the needs of conservative Baptists.

As orthodox churchmen had repudiated the Divinity School in Chicago and founded Northern Seminary, like-minded men lost faith in Crozer Theological Seminary (located near Philadelphia) and organized Eastern Baptist Theological Seminary in 1925. F. M. Goodchild was elected chairman of the Board of Trustees and Charles T. Ball, a southern Baptist, was chosen as president. A doctrinal basis was made mandatory upon trustees and faculty alike. Within a few weeks Goodchild resigned from office because of the incompetence of the president; within a few months the latter withdrew on account of incompatibility within the faculty. Ball proceeded to found Eastern Baptist University in the same city, using the seminary's creed and several of its trustees to govern the new project. When A. K. deBlois became president of the seminary its theological test was moderated and its patronage in the Convention at large increased.

Since fundamentalists have found adequate means of preserving their theological traditions in newly-organized training schools,[39] the denomination has been free from problems involving scholastic tension. When the Baptist Bible Union took over Des Moines University this reactionary body ceased to interfere with the policy of regular church colleges; with a single exception: the 1928 Minnesota Baptist Convention, under William B. Riley's influence, discontinued its affiliation with Carleton College because of alleged Unitarian tendencies in the class-room. A basis of academic tolerance has been reached in the Northern Baptist Convention through a more democratic institutional representation of diverse theological views.

Fundamentalism had run its course when the Northern Baptist Convention met in Chicago in 1927. In preparation for this gathering the executive committee had created considerable harmony. Brougher's presidential address was characterized by a re-emphasis of the historic Baptist faith. The evangelistic note was held uppermost in all the proceedings. Such fundamentalists as could co-operate with liberals received deference in appointment to convention offices. Their party expressed satisfaction with the next year's program and announced that the Convention was returning to a safe and sane orthodoxy. As a matter of fact, con-

[39] In 1927 J. M. Dean organized the Western Baptist Theological Seminary at Portland, Oregon, for fundamentalist purposes.

servatism as a divisive movement was fading out rapidly in denominational life. So friendly had become representatives of liberal and conservative groups that the Chicago Ministers' Conference called upon Professor J. Heindrichs of Northern Seminary to present a paper on fundamentalist status in the Convention; the week following Dean Shailer Mathews set forth the modernist position; and at the third meeting the Conference devoted its entire time to the untrammelled discussion of both points of view.

A survey of the conflict of cultures within the Northern Baptist Convention reveals that participating groups were forced repeatedly to accept a give-and-take basis of social cooperation. The three fellowships that functioned somewhat independently during the most embarrassing days of the controversy became two; the moderate conservatives found their way back into regular channels of Convention service, or they associated with the independent interests of the Baptist Union. A more inclusive policy of evangelical toleration, recognizing divergent theological viewpoints, took expression in selective newspapers, pulpits, colleges and seminaries. The Convention learned to stress evangelism more deliberately, and to proportion the number of conservative and liberal ministers sent to the foreign field. Baptists have learned that their difficulties must be settled by a mutual regard for party differences rather than by the capitulation of one group out of regard for the will of the other. To this extent the exclusive policy of the fundamentalists was repudiated. The dual pride of the denomination, its congregational democracy and its Bible-centered faith, also proved to be its chief disturbances during the period of rapid religious change in America.

While a new harmony has been established by the recognition of certain basic desires of both types of Baptists, the Convention has inherited a more disintegrated structure than obtained when the New World Movement program was launched a decade ago. Besides, it has selected for the most part safe men rather than aggressive leadership to occupy positions of trust on denominational boards. Just here rests the church's present weakness; it has chosen rather liberal principles of evangelical procedure, but it does not have confidence in the men who represent those ideals to lead it forth.

CHAPTER SIX

NEO-CALVINISM IN THE PRESBYTERIAN CHURCH

THE Presbyterian Church is a creedal denomination subscribing to the most elaborate set of doctrines of any ecclesiastical body in America. Constitutionally it requires its presbyters to manage the judicial, legislative and administrative functions of the church according to a closely defined legal system. Since the General Assembly of 1870 this supreme judicatory of Presbyterianism has reserved the right to veto the election of professors to theological seminaries, after their appointment by seminary boards. These three distinctive principles of doctrinal authority, parliamentary polity and direct supervision of theological education, as they were articulated in the denomination, became the occasion of fundamentalism in the Presbyterian Church.

The pages of this church's history are marked with remnants of doctrinal controversy and ecclesiastical trials. A strong minority of conservatives were actively defending the old faith when *The Fundamentals* were published. Nearly one-quarter of the articles in these volumes were contributed by Calvinists. The echo of these documents was officially heard in the famous Five-Points [1] of doctrine adopted by the General Assembly in

[1] Adopted by the Niagara Bible Conference in 1895. See p. 34.

1910. This deliverance provided the church with an orthodox standard that was destined to delegate grave problems to Presbyterians. It read in part:[2]

> "In the present age of doubt . . . the fundamentals of faith and of evangelical Christianity are being assaulted. . . . The General Assembly . . . in the face of these facts, reaffirms adherence to the historic standards of Presbyterianism in the United States, as being the system of truth taught in the Holy Scriptures and to be followed in the future as in the past."

Then followed the statement (with considerable detail of explanation) of the five doctrines. In each case the affirmation was introduced by the words: "It is an essential doctrine of the Word of God and our standards . . . " The fundamentalist cause first voiced itself in this Assembly action. From this time forward the old school party sought means to turn the denomination's course back to the position of their forbears. Perhaps the most effective instruments in this endeavor were *The Presbyterian*, an unofficial paper published in Philadelphia, and its advisory body.

[1.] The Test of Theological Regularity

Every man entering the Presbyterian eldership takes two doctrinal vows: one, "Do you believe the Scriptures of the Old and New Testament to be the Word of God, the only infallible rule of faith and practice?"; the other, "Do you sincerely receive and adopt the confession of faith of this church (the Westminster Confession), as containing the system of doctrine taught in the Holy Scriptures?" Loyalty to these rules signified

[2] *Minutes*, 1910, p. 273.

an aggressive desire to reshape the world in conformity to the glory of God. Conservatives insisted upon literal belief in the Calvinist tenets, and liberals employed latitudinarian interpretation; in either case the clergy served a church in which the test of theological regularity prevailed.

By 1915 the apparent departure from Calvinism had become so marked that one hundred and fifty clergy presented to the church a "Back to the Fundamentals" statement.[8] After declaring for the essentiality of the Five-Points, it begged the ministers to preach them and advised churches "not to call any man save one who unreservedly and heartily accepts the great fundamentals herein enumerated." This announcement was signed by the moderator of the church and three ex-moderators. The next General Assembly reaffirmed its faith in the deliverance of 1910.

Orthodox Calvinism was strengthened further by the spread of Bible conferences during the World War. Evangelists William A. Sunday, J. W. Chapman, Professor B. B. Warfield, Mark A. Matthews and John F. Carson were leaders in the movement. The war mind stimulated reactionism. Some ministers did not hesitate to apply German epithets to liberals in an effort to check new thought. Matthews claimed that "wolves" had entered the pulpits, and, in an effort to arouse his comrades, declared that though "a pernicious activity of the heretic is bad, the criminal inactivity of the defender of the faith is a thousand times worse." General assemblies during the years of international strife advocated a strong patriotic and evangelistic program, and thus de-

[8] *The Presbyterian,* April 22, 1915.

terred the religious malcontents from registering official voice.

Forward-looking churchmen were successful in launching the New Era Movement idea at the 1918 General Assembly. A representative committee was chosen to draft a five-year program adequate to express Presbyterian opportunities following the world's armistice. Although *The Presbyterian* asked conservatives to lend their aid to this project, it warned that "the New Era must begin with and continue on the infallible Bible, or we sink with the Huns into the swamps of man's wisdom and speculation. . . ."[4]

The first New Era agency to suffer heretical charges was the foreign missionary enterprise. At a banquet of the Philadelphia Social Union, early in 1921, W. H. Griffith-Thomas, an Episcopalian clergyman and the guest speaker, remarked that many Presbyterian missionaries in China had broken with evangelicalism. His address and later comments were published in *The Presbyterian*.[5] This journal called for an investigation to determine whether churches should contribute money to missions.

Although Board officials tried to pacify disturbed minds, the Minneapolis Presbytery carried the inquiry to the Winona Lake General Assembly. The committee on foreign missions reported that they had discovered no theological irregularities among their Chinese leaders. However, a moderate liberal moved that the Board be instructed to "examine further into these reports (of heterodoxy) and, if necessary, to take such action as,

[4] Editorial, "The New Era Magazine," op. cit., Jan. 23, 1919.
[5] Feb. 10, 1921.

according to the form of government of the Presbyterian Church, the conditions may demand." The motion prevailed. This effort to keep the testing process within the Board's jurisdiction met with partial success. Distrust of progressives continued to spread through the denomination. The influential First Church, Pittsburgh, organized itself into a foreign missionary society to use its funds where the infallible Bible was believed.

Harry Emerson Fosdick's sermon, "Shall the Fundamentalists Win?"[6] was the signal for a thorough rally of conservatives. They considered that he had assaulted the doctrines of Presbyterianism. The orthodox journals carried contributed articles and editorials to claim the preacher's infidelity. *The Continent* suggested that *The Presbyterian* be fair with Fosdick; the latter replied by asking him to be fair with the church. *The Presbyterian Advance* tried to keep the peace by pointing out that the New York preacher had not criticized any person but "an attitude of intolerance, the very attitude frequently reproved by Jesus himself."[7] In October the Philadelphia Presbytery overtured the General Assembly requesting that the New York Presbytery require Fosdick to bring his preaching into conformity with Calvinist doctrine. The preacher was accused of disbelieving in the Virgin birth. If true, this was a denial of an essential truth of the church.

The doctrinal test was the subject of first concern at the Indianapolis General Assembly in 1923. Although the liberals elected their candidate to the

[6] For circumstances, see p. 70. The sermon was preached in May, 1922.

[7] Sept. 28, 1922, p. 3.

moderatorship (defeating William J. Bryan), the other party imposed on the church a legal definition of the Westminster Confession. The minority report of the committee on the "Fosdick case," was carried after five hours of debate (439 votes for, 359 against), reaffirming the declaration of 1910 and begging the Presbytery of New York to carry out the request stated in the Philadelphia overture.[8]

Liberal evangelicalism was not silenced by this decision. William P. Merrill immediately issued a protest which was signed by scores of sympathizers. He declared that ultra-conservatives were trying to put on the necks of progressives a doctrinal yoke which would never be tolerated. The First Presbyterian Church declined to accept Fosdick's resignation; the New York Presbytery neglected to discipline the congregation. On December 26th one hundred and fifty clergy conveyed their verdict directly to their ten thousand colleagues in a delivery called "An Affirmation." [9]

This Affirmation represented the viewpoint of the progressive party in Presbyterianism. It was "designed to safeguard the unity and liberty of the Presbyterian Church." Its signers accepted the Westminster Confession, though they disclaimed its infallibility. They rejected Scriptural authoritarianism, holding to the guidance of "the Spirit of God, speaking to the Christian believer." The five-point test of orthodoxy had no necessary counterpart in the Bible, and hence did not determine loyalty in the denomination. The General Assembly, in pronouncing a judgment against the New

[8] *Minutes,* 1923, p. 253.
[9] *The Presbyterian,* Jan. 17, 1924, pp. 6–8.

York church, had misused its powers as given in the book of discipline. The delivery closed by deploring the state of conflict among the brethren and calling for a comprehensive church, in which all disciples of Christ might share.

Every agent of fundamentalism replied to this statement. *The Princeton Theological Review* contained articles atacking the doctrine of biblical errancy as the Affirmation had stated it.[10] *The Presbyterian* pronounced its view of church law bolshevistic. The editor claimed that it rejected both revelation and formal reasoning as bases of authority and substituted "the individual subjective consciousness. . . . This . . . strikes at the very heart of Christianity, and advocates a new and antagonistic religion." It would be rather difficult to overstate the dexterity with which the conservatives planned the maintenance of fundamentalist control at the approaching General Assembly. The Denver and Philadelphia presbyteries petitioned the Assembly to act favorably on a resolution that only such men be appointed to church office or seminary faculty as held inviolable the five doctrines affirmed by the judicatory in 1910.

Two significant questions on matters of theological discipline were settled at the Grand Rapids General Assembly. In reference to doctrinal regularity in the church, the permanent judicial commission decided that until a definite interpretation of the Westminster Confession had become legal by the concurrent action of the assembly and presbyteries (and there was none),

[10] "The Testimony of the Scriptures to Their Own Trustworthiness," Samuel G. Craig, XXII, 2, p. 383 f.

the General Assembly had no power to use a doctrinal test with church elders.[11] One desire of the so-called Affirmationists was achieved by this pronouncement.

In the matter of Fosdick's relation to the Church, the judicial commission reported that a Baptist preacher in one of their pulpits was an anomaly and should not continue. The session of the First Church was to confer with Fosdick whether he chose to become a Presbyterian minister or, remaining a Baptist, to withdraw from the New York pulpit.[12] The Assembly confirmed the report, despite the fact that some Calvinists demanded more drastic action. Fosdick tendered his resignation immediately, declining to subscribe to the Confession because it would be for him "a violation of conscience and a moral surrender."[13] The church voted to retain his services until the following March.

Although fundamentalists elected a full quota of their leaders to vacant offices in the 1924 Assembly, they felt that their position was anything but stable in the denomination. Their leaders circularized the churches in December asking them to continue to meet the religious crisis with determined loyalty to the old faith. The Affirmationists met this appeal in a call "For Peace and Liberty,"[14] asking their people "to cherish the ideal of an inclusive Christian Church" and to unite in Kingdom endeavor.

The same group began a quiet campaign to elect Charles R. Erdman as a peace advocate to the moderatorship of the next Assembly. The Presbyterian Con-

[11] *Minutes,* 1924, pp. 197–199.
[12] *Ibid.,* p. 196.
[13] *Ibid.,* 1925, p. 79.
[14] *Christian Century,* Feb. 26, 1925, p. 293.

servatives' Association organized to undermine the faith of commissioners in Erdman, to advance the candidacy of a strict Calvinist, and to discipline the New York Presbytery for its tardiness in releasing Fosdick.[15] Progressive and fundamentalist commissioners met at Columbus in a clearly divided house. However, Erdman for moderator received the approval of a majority. Although he took immediate means to table all overtures treating difficulties in order to avoid Assembly schism, there was an irresistible demand to chasten the New York Presbytery.

The Fosdick case and the familiar policy of ordaining graduates of Union Seminary were too serious grievances for the fundamentalist minority to endure. This Presbytery had ordained recently two young men who refused to confirm belief in the Virgin birth of Christ. This dogma had been one of the Five-Point essentials. The cases were referred to the permanent judicial commission, which presented a ruling that the ultimate control in all matters of ordination rested with the General Assembly, and that it was necessary for all candidates to avow "a clear and positive" belief in the doctrines affirmed by the General Assembly in 1910 and reaffirmed in 1923. The commission chastened the New York Presbytery for ordaining youths who refused to believe in the Virgin birth, "no matter how amiable, educated, or talented (they) . . . may have been."[16]

There was no precedent for this decision in the history of the Presbyterian Church. It seemed so unfair that progressives sought immediate measures to abrogate the

[15] Editorial page, *Chicago Evening Post,* April 25, 1926.
[16] *Minutes,* 1925, p. 88.

statute. The situation between commissioners became so tense that Erdman yielded the chair to the vice-moderator and presented a resolution:

"That a Commission of fifteen members be appointed to study the present spiritual conditions of the Church and the causes making for unrest, and to report to the next General Assembly, to the end that purity, peace, unity and progress of the church may be assured."

The motion was carried and the Assembly concluded its business in comparative peace. The moderator appointed representatives of both schools of idealism to the commission, and defined its purpose to engage in a friendly investigation of general conditions and presbyterial powers and to advise constructive measures.

Meanwhile the New York Presbytery at its autumn meeting put a temporary ban on ordination proceedings. The Affirmationist group, who maintained headquarters in Auburn, New York, sent ten representatives to appear before the commission. They assured the members that there was room in Presbyterianism for ministers of varying theological views, providing that no one tried to retard the thinking of another. A company of one hundred younger ministers also petitioned the commission to consider a policy of doctrinal forbearance.

Following the 1925 General Assembly the fundamentalist cause showed signs of declining strength. *The Presbyterian,* unofficial spokesman for orthodoxy, lessened its efforts to preserve hyper-Calvinism. It turned its readers' attention to anti-evolutionism and other undenominational questions. When the moderator opened the next Assembly, in Baltimore, he decried bitterness and a divided church and asked for a sense of humor in discussing beliefs, over which there was necessarily a difference of opinion. Although a few extreme conservatives were irreconcilable and presented a factious leader for the office of moderator, William O. Thompson's election by a clear margin signalized the commissioners' desire for toleration in the church.

The reading of the report of the commission of fifteen occupied the one important place in court procedure.[17] This twelve thousand word document was a searching appeal for peace based upon complete confidence in the church. It defined five causes of unrest in the church:

> "(1) Such general movements as the Great War, the naturalistic and materialistic thought of the age. . . . (2) Causes coming down from our past history as a Church. (3) Diversity of view on constitutional and administrative questions. . . . (4) Doctrinal and theological differences. (5) Slander and misrepresentation."

The commission continued its study for another year and concluded its report at the next Assembly. It made one important recommendation.[18] The question as to what constituted the essence of the lengthy Westminster Confession had been raised repeatedly in previous years and had been answered in terms of the Five-Points by a popular vote of the Assembly. Fundamentalists used them as a test in several assemblies. The commission ruled that the history of the church did not reveal that the question of essential and necessary articles of faith had ever been settled. General assemblies had a right "to bear general witness to the corporate faith of the church" but they did so at a risk during times of con-

[17] *Minutes,* 1926, p. 63 f.
[18] *Ibid.,* 1927, p. 77 f.

troversy. When an assembly was not in danger of being gravely misunderstood, it might "declare broadly that an article is essential and necessary." However, Presbyterians should always remember that of greater authority than any general assembly was the Westminster Confession, of still greater authority was the Bible, and of greatest authority was Christ himself. As a matter of fact, the final answer in matters of belief was the "Word of God as the Holy Spirit speaks through it." The report was received and adopted.

Two traditions imbedded in the Westminster Confession were given specific articulation here, and one was declared of superior value. The appeal to inner and spiritual authority in deciding rules of faith received priority over the claims of literalistic Calvinism. In this declaration the ideal for which the Affirmationists had resolutely declared received ample justification.

[2.] THE GOVERNMENTAL POLICY OF THE CHURCH

The Presbyterian Church is managed by a republican form of government. Membership in presbytery and assembly, is divided equally between clergy and laymen. Men are elected to office in course or by reason of special fitness, and conduct the judiciary, legislative and administrative work of the denomination at large. When about to act in a judicial capacity, the moderator says, "it (the Assembly) is about to sit as a court of Jesus Christ." Undefined issues may be carried for solution from local presbytery to synod, and, if necessary, to general assembly, the supreme judicatory of the church. The court must abide by the Form of Government. A moderator presides over each session who is honored and obeyed as *primes inter pares*. The commissioners may consider their functions seriously as their credentials invite, or lightly, and serve as a rubber stamp to endorse such policies as boards and commissions recommend. The general assembly numbers about nine hundred members.

During the present century three governmental problems arose to disturb the peace of the church. The first centered in the differentiation of rights of presbytery and assembly in the settlement of points of ecclesiastical misunderstanding. Another was concerned with Board activities in administering service work. The third defined conditions within which Presbyterians could engage in interdenominational projects.

[a.] The Relative Rights of Assembly and Presbytery

For many years graduates of Union Theological Seminary had found it difficult to assure conservative examiners in the New York Presbytery that they were sound in the faith. Owing to the fact that liberal presbyters had a majority, candidates were ordained, however strongly the minority protested. The situation between these parties became so schismatic that an ordination ruling was requested at the 1915 General Assembly. A deliverance making strict Calvinistic doctrine prerequisite was almost unanimously adopted.[19]

At the next meeting of the New York Presbytery three Union men were licensed to preach. Certain members published a two-fold protest. The candidates refused to express their faith in the Virgin birth; and they reserved the right to set scriptural testimony aside in

19 "Report," *The Presbyterian*, June 3, 1915.

deference to the decisions of critical scholarship. Conservative sentiment in the matter was so strong throughout the country that several presbyteries petitioned the General Assembly to have the New York Presbytery disciplined for its misbehavior. Overture 26 took another view. It declared that it was discourteous, unchristian and subversive of proper discipline for one presbytery to pass judgment upon the ordination rules of another.

In unmistakable meaning the Assembly ruled to make personal commitment to the Five-Points essential to ordination. *The Continent* and liberal pulpits voiced their unqualified disapproval of this infringement upon the rights of local presbyteries. It was evident that the relative rights of the two administrative bodies had not been determined constitutionally; at this stage, however, the situation rested during the World War.

The Fosdick case revived the judicial issue in the church. The chief seat of fundamentalism, the Philadelphia Presbytery, petitioned the 1923 General Assembly to require the New York Presbytery to bring Fosdick's preaching into conformity with sound doctrine. Twenty-three clergy and elders in Philadelphia memorialized the Assembly protesting against their colleagues' appeal, for the reason that they did not consider it expedient to call attention to defects in a neighboring presbytery until their own presbytery was managed with more propriety. The Westchester Presbytery solicited the approaching Assembly to take no action on the Philadelphia overture, for the reason that it "deprecates the assumption of one presbytery in attempting to cause intervention of the General Assembly with another presbytery on the exercise of its presbyterial functions."

The Indianapolis General Assembly, controlled by fundamentalists, recognized the Philadelphia overture.[20] This sectional decision naturally intensified the breach between the parties to Presbyterian law. The conservative group and *The Presbyterian* became quite reactionary in their efforts to get supreme control of the church. They organized mass-meetings for the preservation of what they conceived as the time-honored ideals of Calvinism. "Far better an honest conflict than a dishonest peace or compromise," became their rallying slogan. They accused New York liberals of contempt and defiance of the General Assembly. The Fosdick committee in the New York Presbytery tried to moderate feeling by reporting to the latter body in its February meeting that the sermon "Shall the Fundamentalists Win?" did lead to contention, and the section dealing with the Virgin birth was "open to painful misconception and just objection." At this critical juncture the Affirmationists declared for constitutional liberty in the name of the Westminster Confession and the holy Scriptures.[21]

In judicial and legislative proceedings the progressive viewpoint prevailed at the Grand Rapids Assembly in 1924. As has already been mentioned,[22] the supreme court repudiated the right of a presbytery or a general assembly, acting alone, to impose an interpretation of the Westminster Confession upon ministers and elders, and it gave Fosdick an opportunity to choose freely

[20] See p. 103.
[21] See p. 103.
[22] See pp. 104–05.

whether he could become a regular Presbyterian or leave the First Church pulpit.

Constitutionally these dual decisions respecting allied questions were settled in keeping with the historic principles of Presbyterian law. Culturally the situation was otherwise. The law had been affected by liberal influence, but the administrators of the law were fundamentalists who were more concerned with doctrine than with legal orthodoxy. C. E. Macartney defined the main question before his communion as to "whether or not it has the intention and the courage to enforce its own mandates," but pressed the sectional interests of fundamentalism.[23] J. G. Machen cast discredit upon the ministry of the liberals, remarking that "the other (their) gospel has not saved a single soul." Fosdick's departure from the New York pulpit was accompanied by attacks upon him and the local presbytery. While liberal religious journals and secular magazines were sounding the praises of the preacher who kept such poise through the years of innuendo, the conservative press of the Presbyterian Church accused him of being discourteous, defiant and disorderly.[24] The Chester Presbytery overtured the General Assembly to exscind the Presbytery of New York from its fellowship and to appoint a committee to take over its property and form a new presbytery.

The pre-Assembly campaign (1925) of the Presbyterian Conservatives' Association [25] marked the last serious effort of fundamentalists to dictate terms of social

[23] "*The Presbyterian Church in Danger*," *Christian Work*, Mar. 14, 1925, pp. 340–41.
[24] Editorial, "Dr. Fosdick Departs With Noise," *The Presbyterian*, March 5, 1925, pp. 4–5.
[25] See pp. 105–06.

control to the church. Its news for release to the public press on April 25th deliberately misrepresented modernists' intentions. The editorial writer of the *Chicago Evening Post*[26] commented that the dispatch let "the cat out of the bag completely" (*i.e.* revealed its dual motives) when it tried to prejudice the case of the liberal candidate for moderator at Columbus. The next General Assembly broke all precedents in constitutional procedure and supported a decision on the matter of Assembly control of ministerial beliefs.[27] Progressive churchmen could not remain silent in the light of this action. A legal document prepared by progressive commissioners and presented to the Assembly in the form of a protest, pointed out that the ruling had violated many judiciary decisions in the history of the church.

Moderator Erdman's request for a peace commission to determine the basic conditions contributing to schism in the church,[28] marked the beginning of the end of this constitutional conflict between divisive and regular churchmen. Although the Baltimore Assembly was silenced by the comprehensive scope and challenge of the report as read, C. E. Macartney rose to object to a section which permitted one General Assembly to reverse the ruling of another. Obviously this was the last stand for strict ecclesiasticism. The speaker's brother rose and said, "I am for this report from cover to cover, not so much for what it says or does not say, as for the spirit that pervades it." This family difference con-

[26] April 25, 1925. Note also, "A Question of Ethics in Religious Propaganda," editorial in Portland *Telegram* (Oregon), as reprinted in *Christian Century*, May 28, 1925, p. 711.

[27] See p. 106.

[28] See p. 107.

tributed markedly to the liquidation of the reactionary movement. Then Mark A. Matthews spoke in favor of the commission and its findings; this militant fundamentalist of former days pleaded with his brethren for peace and unity! The cause of Presbyterian fundamentalism nearly collapsed with this unexpected generosity. A single "No" was registered against the report when the vote of acceptance was taken.

Macartney remained the only commanding leader to defend ultra-Calvinist law in the councils of the church. Two approaching episodes marked the decline of his influence. When he accepted an invitation from President Henry S. Coffin to address the students of Union Theological Seminary and preached a well-tempered sermon, he gave evidence that his uncompromising attitude had changed to one of toleration.[29] And when he retired from the center of denominational reactionism in Philadelphia and accepted a call to the First Church, Pittsburgh, he surrendered party control in a losing cause to assume a burdensome, though attractive, task in one of the great churches of the country.

The fundamentalists failed to develop a 1927 pre-Assembly campaign. However, one important legal judgment was reached; the court corrected the notably false impression regarding presbyterial powers of ordination made two years previously. It asserted that a local judicatory was competent to license and ordain men for the gospel ministry. Should a General Assembly desire to review a particular judgment, it must decide the merits of the case by the evidence in the presbytery's official record only, providing of course

[29] Sermon printed in *The Presbyterian*, Dec. 9, 1926, pp. 6–8.

that the lower court showed constitutional procedure. A fundamentalist effort to discipline the New York Presbytery at the 1928 Assembly, and thus contradict this decision, was voted down. The fundamentalists' repeated efforts to coerce the courts to settle legislative questions by a direct plea for loyalty to the standards of the church, rather than by recourse to ecclesiastical law, met with defeat.

[b.] The Administration of Church Boards

Early in 1919 the New Era Movement was introduced to the churches as a strong evangelistic, missionary, educational and financial program. Conservative and liberal papers joined in loyalty to the undertaking. Following the General Assembly the same year, at which commissioners criticised modernist tendencies, the Philadelphia periodical expressed doubt regarding the New Era scheme. It thought the election of a layman as moderator magnified the laity unduly and threatened to commercialize the church. Besides, the contrast between the annual financial and evangelistic reports was an evidence of unfavorable change in ideals. A year later a more obvious disapproval of the Movement was apparent. In transferring big business methods to the church, it was said that secularism was displacing spiritual standards. To some it appeared that the missionary forces were attempting to democratize oriental governments rather than to bring sinners into personal relation with Christ. A few months later Griffith-Thomas added fuel to the fire of discontent.[30]

The Continent and *The Presbyterian Advance* came

[30] See p. 101.

to the defense of the missionaries and accused *The Presbyterian* of exercising bad faith. The first paper asserted that the Episcopalian's remarks were based on sheer inference, and the second called his charges reckless, and described his attitude as "a recrudescence largely due to the disturbed conditions of the past few years."

When the General Assembly convened at Winona Lake in 1921 the New Era program commended itself to the progressives only.[31] This Assembly had received fifteen hundred overtures from the presbyteries signifying unprecedented restlessness throughout the church. The Board of Foreign Missions issued a pamphlet to the churches on the subject of evangelism in an effort to allay suspicion. The circular began, "it has been claimed by some, even the friends of missions, that purely evangelistic work is being side-tracked on the mission field for the more attractive, perhaps medical, higher educational, social and other forms of work." The Philadelphia weekly, quoting this remark, declared it was unequivocably "true. . . . These secretaries attempt to cover this question by widening the definition of evangelistic work so as to include relief, education and industrial work." In *The Princeton Theological Review* Griffith-Thomas urged churches to compel their Boards to send out only such men as were sound in the essentials of Christianity.

The attention of the Des Moines Assembly was focused upon the reorganization of the denomination's Boards. The report of a special committee called for the consolidation of thirteen of them into four adminis-

[31] See p. 101.

trative bodies within a General Council; the plan was received at the first hearing and was approved despite much dissatisfaction. A year later, when final action was taken, the report was adopted by a majority of two only. Immediately men claimed that the new plan permitted overcentralization, and accused the secretariat of expunging the liberties of the church. The Presbyterian Church had contracted over a million dollars of debt owing to widespread distrust in its service agencies.

In the autumn the Philadelphia Presbytery reopened the foreign missionary dilemma. It threatened to memorialize the General Assembly to make the Five-Point statement binding upon all persons holding office under the Mission Board or General Council. Robert Dick Wilson had just returned from five months of Bible conferences in the Orient. He found fault with the secretaries for entering into entangling alliances with evangelicals of dissimilar faith. He saw no reason why the Board should oppose its missionaries joining the Bible Union of China, for Calvinists and the Union held almost identical confessions of faith.

When the chief offices of the church passed into the control of the fundamentalists at Grand Rapids,[32] William P. Merrill was refused re-election to the Foreign Mission Board, an office which he had held many years and with great devotion. Men "in every way loyal to the Bible and the standards of the church" were chosen to fill vacancies on the Board. The General Assembly accepted a resolution ordering the Foreign Mission Board to withdraw support from oriental union schools which taught doctrines other than those contained in the

[32] See p. 105.

Westminster Confession. The New Era Movement closed its five-year term and called forth from the editor of *The Presbyterian* the following remarks: "Thus another of the expensive ephemeral movements which have consumed the Church's time, strength and money, and revealed their inherent weakness and opposition to sound principles, has passed away, leaving a large legacy of debt." [33]

Though the progressive forces were silenced in the administrative work of the Boards, they were determined not to submit to an exclusively fundamentalist purpose. Leaders in pulpit and press worked to keep church loyalty from suffering sectional siege. A national Presbyterian conference was called in Philadelphia in February to check divisiveness and to commend the cause of the General Council; a similar meeting was held in Chicago. A strenuous effort was made to engage every local congregation in an evangelistic ministry and a financial campaign. This modern high-power method of denominational work did not commend itself to conservatives. For them, it lacked the spiritual element that used to characterize such meetings. For that reason a strong minority of churchmen looked with disfavor upon the work of the Council and accused it of inefficiency and imperialism.

The denominational decision at the next General Assembly [34] also shifted in measure the leadership of the Boards and introduced a more constructive program. A year later at Baltimore the Assembly adopted a recommendation establishing a modified form of rotary system

[33] Editorial, June 5, 1924, p. 12.
[34] See p. 106.

for membership on the Boards. Since then no acute problems in the administrative work of the denomination have developed.

[c.] Inter-Denominational Procedure

Constitutionally there has never been any barrier to prohibit Presbyterians from entering into close working relations with other evangelical denominations. The 1918 General Assembly appointed a committee to consult such churches as to possibilities of organic union. At the same time this body voted to assume a shared responsibility in the Inter-Church World Movement.

In 1920 the Committee on the Plan for Organic Union for Evangelical Churches in U. S. A. (composed of appointees of twenty-three different denominations) made its findings public. The subject was debated keenly at the Philadelphia General Assembly. Though this body approved tentatively the recommendations of the Plan, controversy had become rife within the denomination and one presbytery after another rejected the proposed union. The next General Assembly abandoned it.

Fundamentalist influence was also determinative in the Presbyterian attitude toward the Inter-Church Movement. Early in 1919 the Philadelphia journal began to speak of the organization as a superman and as contrary to apostolic ideals. Certain delegates to the General Assembly considered the Movement irregular and begged their associates to join them in its abrupt dismissal. The Assembly compromised by voting to support the cause only as it chose to function through strictly evangelical churches. Criticism continued. The Movement was called an unowned child, born out of wedlock, without legal right to name or existence. A stirring controversy punctuated the report of the commission on the Inter-Church Movement at the Philadelphia Assembly. It was recommended that the Presbyterian Church terminate its relationship with the said organization, but finally voted that the matter be left to the executive commission of the Assembly for further consideration. The Movement collapsed in the autumn for want of adequate finances.

A fundamentalist esprit-de-corps developed across denominational lines soon after the World War. There was evidence of this in the editorial columns of *The Presbyterian* in 1919. Men reacted against the Y. M. C. A., the Child-Labor Amendment, prohibition, evolution, but reinforced the interests of Bible conferences and Bible schools. William J. Bryan and the church's evangelists became spokesmen for interdenominational phases of orthodoxy.

Bryan's influence in Presbyterianism was undoubtedly great. Besides his party interests, he injected nonecclesiastical elements into the controversy.[35] His antievolution gospel (late 1922) was made the campaign issue for a restriction in collegiate policy at the Indianapolis Assembly. As a matter of fact, the dogma of evolution was beginning to supplant more strictly Presbyterian subjects and furnished one of the clearest indications of the retirement of fundamentalism from the Presbyterian Church.

[35] *The Presbyterian,* May 31, 1923, p. 5.

[3.] The Limited Freedom of Theological Schools

When the Old and New School Presbyterians reunited in 1870 the church took the prerogative to control the election of professors in theological schools with a view to protecting the faith. Thereafter a denominational seminary could appoint teachers, but the General Assembly had the power to veto the appointment.

Union Theological Seminary caused orthodox Calvinists great concern during the nineties. The stone of stumbling was the question of the errancy of the Bible. The Briggs case went to the church courts and eventuated in the Assembly suspending him from the office of a minister because it was alleged that he had violated the ordination vow. A significant minority of commissioners protested against the decision of the church's judicatory and announced their disbelief in the inerrancy of the original autographs of Scripture. Union Seminary rescinded the compact of 1870 and became legally a free school in 1893.

The doctrine of an infallible Bible would not remain intact. Liberals in seminary and pulpit were teaching another view. The 1894 General Assembly made an example of Henry Preserved Smith of the Union faculty when it unfrocked him as a Presbyterian minister.[36] Five years later the Assembly gave A. C. McGiffert of the same faculty the choice to reconsider questionable views set forth in a lately published volume, or peacefully to withdraw from the Presbyterian ministry. He asked that his name be removed from the roll of the New

[36] Henry Preserved Smith, *The Heretic's Defense* (New York, 1926).

York Presbytery;[37] the request was granted, and the theological school was saved from further discipline.

Union Seminary embarrassed conservatives in the New York Presbytery. Its graduates did not give ordaining examiners the assurance that they were fit to carry forward Presbyterian traditions. The matter was brought to the attention of the General Assembly in 1911 and the issues between the liberal school and local conservative presbyters were debated for several successive years. The 1915 General Assembly received a committee's report bearing on the denominational status of the institution of learning. Henceforth this school "may not, in the opinion of your committee, introduce into the curriculum subjects and teachings antagonistic to or subversive of such doctrinal basis (the Westminster Confession)." The Assembly acted favorably upon the report,[38] though it had no constitutional power to do so.[39]

The lack of confidence which the signers of the Back to the Fundamentals statement[40] and the General Assembly evinced, led the Seminary to publish "A Statement" expressing its view of the doctrinal situation. It contradicted the claims of the Assembly's action and maintained that the charter of the institution granted it full liberty to change the type of its teaching. Much to the disturbance of the conservative party, *The Continent* made claims that Union was a real Presbyterian school. The Philadelphia journal interpreted the pamphlet, first, as an effort on the part of the Board to

[37] His letter printed in *The Independent,* April 19, 1900, pp. 970–71.
[38] See p. 110.
[39] See pp. 115–16.
[40] See p. 100.

tell the General Assembly the nature of Presbyterianism; and second, as a defense of Ritschlianism, a theology that substituted subjective experience for the authority of the Book, and hence "one with the teachings of Thomas Paine and Robert Ingersoll."[41]

During the World War, when German destructivism in the political state and liberal thinking in theological circles were associated in conservative minds, fundamentalists issued their protest against signs of the new learning in every seminary.[42] Professors Youtz and Crelman of Auburn Seminary were placed in a class with the most heretical in Union. The orthodoxy of McCormick Theological Seminary was questioned when it elected John H. Boyd to its faculty. Only Princeton, Lane and Omaha theological seminaries were catalogued as loyal to the historic faith.

When William J. Bryan raised the evolutionary question, many Presbyterians were prepared to accept his gospel and to discipline church schools. He carried the matter to the floor of 1923 General Assembly and proposed a ruling to prohibit funds from falling into the hands of institutions that taught "either Darwinism or any other evolutionary hypothesis that links men in blood relationship with any other forms of life." The orator adduced biblical proof-texts to defend his thesis. The men who taught evolution were *the* disturbers of the Presbyterian peace. The Assembly tried to table the resolution. After three hours of spirited debate a substitute position was drafted, requiring test cases to

[41] Editorial, Nov. 25, 1915, p. 6.

[42] As an illustration, editorial, *The Presbyterian*, Nov. 22, 1917, p. 4.

determine whether a school was teaching "a materialistic philosophy of life."[43]

When the fundamentalist controversy in the Presbyterian Church was at its height, Union Seminary (the most liberal school) passed out of the focus of interest and Princeton Seminary (the most conservative) took its place. This school suffered from disharmony within the faculty. J. G. Machen championed militant orthodoxy, and Charles R. Erdman was the progressive party's candidate for moderator. During the pre-election campaign Machen had shown pronounced partiality toward the fundamentalist candidate.[44] Erdman wrote *The Presbyterian* that he was not aware of any departure from the faith on the part of seminary instructors, but that he was painfully conscious of a heresy of the spirit within the faculty, and he made a cloaked reference to Machen as the source of the trouble. This led the accused to answer that there was a very serious doctrinal difference betwen him and Erdman.

Conflicting student policies within Princeton Seminary on matters of sound doctrine intensified the problem throughout the church. Machen encouraged the student body to promote a fellowship within conservative seminaries, while Erdman, official student advisor, discouraged the schismatic movement.[45] President J. Ross Stevenson supported the latter's judgment. Under

[43] *Minutes,* 1923, p. 213.

[44] Subsequently rather strained relations developed between the two men, when Erdman succeeded Machen as preacher in the First Presbyterian Church, Princeton, in January, 1925.

[45] Fred Eastman, "Disgracing Princeton Seminary," *Christian Work,* April 19, 1925, p. 486.

the influence of Machen, the student government voted to dismiss Erdman from his time-honored position of faculty counsellor and proceeded to form a "League of Evangelical Students." This action was reported to the denomination by the fundamentalist press as a striking evidence of the superior leadership of Machen in the seminary, and as a prophecy of the Presbyterian trend in theological circles.

The situation came to a climax in the Baltimore Assembly when it was recommended that this body approve the appointment of Machen to the Stuart Jessup Chair of Apologetics and Christian Ethics at Princeton. Not a few commissioners distrusted the leadership of this militant man. They had observed his appeal to crowd psychology in his use of the subtleties of Calvinistic logic. They had witnessed his public stand against the Eighteenth Amendment, and had read his uncharitable remarks about his colleagues. One of the strong men of the denomination accused the instructor of displaying "temperamental idiosyncrasies" and moved that his conduct in Princeton be investigated. The Assembly appointed a committee to make a sympathetic study of the conditions affecting Princeton Seminary; in the meantime it would refrain from approving or disapproving Machen's election.

This commission recommended to the 1927 Assembly that the plan of seminary administration be reorganized to permit of one board of governors rather than two. The difficulty within the faculty had introduced corresponding differences between the Board of Trustees and the Board of Directors, with consequent embarrassment in governmental functions. The liberal church press and the Affirmationists favored the recommendation but a strong opposition resisted. Another committee was appointed to make further study. Meanwhile the Assembly refused to confirm the elections of Machen to the Chair of Apologetics or of O. T. Allis to the Chair of Old Testament Literature.

The Princeton problem was a constant topic of controversy throughout the Presbyterian Church during 1927–28. A Princeton Committee of One Thousand presented a lengthy petition to the Tulsa General Assembly discouraging the proposed plan for reorganization of the seminary's boards. Major and minor reports were presented by the investigating committee. The major one constituted forty closely printed pages setting forth a proposed amendment to the charter of the seminary, a proposed new plan of organization, and other recommendations. The General Assembly did not feel there was sufficient unanimity of opinion to warrant acting directly upon the report. It voted to continue the committee another year and to charge the Board of Directors of Princeton to compose the difficulties within the seminary.

Notwithstanding the Assembly's expressed wish for silence on the controverted subject, the editor of *The Presbyterian* declared for a Simon-pure Calvinist school at Princeton.[46] He witnessed in the proposed plan an effort of modernists to shift Princeton from its historic position both doctrinally and administratively. This seminary could never represent the theological interest

[46] "The Majority Report of the Committee of Eleven on Princeton Seminary: Its Misinformation, Its Misunderstandings, Its Legal Impossibilities, and Its Unwisdom," March 7, 1929, pp. 3–15.

of the whole church, as its president had insisted. The school had always been committed to the "unmodified Calvinism of the Westminster Confession." If any change in policy or government were voted by the Assembly, his party would immediately resort to litigation in the civil courts of New Jersey. This article represented the position of the Princeton Committee of One Thousand.

At the 1929 General Assembly the commissioners voted to accept the majority report submitted a year previously. Machen and his supporters threatened to withdraw from Princeton and to inaugurate a school which would be true to the ideals of historic Calvinism, a threat he has since carried out in the city of Philadelphia.[47] Associated with him on the teaching staff are three former members of the Princeton faculty. Meanwhile the New Jersey institution has been peacefully clearing up its administrative problems.

A conflict of theological ideals in the Presbyterian Church is a rather serious matter. Its members rest the cause of Christianity upon the Bible and certain basic convictions which form the foundations for a highly important superstructure of religious beliefs, the Westminster Confession. It was natural that the new learning should lead some men to question the literal veracity of the Confession, and other men to protest out of loyalty to traditions.

The first dogma to suffer questioning was the inerrancy of the Scriptures. For a half century this subject troubled the New York Presbytery, and indirectly

[47] The new school is known as the Westminster Theological Seminary.

the whole church. In 1910 the conservatives' problem shifted from the Bible as a book to such beliefs about it as were conceived to be fundamental to the Calvinistic system. While liberals held to a latitudinarian interpretation of church ideals, conservatives chose Five Points as essential. They sought to apply these as a rigid test in seminary, at ordination and on official occasions of denominational action, in an effort to check theological irregularity. In 1910, 1915, 1916, 1923, 1925 the General Assembly voted to make conformity to them binding upon the Presbyterian ministry. They succeeded somewhat in compelling the church to resist change and to preserve "the truth once for all delivered to the saints."

The controversy reached a climax in 1925. When the fundamentalists were determined to regulate Presbyterianism, the Affirmationists claimed their right to the constitutional liberties which their faith had bequeathed them. The latter group began a steering campaign in the councils of the church. (It should be noted that the fundamentalist problem was forced completely at this juncture from theological questions to the issue of ecclesiastical law.) The defenders of the faith attempted to establish their rules without due regard for the processes of parliamentary procedure. One presbytery could not meddle in the affairs of another, according to the Discipline of the church and the insistence of the Affirmationists. The same standards forbade a general assembly coercing a local judicatory to do its bidding under any circumstance, as the fundamentalists had attempted. Thus the judicial commission ruled, and its rulings represented the supreme law of the church. The fundamentalists' cause lost in the courts of the church for the reason that its sponsors depended upon an appeal to loyalty to historic traditions at the expense of pursuing proper legal methods. Since 1925 the progressive group, as constitutionalists, have inspired the religious ideals of the church.

The widespread appeal for peace in 1925 was another important factor determining a change in Presbyterianism. Lay people had become weary of prolonged controversy. The Affirmationists' request and the motion for a "peace" commission to make a careful study of conditions throughout the church met with hearty responses. The commission's reports in 1926 and 1927 expressed confidence in the spiritual integrity of the Presbyterian Church and neglected entirely any doctrinal definitions. A pre-Assembly conference on evangelism prepared the atmosphere for the latter meeting. Robert E. Speer was the undisputed choice for moderator; his stirring inspirational address on the closing day on the mission of the Cross added to the healing ministry. The center of gravity in controversial questions had shifted entirely from the fundamentalist desire to control the whole denomination to a militant group's effort to manage Princeton Seminary.

It is not surprising that Princeton should have become a centre of siege for the fundamentalist party. This group witnessed all the other important seminaries adopting the heritage of the new learning. They knew that the perpetuation of the old faith depended upon their possession of this historic school. That right having been denied them by the 1929 General Assembly, a few irreconcilables have chosen to continue their testimony through an independent theological training school. With this resolution of conflicting ideals the problems that menaced the well-being of the denomination for decades have been shifted from its centre to its circumference.

CHAPTER SEVEN

THE "RESTORATION MOVEMENT" IN THE DISCIPLES' DENOMINATION

OVER a century ago in western Pennsylvania, a group of devout people retired from the Baptist and Presbyterian denominations to form a fellowship in quest of primitive Christianity. They harked back to the simple gospel of Jesus as found in the New Testament, and called themselves His "disciples." Their corporate effort they designated the restoration movement; it was a plea to restore to the world the unity of the church as they conceived it. The great commission summed up the will of Christ: to disciple all people and to immerse all Christians in the name of the Trinity. Both sinners and misguided sectarians needed this full evangel. To neglect the baptismal prerequisite to church membership was tantamount to disloyalty to the Son of God and a signal of incompleteness in His communion of the redeemed. With such incentives "churches of Christ" were established, and their common ideals served by a loosely organized Convention of such churches. Strongly class-conscious, this missionary cult grew rapidly in the open-country and small-town areas of the Mississippi valley. About their distinctives a serious conflict has gravitated in recent years.

Towards the close of the last century some Disciples

began to stress Christian unity above "restoration" in their ministry. They substituted the values of progressive thought for the sectional claims of a literal biblicism. In 1896 the influential Aetna Street Church, Cleveland, proposed an open-membership plan for the reception of unimmersed believers. The same year a select fellowship, called the Campbell Institute, was organized: "These men were drawn together by their common experience of having felt the impact of the larger world of culture upon their religious inheritance."[1] Through the medium of the Disciple Divinity House, located at the University of Chicago, fearless teachers initiated the critical study of the Bible. The *Christian Century* and the *Christian Evangelist*,[2] weekly papers, exercised a provocative influence for liberation in the church.

The basic demands of the restoration movement preserved a vigorous conservative testimony within the denomination. The *Christian Standard*, a weekly published in Cincinnati, became its organizing herald. A generation ago this organ began to call attention to church irregularities and to disagree with the Chicago weekly in interpreting Disciple policy.[3] Periodic doctrinal congresses were instituted at which churchmen discussed questions pertaining to biblical criticism, open-membership and mission compromise with so-called sects, which interrupted the peace of the denomination.

[1] H. L. Willett (editor), *Progress* (Chicago, 1917), p. 37.

[2] The author regrets that he has not had access to the files of the *Christian Evangelist* in the preparation of this study. Its editor, James Harvey Garrison, exercised an important moderating influence throughout the church for a quarter of a century. *Christian Century*, Jan. 28, 1931, pp. 128 f.

[3] *e.g.*, The Jordan and Sarvis missionary incidents.

In 1916 the Des Moines Convention appointed a committee of five to confer with representatives of the church's societies, boards and journals, with the hope of establishing better understanding between contending parties. The Disciple household was clearly divided.

[1.] The Pattern of Primitive Christianity

The commanding purpose of Disciples had been to reinstate primitive Christianity in an American fellowship. The pattern was found in the New Testament. However, as students examined the Scriptures historically, they discovered that there was no approved plan, but a variety of experiments. Besides, as they compared their plea with the position of other sects they learned that ideals that separated communions were not as important as those that related them. Progressives began to teach a socially-conditioned Bible and to practise comity with leaders of other denominations. Orthodox members disclaimed compromise with sects and defended the dogma of biblical infallibility.

Among the first centers of controversy were Transylvania College of Arts and the School of the Bible, located in Lexington, Kentucky. These schools had pursued a conservative policy until the coming of President Crossfield. In 1916 the *Christian Standard* charged that they had modernized the Scriptures and destroyed Disciple testimony. The editor declared that the so-called new theology led youth to assume a better-educated-than-thou attitude toward the older clergy and a skeptical view of the restoration movement. Although the Kentucky schools issued a statement declaring their loyalty to Disciple standards, many senior ministers discounted the trustworthiness of their witness. The local state Convention became divided over the question. The uncompromising party became a self-appointed Christian Bible College League, which defined its purpose to recover the College of the Bible from the control of destructive critics and to guard the traditions in all Disciple colleges.

While the League was fostering a sectional campaign in churches, progressive leaders conceived the advisability of merging Disciple agencies into the United Christian Missionary Society. Obviously this anticipated departure from the historic method of voluntaryism was interpreted by some as giving centralization of power to liberals and putting politics into the conventions. One hundred and eighty-three men announced a "Call" for serious action on behalf of time-honored principles. It was delivered to the churches in advance of the general Convention (at St. Louis) and read in part as follows:[4]

"That there is in the brotherhood of the Disciples of Christ a well-intrenched propaganda to encourage unsound teaching in our colleges, and to force upon our congregations the 'open-membership' plan; no one who has kept up with events can doubt. . . .

"Our program at St. Louis will have on it no place for 'compromise' or 'diplomacy'. . . . We shall plan to meet in St. Louis at a common rendezvous the day before the Convention begins, to plan the campaign and should the plan for which we stand be defeated on the Convention floor, we shall call a meeting and confer respecting a future policy."

The conventions were cancelled owing to the influenza epidemic. The Call served its purpose, however, for it

[4] *Christian Standard,* Sept. 21, 1918.

precipitated a general protest against progressivism. The protestants called a pre-convention Congress in Cincinnati the next year, to consider advisable action. This city was the strong center of *Christian Standard* activity. Literally hundreds of clergy and laity subscribed to the meeting. The leading figures were Russell Errett, Z. T. Sweeney, K. D. Kershner and W. N. Briney. A truculent temper marked the proceedings. The resolutions drawn up included a rather thorough review of party criticisms.[5] The group reasserted its faith in the plea for the restoration of the New Testament church, and condemned the open-membership principle and the substitution of "human creeds" for "the simple creed of the New Testament." When the controverted subjects were introduced at the regular Convention scenes of indecorum followed. Missionary secretaries were forced to answer publicly to inquisitive doctrinal questions.

Later the resolution committee presented a report to the Convention bearing on the problems of party conflict.[6] The framers took care to preserve the only reasonable basis of authority in such a democratic body as the Disciples, neglected the appeal to ecclesiastical censure which the orthodox party demanded, and enunciated the right of local autonomy in Disciple churches. They also denied the validity of a creedal test in their communion.

During the following year restorationists centered their criticism upon the United Christian Missionary Society with a view to arresting the practice of open-

[5] *Christian Standard,* Oct. 25, 1919, pp. 16–17.

[6] *Ibid.,* p. 6.

membership on Chinese mission fields. Frequent articles in the *Christian Standard* declared the unwarranted departures that missionaries had taken. The Society circulated an irenic letter hoping to mollify the disturbed party, but they were unsatisfied and proceeded to make the baptismal question the touchstone of the gospel at the St. Louis Convention. A resolution to enforce a strict doctrinal test was defeated and a modified one adopted. According to this Medbury ruling, the executive committee was not to approve "of the advocacy or practice of open-membership among the missionaries or mission stations supported by the foreign society." This position necessitated Chinese conformity to American orthodoxy; it also gave the impression that the home churches were all close immersionists.

Frank Garrett, secretary of the Chinese work, was present at the 1921 Convention to plead the injustice of the resolution. The delegates rescinded their action of the previous year by a vote of four to one. The restorationists were so dissatisfied with this action that they convened in Louisville and instituted the New Testament Tract Society to carry forward their divisive missionary purpose. The important First Church, Canton, Ohio, voted to withdraw its financial support from the United Society until it committed itself doctrinally to the necessity of baptism by immersion. Other churches followed this example.

This move so alarmed the officials of the United Society that the Board compromised with the conservatives in order to safeguard their program. They adopted a creedal formula, signed it themselves and sent it forth to the missionaries for their signature. Meanwhile, the

Tract Society began to issue pamphlets setting forth denominational disorders and the essentials of the New Testament Church. At the same time the Campbell Institute announced a tractarian movement in behalf of progressive Christianity. The one sponsored a Congress for malcontents and the other a forward-looking program for the regular Convention. The influence of congress sentiment upon the 1922 convention policy was so strong that the United Society continued its doctrinal test, despite the efforts of the liberal wing to the contrary. A Sweeney resolution recapitulated the principle formerly in force in the Medbury statement.[7] The First Church, Canton, immediately reversed its plan and voted to do some of its missionary work through the United Society.

The restorationists did not feel that their ideals would be completely safeguarded until the Society was dissolved into its constituent agencies. This action would unseat the progressive secretaries. The *Christian Standard* used the testimony of a reactionary evangelist to give a history of the Society's foreign service as an illustration of its repeated failure to keep faith with the historic plea. This weekly encouraged the development of home missionary projects in direct contradistinction to the regularly organized work of the Society. The divisionist party had won such recognition in the churches that it gave only passing attention to the Colorado Springs Convention in 1923. The liberals carried forward a non-committal (doctrinal) program until a year later when they insisted upon attempting a reconciliation with the other group. In "a sincere and prayer-

[7] Quoted in *Christian Standard*, Sept. 14, 1922, p. 1138.

ful attempt to avert a breach which threatens to open in our holy cause," a group of twelve men representing both parties in the conflict deliberated and brought forth the following resolution, which was duly presented to the next Convention and adopted:[8]

"Whereas, A serious misunderstanding has arisen between the management of the United Christian Missionary Society and many brethren and churches who oppose its members . . . therefore,

"Be it resolved, That a committee of five brethren, all of whom shall be well-known for their loyalty to our organized work, and also the cause of New Testament Christianity, shall be appointed by the president of this Convention to act as a peace conference committee. . . ."

Orthodox extremists were quick to hold up this overture to ridicule: it permitted of a packed committee which would favor the will of the Society. The steering committee changed the resolution to read that two members should represent the agencies, two "the brethren who disagree with them," and the fifth, the appointee of the executive committee of the Convention. Notwithstanding this cordial effort to work harmony in the denomination, the *Christian Standard* refused point-blank to co-operate with the perpetuated missionary society. On the contrary, it assembled six hundred associates in December and organized an independent service agency, called "the Christian Restoration Association."

Not content with its strong constructive program to redoctrinate the brethren in the fundamentals of the faith, this fellowship kept up a constant criticism of the

[8] *Christian Standard,* Nov. 15, 1924, p. 9.

official program of the Convention. Five representatives, meeting with the Convention committee, recommended that the Oklahoma City Convention retract in 1925, and presented for its consideration a long and creed-ridden set of resolutions. After five and a half hours of debate, the Convention voted to favor the proposals. These included a recall of 'open-membership' missionaries, the appointment of a commission to investigate foreign missions, and other claims.[9]

The Board of Managers of the Society went into conference immediately to put an official interpretation upon the document. One resolution provided that no person could be employed by the United Christian Missionary Society who had committed himself to belief in the reception of unimmersed persons into church membership. The Board interpreted the expression 'committed to belief in' as "not intended to invade the right of private judgment, but only to apply to such an open agitation as would prove divisive."[10]

This commitment was considered by forward-looking Disciples as the most threatening move to defeat progressivism in the church's history. Fifty of their number convened in Columbus to discuss the situation. They insisted on the historic right of religious liberty, and set out to enlist all free Disciples in a crusade to interpret the New Testament and God's will for themselves, and to revoke the coercive laws. Burris A. Jenkins founded a paper, *The Christian,* to give publicity to their ideals. The other faction met in midsummer, appointed a committee on future action, and announced

[9] *Christian Standard,* Oct. 24, 1925, p. 1.
[10] *Christian Century,* Dec. 17, 1925.

a pre-convention Congress at Memphis to meet a crisis within the communion.

The commission investigating missionary work in the Orient published their report in a typewritten document of thirty-one pages. They did not find evidence of non-immersionist practice and commended the policy of the United Society. The *Christian Standard* questioned the veracity of the report, as did the speakers at the restorationist congress. These traditionalists made a supreme effort to possess the organized work of the Disciples at the convention which followed. When the mission report was introduced the session became panicky. The inquisitors did their best to break down the value of the commission's evidence and to disqualify its personnel. Nevertheless, the Convention sustained the report by a four-to-one vote. General distrust in the position of the divisionists broke their morale for the remaining sessions. They retired from the Convention quite disheartened for the well-being of the church at large. The Oklahoma creedal statement, as interpreted by the Board of Managers, was reaffirmed by the Society in a vain effort to preserve inter-sectional harmony.

Since this occasion the orthodox party has pursued their separate interests through the channel of the Christian Restoration Association and the regional congresses which their committee on future action have sponsored. The committee arranged a rally of national dimensions at Indianapolis the following October. It was known as the first North American Christian Convention and was patronized widely. The changed situation had driven the speakers to doctrinal disputation; they defended the Deity of Christ, the integrity of the Scriptures, New Testament baptism and similar topics.

These emphases marked a notable departure in Disciple policy on the part of the restorationists. They found a basis for unbroken peace and fellowship by retiring from the denominational program which conditions in recent years had made necessary, and by rededicating their lives to the elemental truths of primitive Christianity. The service phase of their cause was cared for through the ten delegated bodies within the divisive Christian Restoration Association. This action has apparently given the conservatives adequate opportunity for self-expression and the perpetuation of their orthodox faith.

[2.] The Democratic Method of Church Procedure

In 1917 the Kansas City Convention of Disciples adopted a constitution and provided for free democratic procedure in the denomination's work.[11] Rather than an authoritative agency, the Convention served as a corporate influence throughout the churches and as an official clearing-house for Disciple business. Such members of churches as attended and enrolled at the Convention compose the annual assembly.

This more business-like policy was sponsored chiefly by men who were Campbell Institute members. Naturally also executive leadership was drawn from their ranks. The *Christian Standard* party believed that this was a departure from apostolic practice and a copy of humanly-devised denominationalism. The paper criticized the editorial policies of *The Courier* (of Texas),

[11] B. A. Abbott, *The Disciples* (St. Louis, 1924), pp. 198–99.

The News (of Iowa), the *Christian-Evangelist,* the *Christian Century,* and the *Union Christian Quarterly,* terming them the propaganda type of Disciple literature because they favored the structural policy of the Convention.

At their Centennial Convention in 1909 Disciples had nominated a committee to consider the feasibility of reorganizing the missionary and philanthropic work of the churches. Owing to the fact that conservatives already feared for ecclesiasticism within the fellowship, it was four years before the first ideal was consummated in the "Men and Millions Movement." This project, similar to the New World and New Era movements of their sister churches, broadened the horizon of Disciples and gave them a more adequate evangelistic, educational and missionary program. They enlarged their budget to compass the new challenge, and improved methods of finance in local churches.

Soon after the International Convention was constituted, another ideal found fruition in the proposed United Christian Missionary Society. It was this additional accommodation of Disciple work to American business methods in war-time, that led a company of protesters to issue their Call to retrenchment.[12] They considered efficient churchmanship incongruous with spiritual Christianity. R. H. Welshimer of the First Church, Canton, Ohio, informed the readers of the *Christian Standard* that the disturbing agent in brotherhood work was the Campbell Institute, for four of seven on the executive committee of the Board of Education, seven college presidents, seven college deans . . . the president and secretary of the Convention and four

[12] See p. 135.

members of its executive, were members of this Institute. He believed that this "diplomatic corps" had seized the Disciples' seats of administration.

Despite the protracted opposition that the *Christian Standard* forces carried on, the United Christian Missionary Society was set up at the 1919 Convention. This instrument correlated the work of six national agencies under the direction of a Board of Managers numbering one hundred and twenty men and women. Because of the intense rebuke of some conservatives, the three boards whose projects were least in harmony with the ideals governing the plea, were not included within the new jurisdiction. These were the Board of Temperance and Social Welfare, the Association for the Promotion of Christian Unity and the Board of Education. The Society became a legal body, independent of the Convention, though meeting annually in conjunction with it. In reply to Congress' proposals [13] the Convention extended one gesture of compromise (however clearly its formation of the United Society may have contradicted it). It affirmed: "We declare ourselves in favor of a more democratic form of organization."

The United Society had not served the denomination five months when the Cincinnati organ accused it of putting "the steam-roller over everything and anything that may get in its way. Already it is boldly asserting its right to brush aside history-honored custom, to usurp authority, and to bend, and even break, its own constitution to attain its aims." After the restorationists had dictated the Medbury policy [14] (a popular vote, fol-

[13] See p. 136.
[14] See p. 137.

lowing a spirited debate constituting for them the divine will for the mission field[15]), they chose what they termed was a constructive program for 1921, in which old-fashioned evangelism received nation-wide attention. As a matter of fact, the chief purpose in this crusade was to suppress supposed apostasy lingering in the churches and to indoctrinate all in loyalty to the restoration movement. The orthodox party added many converts to their churches, while an increasing number of liberal congregations voted to admit evangelicals to membership without their re-baptism. The spirit of toleration manifested itself in the next Convention and that of intolerance in the meeting of the independent New Testament Tract Society.[16]

The Tract Society imposed heavy demands upon the United Christian Missionary Society doctrinally and administratively. The latter's Board of Managers became so alarmed for the work of the denomination that they acquiesced to nearly every request. They recommended that opportunity be given Disciples to amend motions and resolutions from the convention floor; they disclaimed any desire to interfere with the autonomy of an agency; and they disavowed an intent to subject state societies to their oversight. This approbation left the regular work of Disciples without any orderly principles of control. The *Christian Century*, in a searching editorial entitled, "The Gospel According to the Board of Managers," described the situation in these terms:[17]

[15] Note the editorial (*Christian Century*, Nov. 24, 1920) that described the group's method of securing its ends.

[16] See p. 137.

[17] Op. cit., Feb. 9, 1922. About this time the paper became an undenominational journal of religion.

"The greatest danger in the present issue is not theological reaction, but moral disintegration. An ethical obscurantism is inevitable where convictions of truth are played with in the fashion that has been growing upon the Disciple official mind for nearly two decades."

The Board of Managers' good intentions miscarried. The Tract Society proceeded with its divisive program. It endorsed as thorough a policy of reindoctrination for home missions as for foreign work. The Clarke Fund [18] had accumulated sufficient reserve to express the desires of the non-co-operative party. The Fund's evangelists preached biblical legalism in opposition to the emphasis of the Convention's home missionaries. Open conflicts between intruding preachers and state secretaries were not infrequent. As a further effort to placate the feelings of the disaffected group, the United Society elected P. H. Welshimer, President of the New Testament Tract Society, to membership on its executive committee. The Canton minister resigned immediately, explaining that the only way out of convention distress was the dissolution of the United Christian Missionary Society. Welshimer's church, which served as a good barometer of restorationist policy, notified the Society that it would henceforth exercise custodianship of all its missionary funds.

At this juncture a fully qualified counter-movement asserted itself within the Disciples' denomination. The Clarke Fund and the New Testament Tract Society merged into the Christian Restoration Association. It

[18] This Fund consisted of money left by Sidney S. Clarke, "in trust forever for the preaching of the gospel."

stated as its distinctive purpose, "to exalt the local church as the fullest flower of the Kingdom of God on earth, free and untrammelled by any agency of man's making." Thereafter the United Society supervised its missionary and educational program, while the Association administered ten orthodox agencies of its own construction. The former party sought to promote peace and tolerance throughout the fellowship; the latter took an exclusive attitude.

The Christian Standard Publishing Company proceeded to give adequate publicity to the Association. It committed the function of constructive work to the regular Cincinnati weekly, and designed a new periodical, *The Spotlight,* to engage in militant propaganda.[19] The first copy of the latter was released in time to have its desired effect upon the approaching Convention. In the resolutions adopted by the Oklahoma City body,[20] the Convention was asked to revise its constitution to limit the powers of the committee on recommendations; the United Society was commissioned to open its books for inspection at the request of any contributing church; and both agencies were to exercise care not to prejudice local churches for or against any field agents engaged in Christian work. These restrictions virtually dissolved the powers of official denominationalism and converted the Disciple cause into an innocuous association of local congregations.

Liberal strategy to keep the denomination facing

[19] "A New Adjunct to the 'Standard' Journalism," *Christian Standard,* August 8, 1925. "*The Spotlight* will aim to expose and counteract the evils which disturb the peace of the brotherhood."

[20] See p. 140.

forward had been entirely outdone. The *Christian Century* expressed a devout hope that the restorationists would withdraw completely from the brotherhood. But since they had accomplished their purpose in large measure, the burden of action rested on the progressive forces. The *Christian Courier* of Texas predicted that free Disciples would form a new fellowship rather than obey the letter of the Oklahoma City law. Liberal leaders and the Board of Managers of the United Society insisted upon holding the principles of progressivism which history had made dear to them.[21] They proceeded to direct the official work of the churches quietly, but without conforming to the demands of the extremist party. Meanwhile *The Touchstone* formerly *The Spotlight,* was filled with such material as would tend to undermine completely the morale of the churches in regular Disciple work. It claimed that the interpretation which the Board of Managers put upon the late Convention resolution was one that rendered it null and void for their corrective purposes; hence the Call of the committee on future action, the political part of which reads as follows:[22]

"This is *the emergency* concerning which we address you. What shall be done about it? Unquestionably we are at *a crisis. Quick action is required. . . .*

"Our aim is merely to turn on the light. This done, we are willing to abide the results. We most earnestly urge upon all to be in attendance at Memphis, November 9–17 inclusive, to *aid in the protection of the interests now in jeopardy,* and in the rededication of them all, and of ourselves, to the service of Christ and His gospel." The *italics* as printed.)

[21] See p. 140.
[22] Supplement of *Christian Standard,* Aug. 14, 1925.

The Memphis proceedings in congress and convention have been reported in so far as they serve the present purpose.[23] This occasion marked the high point in restorationist reaction to progressive leadership and ideals in the Disciple denomination. The restorationists met in independent sessions simultaneously with convention meetings to enlist militant strength for the pending administrative test of power. These men had undoubtedly come to Memphis to dissolve the United Society into its several parts and to elect controlling officials of their own kind. When the test was made in the acceptance of the report of the missionary investigating committee,[24] they suffered such a reverse[25] that they have remained aloof from conventions since that time. The defeat of this partisan movement was the equivalent of a vote of faith in the Board of Managers of the United Christian Missionary Society. Frederick W. Burnham was reelected president of the Society for the seventh term and received a hearty welcome when he resumed his office.

The Christian Restoration Association has continued to enlarge its powers. It has added evangelists to its field forces, accepted the supervision of other mission stations, and increased its tractarian service. In the North American Christian Convention, which the Association called annually to incite loyalty for the separatist cause, the orthodox ideals of this primitive church

[23] See p. 141.
[24] *Ibid.*
[25] For the *Christian Standard* reporter, it was "a convention of bad faith . . . at Memphis a host of brethren found themselves ashamed to be considered any part of the United Christian Missionary Society." Editorial, *Christian Standard,* Nov. 27, 1926.

group have been exploited. These people believe that they are called of God to make over all Christian sects, including the modernist Disciples, into a genuine brotherhood of Christ.

Since 1926 regular denominationalists have been waiting an opportunity to reorganize the constitution of their Convention to permit of a delegate basis of representation at the annual meeting. They desire to provide for a more just and democratic government of the churches at large. The restorationists' opposition to the departure, has led liberals to believe that it is not yet the part of wisdom to insist on the change.

[3.] Missionary Rules of Christian Discipleship

The effort to maintain literally the rules of Christian discipleship [26] in America and on the foreign field has provoked problems of far-reaching dimensions. The main difficulty became defined as the open-membership issue. In its applied form, the immersion dogma became a test of Christian union with evangelical sects.

A generation ago some Disciple leaders had concluded that baptism by immersion was not a Christian essential. They encouraged a more democratic attitude towards other sects in the promotion of New Testament ideals. Their number increased rapidly during the next two decades. When the World War threw its shadow across the churches of America, liberal Disciples insisted the more upon loyalty to primary values which should hold all Christians in harmony. The *Christian Century* presented frequent editorials in favor of open-membership practice; the *Christian Standard* denied the biblical

[26] See p. 132.

basis of its contemporary's plan. This subject had become a controversial one at practically every meeting of the Convention.

If the literalists and liberals could not agree upon fundamentals of ecclesiastical procedure among themselves, much less could they agree upon those between their denomination and other evangelical groups. The liberals cultivated the goodwill of Protestant bodies and secured Disciple membership in the Inter-Church World Movement; the restorationists maintained that this participation contributed to disunion, for they fellowshipped with people who compromised on a subject of scriptural orders. The basis of action was considered a new idea and a part of the infidelity of the times. The *Christian Standard* conducted a lengthy weekly symposium on this compromise issue.

When the advocates of the plea learned that their missionaries were practising open-membership methods, their dissatisfaction with denominational policy became resolute. At a sectional congress in the autumn of 1919 [27] they hinted at the possibility of organizing an independent society to carry forward their apostolic interests. They did make a strong protest. Open-membership practice had to cease! As for the "Inter-Church combination," to continue membership in it was to become a denomination, a human device which the true brotherhood had vetoed from its inception.

The General Convention advanced a more progressive program instituting the United Christian Missionary Society under liberal leadership. One member of its executive resigned because of open-membership prac-

[27] See p. 136.

tices in China, and carried his protest to the churches through the vehicle of the *Christian Standard.* He suggested that the next (partisan) congress "devote itself to the democratization of the administrative agencies of our brotherhood." R. E. Elmore lent his support to conservatism by presenting a caustic criticism of Chinese missionaries. The *Christian Century* inadvertently added zest to the divisive movement when it stated editorially, "Most, if not all, of the mission churches of Disciples in China have been for some time receiving unimmersed Christians into their membership. They feel that, under God, they can not do otherwise."[28]

When the General Convention met in St. Louis in 1920 the restorationists raised the immersion question. Representatives of the executive denied that open-membership was practised in China, whereupon C. C. Morrison was called upon to explain his editorial in the *Christian Century.* He read excerpts from missionary letters to affirm that such practices did prevail in the Orient. Forthwith, a reactionary group retired from the Convention to meet in private. They appointed an emergency committee to take any special action deemed advisable in case the United Society failed to clean house, and they were responsible for insisting upon the undemocratic demands made in the Medbury resolution.[29]

A year later Frank Garrett explained to the Winona Lake Convention how impossible it was to pattern Chinese churches after American institutions. For instance, to have made immersion an essential to Christianity would cast a stone of stumbling in the way of

[28] Editorial, "A Passing Dogma," Aug. 26, 1920.
[29] See pp. 137, 144.

native Presbyterian and Methodist Christians. He appealed for charity permitting of interchange of converts among Chinese churches. E. S. Ames and J. B. Briney debated the relative merits of open-membership in the denomination. The Convention approved the missionary's position, but the United Society, sensing a reaction in the organization of the New Testament Tract Society, was forced to retract in its policy.[30]

Meanwhile a travelling evangelist who had served on the executive committee of the Foreign Missionary Society for years, asked permission to visit China and the Philippines in the interests of the gospel. His request was not happily received, for some of the committee looked upon his attitude with suspicion.[31] Since the gospeler pressed his claims repeatedly, one member of the executive offered to pay his expenses on the tour. He accepted the favor and returned in time to report his findings to the 1922 Convention. The subject of open-membership was the principal question of debate again. Liberal leaders tried to expunge the Board of Managers' ruling on baptism from the church's prescribed order. Caucuses of conservatives insisted upon a leave-it-alone basis. The evangelist gave a favorable report of missionary practice in China and urged the Disciples to lend their support to the United Society; besides, E. K. Higdon, minister in Manila, tried to force the will of the orthodox party by addressing a letter to the Convention inquiring if he should resign from his post, for he refused to permit the Board to bind his con-

[30] See pp. 137, 145.

[31] Note the confidential letter written by S. J. Corey to supporters of the United Society, intercepted by the *Christian Standard* and published March 1, 1924, p. 8.

science on the immersionist question. Albeit, in the interests of peace the delegates chose to require that "only those who are immersed, penitent believers in Christ" were eligible for membership in mission churches.

The United Society made a short and expensive peace. The evangelist who had visited the church's mission fields changed his mind and insisted that "sprinkled" believers did join Disciple churches, and that several missionaries had informed him that they were in full accord with the open-membership policy. That the Cincinnati organ was using this man to help break down the United Society became increasingly apparent. He wrote a sequence of articles for the paper on the general theme, "Three Years a Member of the Executive Committee, and Why I Resigned," telling the intimate story of tensions and divisions in the Disciples' benevolence work during the Society's short term of trial. In May the Board accepted his resignation. Immediately, he begged the dissolution of the United Christian Missionary Society and stood for re-election on that principle.

At this period, when conflicting interests were so tense in all the evangelical churches, the restorationists began to sense an affiliation with the fundamentalists of other denominations. However inconsistent their attitude, they were constrained to join in the general reaction to liberal religious thinking and progressive churchmanship. The *Christian Standard* opened its pages to such writers as William B. Riley and William J. Bryan. The editor belittled the preaching of Harry Emerson Fosdick and commended that of John R. Straton. The World's Christian Fundamentals Association was recognized. In close harmony with fundamentalists the editor of the *Christian Standard* wrote: [32]

"... we wish to draw attention to the peculiar relationship that exists between the fundamentalists and the restorationists. In so far as the fundamentalists accept the Bible, and the Bible alone, as the rule of faith and practice, the deity of Jesus as the Christian creed, and faith in the Lord Jesus and unreserved submission to Him as the true test of conversion, we are wholeheartedly their brethren in Christ."

Later, as if to out-fundamental the fundamentalists, the editor warned:

"Fundamentalism as espoused by the denominational world, is modernism in sombre garb. . . . When we get back to facts it is found that our fundamentalist-denominational friends who are rising up in their wrath against the modernist are children of the creed-making hierarchs who centuries ago sat in ecclesiastical conclave and substituted man-made articles of faith for the all-sufficiency of the Scriptures given by inspiration of God."

This extreme conservatism marked the complete decline of restorationist interest in the official work of the Disciples' denomination, and the development of the factional Christian Restoration Association. A Philippine incident arose to widen the gulf between them. A veteran missionary in the Philippines had refused to abide by the principles for which the Society stood, and was recalled late in 1925. He declined to come home but continued to preach a gospel that divided mission loyalties. A colleague and forty native congregations took the part of the senior evangelist. The Association intervened and adopted these people, thus gaining an-

[32] Sept. 16, 1922, p. 10.

other evangelistic field for its supervision. The *Christian Standard* published the episode as a defeat of the Society and a victory for the Association.

During the last few years the restorationists have continued unabatedly their testimony to primitive Christianity. They have never ceased to make claims for the binding authority of baptism by immersion. In preparation for the second North American Christian Convention, the committee on future action introduced scores of their missionaries, who formerly were members of other sects, to the churches through the columns of the Cincinnati paper, and used these individuals to prove that the restoration movement was the meeting-place of all true believers in Christ. The editor estimated that one thousand ministers (fully one-tenth of all Disciple clergy) had forsaken "human" creeds and sects and adopted New Testament Christianity.

[4.] The Independence of Disciple Schools

The Disciples shared rather extensively in the founding of small colleges during the nineteenth century. Their schools had indoctrinated youth in the standards of the brotherhood without any question until the new learning was advanced, when some institutions changed their scholastic attitude to that of open-minded search for truth. The Lexington schools took a stand for a broad Christian culture in the South.[33] The Disciple Divinity House in Chicago cherished ideals similar to those of the Campbell Institute, and has probably been the largest single factor in spreading liberal thought through the churches.

When President Crossfield of the Kentucky schools

[33] See p. 134.

added to his faculty E. E. Snoddy, W. C. Bower and A. W. Fortune, a more latitudinarian influence began to express itself in the class-room. These men applied the evolutionary hypothesis to the history of man and the Bible. In January, 1916, the Curators of Transylvania College and the Trustees of the School of the Bible endorsed the administration and faculties, which were suffering widespread suspicion. The executive committee of the Disciple Board of Education circulated a pamphlet on Christian nurture among the ministry in order to allay fears for the safety of the church's colleges. The *Christian Standard* accepted the announcement as a defense of Lexington and replied editorially that "this superlative nonsense (higher criticism)" was being absorbed in theological class-rooms, as though it were necessary for re-interpreting Christianity.

The same month five students drafted a complaint against certain instructors at Lexington. They had taught that "the first chapter of Genesis is poetry," that Jehovah was "the tribal god of the Jews," and so on. These teachers were "opposed to Professors . . . who hold to the old principles of the College." The teachers under criticism replied that the document was in part false, and calculated to destroy the interests of free education and the fundamental ideals of the Disciples of Christ. Eighty-seven per cent of the student body communicated to the public their confidence in the integrity of the men. Besides, they protested against the censorious attitude of their fellow-students. Dean H. L. Calhoun defended the claims of the orthodox minority of students. Conflicting sentiments prevailed within faculty and student body.

The *Christian Standard* conveyed this information to

the churches in such a way as to incite far-reaching distrust in the Lexington schools. It was claimed that since these institutions participated in the Men and Millions Movement, they should abide by the theological wishes of their benefactors. Many restorationists cut off their subscriptions to the church's budget. The *Christian Century* urged the administration to announce its progressive purpose in terms of the new freedom and the scientific temper.

In May Calhoun resigned from the faculty and published his reasons in a series of articles in the Cincinnati paper. A month later the Board of Trustees, on the basis of a careful survey of conditions, assured Disciples that the School of the Bible was in harmony with the ideals of the brotherhood, as they related to the inspiration of the Bible, the divinity of Christ, and the plea of their people. Owing to the administrative independence of Disciple colleges the orthodox group could not use the General Convention to discipline the institution. They discovered an effective indirect method in the organization of the Christian Bible College League.[34] Restorationists carried their rebuke of modernist learning further by founding new schools to testify to orthodox biblicism. T. W. Phillips had established a university in Oklahoma and a Bible institute in Ohio, each school bearing his name. Angola and Bethany Institutes, in Indiana and Virginia respectively, were added by the gifts of conservative laymen. The *Christian Standard* commended these, while it repudiated the doctrinal positions of Transylvania, Drake, Hiram, Eureka, Butler, William Woods, Atlantic Christian, and

[34] See p. 135.

Canton colleges. Although the presidents of these institutions of higher learning were members of the Campbell Institute, the editor flattered it when he credited it with the liberalization in Disciple policy of collegiate education.

Meanwhile, the Kentucky schools remained the chief center of conflict. In a College of the Bible *Bulletin* (1919) E. L. Powell defined the basis of spiritual authority in the denomination and showed its bearing on the local situation. The writer remarked that the issue was academic liberty versus ecclesiastical authority. He challenged the school's critics to produce any creedal formula that could represent the historic genius of the Disciples. Powell reminded them that his people had always committed their cause to the Christ of conscience; this source of inspiration the administration honored, and for that reason the schools were loyal in teaching and preaching and practice to the historic faith.

The *Christian Standard* published a digest of the Powell article in order to give Professor A. Fairhurst, a former trustee of Transylvania who was asked to resign on account of his incompatibility on the Board, an opportunity to set forth the counter position. He interpreted the preamble of the *Bulletin* statement as a word of contempt. As to the basis of authority in the church, the writer rejoined that "they (college executives) indulge largely in uncanny words and epithets for creating prejudice in the minds of the readers." Fairhurst made no serious effort to meet the Powell challenge. Although criticism continued, the liberal schools have survived; some have found it necessary to restrict their stress upon progressive ideals, especially schools in the South; others have continued their independent course, making their appeal to liberated churches and youth.

In 1923 the trustees of the Clarke Fund announced to the public and opened a non-standardized training (Bible) school in Cincinnati. This institution entered the Disciple field of theological education to provide for conservatives, as the Chicago and Lexington schools provided for progressives. "It is our observation," commented the founders, "that the Restoration movement is suffering at this time from the lack of an on-coming generation of leadership loyal to the New Testament Scriptures, on fire with evangelism and committed to the task of restoring the New Testament Church to the world."[35] When the Christian Restoration Association was organized, it supervised, in addition to the Cincinnati school, the Christian Normal Institute, Christian Bible College of Colorado, Eugene Bible University, and the Minneapolis Bible College. Soon these separatists added mission stations in the Philippines and South Africa, and founded Bible schools in each place to train native evangelists. Their latest addition of orthodox equipment have been Bible institutes in South Dakota and Los Angeles.

At the present time the Disciples' denomination is more seriously divided than is any other evangelical people in America. Since 1925 the restorationists have administered a well-organized counter-movement within

[35] *Christian Standard,* Aug. 4, 1923, p. 1.

the General Convention. This party have independent educational, missionary and secretarial operations; they also possess their own journalistic and convention voices. They maintain a strictly exclusive attitude towards progressive policies within the Disciples' communion, and towards other Christian bodies. The restorationists feel that God has called them to reinstate "the ancient order," which has been defined as a "conversion" experience, an extreme form of congregationalism, and "close" ordinances of baptism and the Lord's Supper. They are not creedsmen as, in the strict sense, are all other fundamentalists. The "gospel of Christ" has been their creed, although they have never succeeded in throwing off completely the doctrinal trappings of traditional Protestantism.

Notwithstanding the clear evidence of division among Disciples, each group is strongly attached to the basic aim of their historic plea. That is, they both desire passionately the unity of Christendom. But they face the anomaly of obvious disunity among themselves. The restorationists have striven to bridge the gulf by asking for conformity to a biblically-defined program; the regular party have sought it by loyalty to New Testament ideals. The latter have believed that progress in Christian culture has necessitated the scrapping of the old prescriptions; hence progressives find that they have more in common with liberal Christians of other denominations than they have with the conservative group in their own brotherhood.

In this conflict of ideals Disciples have enlisted a controversial psychology that has characterized them throughout their entire history. During the clash of secular and ecclesiastical cultures a generation ago, the debating spirit was very marked among this people. Restoration reaction to progressive measures was at full tide in their church earlier than in any other evangelical body. This disputational attitude has permitted Disciples to go to extremes in personal attack and divisive action, such as have not been experienced in other denominations.

Moreover, the mass-meeting nature of their regular conventions was not conducive to the arrest of this corporate failing. Little that was "regular" or convention-like transpired at some annual meetings of the church. Disciples lack constitutional methods of procedure; hence the present desire of the forward-looking leaders to introduce the delegate rule of convention attendance. Repeatedly when significant decisions were made, a crowd-mind registered the official voice. Under such conditions no appeals carry more weight than those made on behalf of sacred tradition, and against new ideas. The *Christian Standard* party have resolutely put forward these challenges. When the liberals refused time after time to comply with orthodox commands conservatives chose an independent testimony, finding it easier to provide a sectional program than to remain within the Convention and to help integrate a reasonable Christian position on a give-and-take basis. The Disciples have lacked a constitutional foundation for their faith and an adequate denominational loyalty to hold their factions together in a period of critical readjustments in American Christianity.

CHAPTER EIGHT

"ESSENTIALISTS" AND THE METHODIST EPISCOPAL CHURCH

American Methodism has been distinguished by four traits: the primacy of a personal experience of Christ, a pragmatic test of doctrine, a system of ecclesiastical connectionalism, and a plan of study courses for inadequately trained ministers. Wesleyans have always made the need for salvation from sin and the desire for the good life the first demands upon the individual. Although a quasi-doctrinal test was written into the rules of Methodism during the gravity of war days in 1864, dogma is subordinate to the promotion of piety.

The Methodist Episcopal Church in America was organized the day before Christmas, 1784. Twenty-four years later the membership adopted a constitution, by which representative "conferences" determined the precepts of Methodist law, and an episcopal order supervised the church's work. Soon the bishops began to project courses of study to serve the need of unschooled clergy, in which the content was mainly scriptural doctrine. In the late thirties the Board of Bishops doubted the advisability of independent theological schools in the church and arranged to supervise their biblical institutes. In 1845 this denomination split geographically over the slave question; this study has to do with the northern body.

[1.] THE RELIGIOUS TEST OF HOLY LIVING

The first chapter of the church's Discipline stresses religious experience above creedal formula. The Bible's portraiture of holy living is the Christian's ideal. A Methodist gives his allegiance to the Scriptures and to the Articles of Religion,[1] whose salient points are universal redemption, entire sanctification, the fellowship of believers and Christian service. The Apostles' Creed and the Articles represent the general doctrine of the church.

Like all other evangelicals, Methodists shared the struggle to reinterpret the Bible in terms of the historical method of study. *The Methodist Review* in the nineties, during the editorship of James W. Mendenhall, conducted an uncompromising controversy with higher critics; the same editor used the *Christian Advocate* also, weekly organ of the church, to awaken preachers on behalf of the inerrant Book. By publication and evangelistic address, L. W. Munhall and William H. Burns defended the orthodox view. Charles H. Parkhurst, the editor of *Zion's Herald,* pursued an open-minded policy and attempted to keep the clergy forward looking. He was supported by certain teachers in Wesleyan colleges who popularized the findings of critical scholarship.

Confusing currents of thought led the Board of Bishops to make a declaration on the biblical question

[1] In 1784 Wesley revised the Thirty-Nine Articles of the Church of England to become the twenty-five authorized Articles of Religion of the Methodist Episcopal Church.

at the 1912 General Conference. The delivery favored orthodoxy: "If there is no Book of God, absolute and unerring as a guide to faith, then there has never been a church of God, after our conception of the phrase. . . ." This official voice did not check liberal views, for their champions looked upon the practical test of loyalty to Christ as an adequate ecclesiastical authority. Conservatives tended to make a standard doctrine of the Bible the primary norm of Methodism.

It was a simple matter for biblicists to apply their test to the Conference Courses of Study. They could read what they considered safe or destructive. Because these courses shaped the ideals of the ministry, literalists surveyed them carefully. The same principle applied to the Methodist Book Concern's publications for the laity. Since 1913 there has been constant criticism of these types of literature. It was alleged that they catered to opinions which ran contrary to the historic truths of the Methodist Church. The main center of distrust was the New Jersey Conference, in which Harold Paul Sloan exercised a commanding leadership.[2] Conservative sentiment has been augmented by a weekly publication, *The Methodist,* of which L. W. Munhall is editor.

The General Conference (1916) failed to satisfy the demands of conservatives for a doctrinal change in the Courses of Study. Not even the revised ritual commended itself to these apostles of orthodoxy. It was different from the old forms! The next New Jersey

[2] Editorial, "The Judgment of New Jersey," *Christian Advocate,* March 19, 1914, p. 384. Note also the disaffection expressed by L. W. Munhall, *Breakers! Methodism Adrift* (Philadelphia, 1914).

Annual Conference characterized the current Courses as "a mere system of ethics with certain religious sanctions," and insisted upon a revival of the teachings of the Articles of Religion. The resolution with definite criticisms was printed in the regional *Christian Advocates*. There arose between Sloan and the Commission on Courses of Study a controversy that continued throughout the rest of the quadrennium. Other annual conferences joined in discrediting the official position.

The New Jersey Conference felt obliged also to call the churches back to pure religion. It reported that the discipline governing sinful amusements was being violated: theatre-going, dancing and games of chance had intervened in parish life. These practices were "antagonistic to vital piety, promotive of worldliness and especially pernicious to youth." The General Conference was petitioned to forbid these by making additions to the Book of Discipline. Bishop Joseph F. Berry of Philadelphia endorsed the overture, while Bishop Thomas B. Neely declared that secularism had swept the church. It needed a new baptism of the spirit supported by applied authority. These parties made a serious effort to arrest the processes of social change in a shifting religious culture.

The editor of the *Christian Advocate* testified how clearly the councils of the church were divided on controversial questions at the 1920 Conference.[3] Majority and minority reports attended problematical questions. Keen interest was manifested in determining whether or not the question put to prospective church members

[3] Editorial, June 10, p. 781.

was constitutionally a doctrinal test.[4] By sheer perseverance of the conservatives, the Conference upheld its constitutionality.[5] Customary attachment to this tenet and fear for the consequences of an experimental attitude, prevailed more strongly than legal procedure in the decision of the Conference.

The Buckner incident in Nebraska accentuated theological issues throughout the church. An Aurora minister had preached doctrines which the presiding bishop, Homer C. Stuntz, considered untrue. Though the superintendent reprimanded his fellow-minister, the latter continued to assert his personal freedom until officers feared for the peace of the church and retired him at the next Conference.[6] This led William H. Shipman to renew his campaign against the constitutionality of a doctrinal test. He denied the legality of the Nebraska decision, and claimed that a man should enjoy the right of private judgment in the interpretation of the Scriptures. The test was good in its historical meaning, but not as a regulative norm.[7] Bishop L. B. Wilson was constrained to trace the history of the test and to approve its current function. Shipman replied that neither Jesus, Paul nor Wesley had ever used such a religious standard, and Ernest F. Tittle commented that a man might meet successfully the doctrinal test but show no tolerant spirit toward his fellows.

While some conservatives held steadfastly to the

[4] The question: "Do you believe in the Doctrines of the Holy Scriptures as set forth in the Articles of Religion of the Methodist Episcopal Church?"

[5] *Daily Christian Advocate*, 1920, p. 501.

[6] Pamphlet, J. D. M. Buckner, *How I Lost My Job as a Preacher.*

[7] Monograph, *The Doctrinal Test.*

general principle of doctrinal authority, others applied it to the Courses of Study. This was the concern of the New Jersey group. Their 1923 Conference referred a memorial to the General Conference in which they catalogued the heterodoxies of the educational system. The *Christian Advocate* considered the overture was "a declaration of distrust" in the administration of the Methodist Church. Meanwhile the "sinful amusement" question was raised in anticipation of another liberal effort to change paragraph 280 in the Discipline. At the request of the *Methodist Review,* Frank Neff wrote in favor of strict conformity to the amusement veto, and Bishop Edwin H. Hughes in disapproval of the legal prohibition. The first writer considered the clause a great deterrent to tempted persons; only eternity would reveal how many souls had been helped in their struggle against enemies of the spiritual life. The bishop felt that there was a moral disproportion in the disciplinary clause; the penalty was one for a Methodist circus-goer and a saloon frequenter. It had become a threat or a bogie, and should be removed.

The three subjects which had precipitated wide discussion became the occasion of tension in the legislative halls of the 1924 General Conference. As a result, a few of the most criticized texts were removed from the Courses of Study. Sloan bent his main effort to retain the doctrinal test. He introduced a motion that the Conference declare "the binding authority of our Articles of Religion and other established standards of doctrine."[8] There was considerable debate. A committee reported back asking for the removal of the old candidature question and in its place to insert a pledge

[8] *Daily Christian Advocate,* 1924, p. 452.

of loyalty to Christ, to "the Christian faith as contained in the New Testament of our Lord Jesus Christ," and to the Methodist Episcopal Church. Sloan moved an amendment that the phrase, "and summarized in the Apostles' Creed," be added to the second object of loyalty. This would have bound the church to an explicit confession of faith. After further debate, the amendment was lost and the report of the committee adopted.[9] As for the third subject of controversy, the Conference ruled to substitute the Wesleyan principle of conscience for the amusement paragraph.

The conservatives had become sufficiently group-conscious early in 1925 that they organized themselves into "the Methodist League for Faith and Life." They described as their purposes,[10] "to reaffirm the vital and eternal truths of the Christian religion, such as the inspiration of the Scriptures, the deity of Jesus, His Virgin birth . . . , and so on." The League set forth a program of reaction wherever theological orthodoxy was endangered. A monthly organ, *The Call to the Colors,* kept its members acquainted with prevailing issues. The League's centers of strength were the New Jersey, Philadelphia and Baltimore Conferences. Copies of official information were distributed among the *Advocates* of the church, but they refused to give them space. This denial of recognition was interpreted by the League as adequate evidence of the necessity of their sectional work, for was not the denomination controlled chiefly by "modernism"?

Bishop Edward Blake, in opposition to League propa-

[9] *Daily Christian Advocate,* 1924, pp. 629–31.

[10] Pamphlet, *A Call to the Colors.* President of the League, Harold Paul Sloan; Vice-Presidents, Clarence True Wilson, Clarence D. Antrim, Henry P. Delaney and Charles L. Kingsley.

ganda, informed Methodists that he considered neither the Apostles' nor the Nicene Creed was an authoritative document.[11] Rather, they were historical pronouncements in a progressive Christianity. He affirmed the inconsequential nature of the Virgin birth dogma. As the founder of Methodism asked his followers to "think, and let think," so Christians were invited to interpret their faith in terms of their experience. Protests emanated from many quarters in the communion.[12] For some timid souls, Blake had exploited the Christian faith. They decided that if men wanted to support a church based on modern doctrine, they should go apart and found one; but the Methodist church should remain unshaken. Professor J. A. Faulkner of Drew Seminary regretted that evangelicalism had fallen upon such evil days. He was afraid that should men begin to doubt the supernatural character of Jesus' birth, they would soon deny his divinity.

Bishop Blake did not spare his brethren in his reply. He said that he had been accused of apostasy by those who suffered "the obsession of the so-called heresy-hunters." He repeated that the inerrancy of the Scriptures was indefensible. The acid test of Christianity was not a type of belief about Christ, but Christ-likeness in living. The battle for righteousness was more imperative than conflict over creeds. As a matter of fact, the bishop was re-directing the church's attention from un-Methodistic stress upon right belief to the Wesleyan distinctive of religious piety.

[11] "The Authority of the Creeds," *Christian Advocate*, Jan. 21, 1926, pp. 57–58.

[12] Note the editorial, "What is Disturbing the Methodists?", *Christian Century*, May 20, 1926, pp. 637–40.

The League for Faith and Life celebrated its first anniversary by conducting a national campaign for new members. It used the Blake confession to prove the unsafe leadership of Methodist officials. Schoolmen in the Drew and Garrett theological institutions were placed in the same category. The League called its members Essentialists, changed the name of its publicity organ to *The Essentialist,* and asked for a greatly increased membership. The League's paper informed readers that three essentialists for every modernist replied to the letter of invitation to join. The editor used the replies from liberals to prove their pseudo-denominational position. The League was "the true Methodist Church within the Methodist Church."

The essentialists caused the Church considerable disturbance during the next year. They promoted a spirited program to enlist League chapters within the various conferences. The New Jersey agents charged Henry H. Meyer, the editor-in-chief of Sunday school publications, with employing a unitarian policy. L. W. Munhall engaged in constant and bitter criticism of the Courses of Study for young ministers. So far-reaching had the controversy spread that the editor of the chain of *Christian Advocates* begged the apostles of the church to keep "a Thanksgiving Armistice."[13] He granted that, however ruthless modernists had been in their criticisms of the Bible, they were also possessed of an abounding quest for truth; fundamentalists, on the other hand, though sometimes intolerant, were making a sturdy witness for Christ. All Methodists should honor Christ by uniting in a Te Deum during the national

[13] Op. cit. Nov. 18, 1926, pp. 1547–48.

holiday season. Sloan rejoined, "Can we sacrifice faith for peace?" He saw no possibility of an armistice with what he considered were two religious interpretations competing for the mastery of Methodism.

The gentle appeal of the *Advocate* was followed by a stern refusal to publish further League items of information or advertisements. Leading churchmen began to assert similar suppressive measures. Henceforth the orthodox cause continued in the face of strict disapproval of Methodist leadership.

The minor part that the League for Faith and Life played in the 1928 General Conference at Kansas City proved the limited sphere of aggressive orthodoxy in the church. Sloan carried to the legislature a petition bearing ten thousand signatures from churches in forty-one states, asking for a committee of fifteen to investigate seminaries, pulpits and Sunday school literature for flagrant evidences of disloyalty to Methodist doctrinal standards. The house refused by a two to one vote to give his request any consideration. Of the twelve correctional objectives which the League entertained for the General Conference, not one sectional appeal received the church's approbation.

The only possible correlation between orthodox agitation and Conference action was the general sentiment in the Sloan petition and the "Declaration on Spiritual Life and Standards of Faith" presented by the committee on the state of the church.[14] The latter document asked churchmen to observe diligently certain doctrines which the Episcopal Address had mentioned, but reminded them that theological regularity was not a

14 *Daily Christian Advocate,* 1928, pp. 329–30, 465–66.

sufficient guarantor of discipleship in Methodism. They were "to translate into holy living the things that we believe." In this verdict the Methodist Episcopal Church repudiated the essentialist emphasis and restated its loyalty to the historic principles of Wesleyanism.

[2.] The Episcopal Control of Ecclesiasticism

Methodism is noted for its remarkable connectional system of church administration. This is supervised through the episcopal office. A general superintendent or bishop presides over each annual Conference, names district superintendents, and in consultation with the latter, places ministers in their respective parishes. By this arrangement no parish is independent of the direct supervision of elders. The plan also allows for a close interdependence of laity and clergy, and clergy and officials. The Board of Bishops meets semi-annually to consider policies affecting the practical and spiritual well-being of the church. They have no vote in the General Conference. By means of a chain of *Christian Advocates* with an editor-in-chief and six pages of syndicated materials, the ideals and interests of the communion are kept before all its members.

Legislative affairs are cared for in annual (one hundred and three areas) and general conferences. The later are called quadrenially and hold the major juridical rights under a few restrictive regulations. It is composed of an equal number of laity and clergy. When this body hears reports from the judiciary committee and acts upon them, it sits as the supreme court of the church. When an individual feels a grievance he appeals to the local superintendent for redress; when a church or group of churches is dissatisfied with a situation, they petition the annual or general conference for a correction.

The New Jersey Conference filed a protest with the 1916 General Conference against the operating policy of the commission on Courses of Study. The allegation declared that its members leaned far toward liberalism. The Quadrennium met the request by restating the Discipline to allow the Board of Bishops to appoint the commission, which included two bishops, two educators, two regular ministers and the book editor of the Methodist Book Concern. This measure failed to comfort the conservatives, for they disowned the views of the educators and editor. At the next meeting of the New Jersey Conference delegates voted in favor of abandoning the commission plan and returning the powers of text selection to the bishops. Oregon Methodists agreed. The Ohio Conference condemned the practice of discontented conferences sending communications to other conferences inviting similar criticism, and they begged the General Conference to continue its democratic policy governing Courses of Study.

More than thirty annual conferences petitioned the 1920 General Conference to modify the Courses in order to protect the faith of young ministers. The committee on education presented divided opinions to the legislative body. One report favored continuing the regular policy; the other considered that since the doctrinal fidelity of future courses was not assured to the church, the bishops should have full supervisory power to amend. Sloan desired to see the disturbed church reassert its confidence in sound doctrine, and spoke on behalf of the latter alternative. D. G. Downey claimed that only a few propagandists, who used innuendo and imputation, were agitating the forces of Methodism; he asked his brethren to leave the commission alone. The motion to lay the second report on the table was first rejected, then adopted (481 to 286). Subsequently the same recommendations were lifted and, with slight amendment, accepted by the house.[15]

The Des Moines churchmen also divided on the question of the constitutionality of the doctrinal test as applied to prospective church members.[16] Fourteen members of the judiciary committee claimed that since the question was doctrinal it was unconstitutional. Five members maintained its regularity; they insisted that should the majority decision be followed to strike the question out of the Discipline, "it would make of our Articles of Religion merely a set of recommended doctrines with no authority over the faith of the people, and any person, no matter whether he were Jew, Mohammedan or pagan, could claim membership in the Church with impunity." When the question was put to the delegates, the majority report was adopted (390 to 369). Because considerable dissatisfaction was expressed by the literalists, the question was reopened. A confusion of motions and points of order threw the house into parliamentary disorder. It was finally decided to print the ayes and noes as officially given and allow any who desired to change their vote to do so within a stated time. By this method the decision of the Conference was reversed (364 to 451) and the doctrinal test remained.

A general superintendent's method of treating the

[15] *Daily Christian Advocate,* 1920, pp. 554–57.

[16] See pp. 166–67.

post-war harvest of premillennialism illustrates the success with which a Methodist irregularity is suppressed in the local parish. The Los Angeles Bible Institute was responsible for stirring up interest in the dogma among California ministers. Bishop A. W. Leonard instructed his district superintendents to discipline any man who preached the doctrine, and if that were not sufficient, to refuse him fellowship in the Conference. The Buckner case also signifies the power of the episcopal office for this purpose.[17] Bishop Stuntz sent the preacher a word of counsel asking him to conform his utterances to orthodoxy and used the episcopal office to threaten him. The minister continued his freedom in the pulpit and was called before the Bishop and his cabinet. They employed the retirement clause and put Buckner aside, despite his repeated requests for a legal trial. The editor of the *Christian Advocate* called the attention of the church to the injustice of the Nebraskan action.[18] The bishop quoted the Discipline to prove that he was within the law, and that the editor had prejudiced the case for the purpose of good journalism. Though several bishops disagreed with their colleague, the Buckner decision stood.

The 1923 New Jersey overture to the General Conference raised other questions of ecclesiastical prerogative.[19] It claimed that the commission on Courses of Study had refused to abide by the 1920 ruling, and asked that the Board of Bishops be given the power to appoint the commission. It was further stipulated that the com-

[17] See p. 167.
[18] "The Rights of a Minister," op. cit., Nov. 9, 1922, pp. 1394–95.
[19] See p. 168.

mission should announce the book list in the *Advocates,* after which the bishops were to review them for approval. This rule would allow self-appointed censors of the Courses opportunity to present their verdict to the churches in advance of the bishop's reviews. Such surveillance of episcopal integrity was the most unfair feature in the memorial.

At the Springfield Conference the irenic appeals made in the Episcopal Address and the "Declaration on the Spiritual Life" presented by the committee on the state of the church, assured the disturbed party that nothing sacred to Methodism would be surrendered. When the New Jersey overture was presented, it was announced that of the one hundred and three annual conferences, only seven lent it their approval; and some of the seven were among the weakest conferences in the church. It was not strange, therefore, that the committee on education praised the Courses of Study, granting only a few and minor concessions to the petitioners, and complimented the personnel of the commission, and that the Conference adopted the report as read. In this action the strength of the dissenting party in Methodism had been put to its severest test and was found to constitute a weak and ineffective minority.

The measure of success which the conservative party gained at the General Conference together with the moral support which Bishop Berry of Philadelphia gave them in a published article, "The Modernist Drive in Methodism," [20] were the prime reasons contributing to

[20] *Christian Advocate,* Dec. 4, 1924. The bishop claimed that watchful modernists were filling every vacant office in the church with their friends, while defenders of the faith were "asleep at the switch."

the formation of The Methodist League for Faith and Life.[21] Forty men attended the organization meeting in Wilmington, Delaware. Because the *Christian Advocates* had been closing their pages to independent propagandists, the League asked the pressmen to reopen their columns to a free, frank and courteous discussion of questions vital to the welfare of Methodism. Most of the church's papers gave space to the League's publicity. In an editorial, "Kindly Excuse this *Advocate*," the editor of the Michigan *Christian Advocate* declined the use of his paper, explaining that if the promoters of the League were set to give the church an example of holy living he would yield to them, but if they were one with other fundamentalists, he begged to be excused. In the meantime he would wait and see. The editor-in-chief of the *Advocates* was prompted to set forth the latitudinarian attitude of Wesley on matters doctrinal to show that any of his fellowship who sought to establish a strict uniformity of opinion were not bona fide Methodists.

Notwithstanding this opposition, the League reported that it had gained members in nearly every Conference in the Church, and that officers in field and college and many laity were endorsing the movement. The Methodist Preachers' Meeting of the Washington District deplored any further effort to build up the League at the expense of harmony in the Baltimore Conference. It accused the Sloan group of insincerity and of ecclesiastical ambitions.[22] During the autumn, chapters of the League were organized in Baltimore, Wilmington,

[21] See p. 169.
[22] *Christian Advocate* (Washington District), June 18, 1925.

Philadelphia, New Jersey and at Berkeley, California. The Wilmington group changed their constitution to admit members of the Methodist Episcopal Church, South. The Philadelphia chapter numbered one hundred and thirty, including all the superintendents. Two hundred and fifty joined the League at its initial New Jersey meeting.

The Wilmington chapter felt the Course of Study situation had become morally aggravated, and appointed a committee, which was later enlarged by the League, to wait upon the Board of Bishops and request "a radical revision of the Course to bring it into harmony with the law." The Commission was charged with intentional disobedience. The bishops answered the deputation in a published statement; they were constrained to follow the advice of the General Conference, and extended their approval to the Commission's selection of texts. The episcopate exhorted the churchmen to avoid controversy and to preach the full gospel with characteristic Methodist passion. Sloan considered that the bishops had raised a dust to becloud the issue and replied that the League would tolerate disunity rather than surrender their precious faith.

The League for Faith and Life showed clear signs of limited appeal after twelve months of aggressive effort. During 1926 it asked for men gifted both with vision and decision to enlist in its cause. This crusade for recruits was not more successful than previous ones. The organization altered its constitution to permit of a regular division of its activities in the Methodist Episcopal Church, South. This extension of interests was undoubtedly an unconfessed failure of the Sloan party to carry on advantageously within the limited area of class freedom in northern Methodism. The official regulations of district and general superintendents were constant deterrents to men who otherwise would have spread schism throughout the church.

Notwithstanding the church's repudiation of the League program, its members projected further reformative plans at their second anniversary. Anticipating the approaching General Conference, they challenged the Board of Bishops to use their office to bring about a proper change: "If you appoint a Commission on Courses of Study to enforce the law for a standard course, some of whose most influential members are aggressive Modernists, how can you appear in a better light than the political leaders who appoint men who have been interested in the sale of liquor to enforce prohibition?" The petitioners thought that the church could be saved from its enemies if the bishops would assert their resolute leadership. When the Kansas City Conference actually met, these reformers failed to get a single orthodox issue before the delegates.

In the election of new bishops one test of the essentialists' popularity was registered in Methodism.[23] When the first ballot was taken for nominations, the president of the League for Faith and Life received seventy-one votes out of a possible eight hundred and twenty-three, and stood eighth in order of preference. In the third vote he received one hundred and thirty-five ballots in his favor and held the same relative position. At the fifth test, more than a third of Sloan's supporters dropped his name from their ballot; he withdrew his

[23] *Daily Christian Advocate,* 1928, p. 523 f.

name. Since this Quadrennium has passed, the essentialist organization has renewed its witness to the fortunes of orthodoxy in the Methodist Church, but with prospects of slight reward as far as the will of the corporate body is concerned.

[3.] The Education of the Laity

The Methodist Church has always exercised a zealous interest in the well-being of its lay people. Early in its history it set up the Methodist Book Concern to publish literature for the edification of children and adults. In recent decades this institution has been directed by men of liberal religious views.

The scholarly approach did not bring peace of mind to men enamoured with the ideals of classical orthodoxy. In 1909 William H. Burns published a book, *Crisis in Methodism,* in which he accused the editor of Sunday school publications with teaching that it was the duty of the church to preserve children from sin rather than rescue them from their fallen condition. L. W. Munhall struck a similar note in a volume, *Breakers! Methodism Adrift.* In 1913 the New Jersey Conference appointed a committee to make a careful investigation of the regular Courses of Study and the publications of the Methodist Book Concern, of which George P. Mains was book editor. This committee worked industriously and produced a voluminous report which was adopted a year later and printed in the Conference minutes. Special criticism was brought against Mains, not only because of his influence as an official but also because his book, *Modern Thought and Traditional Faith* (included as a text in one of the

Courses of Study) was claimed to disparage Christian truth.

The book editor ventured to explain why the New Jersey indictment came to be directed against him personally.[24] Sloan who had recently moved to the seaboard state, had promised his western friends that he would "strike many stalwart blows for Methodism," and wanted to make good his promise. The criticism was intended to break down the church's confidence in its book editor. The New Jersey Conference had overlooked the personal factors in the situation and petitioned the General Conference of the Church to change its editorial policy and thus to preserve the faith.

The General Conference gave slight regard to repeated criticisms of the religious education material at its 1916 and 1920 meetings. At the next Quadrennium it paid more serious concern to the complaints of the minority group. After a lively debate the delegates instructed their editor and his staff "to studiously avoid the use of such expressions as disturbed the religious sensibilities of lay people and to keep every instruction in accord with the church's faith." This denominational gesture was happily received by Harold Paul Sloan, spokesman for the disaffected party; for, soon the Methodist League for Faith and Life originated and insisted, as one of its six objectives, upon the omission of all destructive criticism of the Bible from Sunday school helps.

The most daring effort to convert the church's publishing policy to conservatism was introduced into the 1927 New Jersey Conference. League members under-

[24] "A Recent Conference Episode and its Partnerships," *Christian Advocate,* March 26, 1914, p. 410.

took to discipline Henry H. Meyer, the editor-in-chief of Sunday school literature.[25] Bishop William F. Anderson of Boston presided at the Conference and Meyer addressed a session. The speaker referred to the prevailing divisive spirit that endangered Protestantism and regretted the condition. No sooner had he retired from the rostrum than the president of the League took the floor, paid a tribute to Meyer's scholarship, and then told him that the divisiveness in Christianity was due to the fact that certain men, who had pledged their faith to Christian essentials, were now assaulting them. Sloan then presented a resolution, which Bishop Anderson interpreted as an insult to the guest speaker. The chairman ruled that if Meyer were to be tried for heresy it would have to be done in his own conference. He blamed the essentialists for bringing the factional spirit into their Conference. Besides, the bishop intimated that phases of the old theology had been discounted on good grounds, and for that reason Sunday school men were drawing more and more upon progressive scholarship to interpret the Christian life.

The propriety of this parliamentary act of the bishop was questioned by members of the Conference. To avoid further dissension, the chairman tried to steer the brethren into a consecration meeting, but the leader of the League replied that he refused to be forced into an emotional situation. Later Bishop Anderson sought the conference to expunge from their records the resolution bearing on Meyer's work, but the suggestion was not received favorably. The New Jersey Conference had been controlled by League members, who used the

25 Reported in *The Essentialist,* May, 1927, pp. 30–37.

occasion to denote emphatic repudiation of the editorial policy of Methodism and of the episcopal support accorded that policy.

The League for Faith and Life attempted to remove the editor-in-chief from office at the next General Conference. They criticised him for publishing views that diverged from or negated the established standards of the Methodist Episcopal Church: "The Church has given no one a commission to modify its faith by misteaching its babies, when they are too young to know." Eight memorials bearing on church school curriculum were presented to the committee on education at the 1928 Quadrennium. Five endorsed the literature and three disapproved it. The committee weighed the overtures on their merits and agreed to commend Meyer for his fine service to the denomination, though cautioning him that he prepare his papers with "reverent regard for, and loyalty to the historic standards of Methodism." When his name was presented for re-election, he was elected by a large majority over the League candidate.

Though more recent objections have been registered against various Methodist publications, church leaders have given them slight recognition. The essentialists cannot penetrate the church's administration to compel literalistic devotion to the Articles of Religion in its service publications.

[4.] The Theological Training of the Ministry

Methodists have resorted to two methods of ministerial training. A bare majority of leaders receive college and seminary education; the remainder enter the service unschooled and receive instruction in Conference study courses. The teaching function in school and extension work has been committed always to the best scholarship in the church. In common with other evangelical bodies, this people faced a division of opinions when higher criticism was drafted into theological education. Heretical charges were brought against the leading scholars.[26] In 1895 thirty-eight students of Boston University petitioned the trustees to discipline Professor H. G. T. Mitchell because it was alleged that his teachings leaned far toward Unitarianism and naturalism. Borden P. Bowne of the same institution suffered severe criticism. President William F. Warren publicly defended his own two colleagues.[27] He pointed out that biblical teachers either could keep silence on the question of higher criticism, or frankly present students with the problems involved and leave them free to make their own answer. The first alternative was a cowardly plan; the second, though involving perils, was praiseworthy. Warren addressed himself sharply to "the zealous pastors and revivalists and bishops who from the pulpit abjugate and so doing gratuitously advertise the 'higher critics' and their 'rainbow Bibles.' "

Bowne and Mitchell both faced church trials for their alleged heresy. In 1904 five accusations were brought against the former teacher in the New York East Conference.[28] The charges were supported by copious ex-

[26] *e.g.,* L. W. Munhall, *The Highest Critic Versus Higher Critics* (Philadelphia, 1896).

[27] "Current Biblical Discussions—the Proper Attitude of Theological Faculties with Reference to Them," *Methodist Review,* May, 1899, pp. 368–81.

[28] "The Orthodoxy of Bowne," collated by the editor, *Methodist Review,* May, 1922, pp. 390–413.

cerpts from his writings. The committee appointed to direct the trial gave several hours to receiving evidence from complainant and defendant, after which it retired and agreed that none of the specifications or charges was sustained.

The outcome of the Mitchell case was quite otherwise. The administration silenced the first group of students to petition the trustees. Three years later another group served notice that they were withdrawing from the school, and declared their reasons.[29] The bishops reprimanded the teacher; he was re-elected to the faculty upon a signed promise that he would conform to church doctrine. Unbridled criticism spread and ecclesiastical sentiment forced Mitchell out of his chair. He called for a heresy trial in his own conference. The request denied, he asked justice of the episcopal group. They excused themselves from action by employing a legal technicality. The case was appealed to the General Conference in 1908. The court ruled that the declined trial was unlawful; and, to safeguard bishops in the future, it changed the Discipline to make the local conference, rather than the episcopate, responsible for investigating charges of erroneous teaching in church schools. According to two of the church's historians, this action ended the danger that Methodism might become a heresy-hunting Church.[30]

The 1908 Quadrennium gave forth an epoch-making pronouncement in the form of "The Social Creed of the Methodist Episcopal Church." In it the ethics of Jesus

[29] H. G. T. Mitchell, *For the Benefit of My Creditors* (Boston, 1922).

[30] H. E. Luccock and Paul Hutchinson, *The Story of Methodism* (Cincinnati, 1926), p. 459.

were applied to the conditions of modern life. Four years later the commission on Courses of Study added several texts bearing on social Christianity. When these manuals were circulated through the church, conservatives initiated a campaign of criticism that has not yet ceased. When the book list was published in 1916 a committee from the New Jersey Conference waited upon the Episcopacy to protest against ten texts. In the interests of peace, though granting no evidences of unfitness in the text, the Commission omitted one book.

This degree of compromise did not comfort the New Jersey conservatives. Sloan set forth their grievances and demands in pamphlet form. The commission accused the writer of misquoting materials and of superficiality. The Jerseyite charged that the churchmen were addressing their remarks against him rather than in terms of the denominational difficulty. He and his friends could not endorse the kind of gospel that such men as Bowne, Meyer and Coe were offering in prescribed texts.

The Methodist Church was divided in theological judgment at its 1920 General Conference.[31] The committee on judiciary advised that the commission on Courses of Study follow conciliatory measures in view of the sectarian tensions abroad in the church. During the debate that preceded the approving action of the Conference, Sloan quoted from one of H. F. Rall's (secretary of the commission on the Courses of Study) books to prove that he denied the Johannine authorship of the fourth gospel and consequently robbed Christians of the great discourses of Jesus contained therein.

[31] See p. 166.

President C. M. Stuart of Garrett Biblical Institute took the floor on a matter of high privilege and presented a protest, which was recorded by the vote of the house in the minutes of the Conference, to correct the unjust imputations made against his colleague. The latter had given written pledge, stated the executive, that his teachings were in harmony with the ideals of the church.

The commissioners submitted the book list to the Episcopal Board at their spring meeting in Portland, Oregon. The bishops advised substitutions in the case of three manuals. Sloan published his estimate of the texts in a volume, *Historic Christianity and the New Theology*. He had discovered that thirteen of the forty-seven books supported the so-called new theology and were entirely defective. Their gravest weakness was the negation of the supernatural in the Scriptures and in Christ, and the ignoring of the importance of justification by faith alone. The same writer felt providentially called also to scrutinize articles contributed to church periodicals by Professors Edwin Lewis of Drew and Arthur W. Nagler of Garrett.

The next General Conference at Springfield entertained a memorial bearing on Courses of Study policy.[32] With the purpose of compromise the committee on education recommended that the texts should represent the verities of the faith as established in the Constitution of the Church; and that the Discipline, "with some special emphasis upon the Articles of Religion," and the standard sermons of John Wesley be included in the Courses of Study. The commission was required to communicate

[32] See p. 177.

the outline of the Courses and the texts to any member of the church making request at the same time that they were handed over to the Board of Bishops for their approval.[33]

Soon a self-appointed committee of essentialists waited upon the Board of Bishops to ask for the enforcement of the 1924 mandate. These men protested against five books, two of which were written by Methodists. The Episcopal Board excluded one only. Within two months ultra-conservatives organized themselves into The Methodist League for Faith and Life, three of whose objectives were intended to bring the denomination's theological teachings into harmony with the authoritative Articles of Religion.

Few schoolmen within the Methodist communion gave their moral support to the sectional movement. Professor J. A. Faulkner contributed articles to the League's organ, while its editor named Professor Arthur Holmes of the University of Pennsylvania as an associate. Kimball Theological Seminary only was considered an orthodox institution. At the League's first annual meeting, fundamentalist greetings were conveyed from non-Methodist representatives of Princeton Seminary, Wittenberg College (Lutheran), Eastern Baptist Seminary, and the League of Evangelical Students. Invariably, this interdenominational aspect of conservatism has arisen in a communion when conditions within it did not permit of satisfactory expansion of the orthodox cause.

The League for Faith and Life laid plans to convert the mind of the approaching General Conference to

[33] *Daily Christian Advocate,* 1924, p. 452.

sound educational ideals. *The Essentialist* listed schools, scholars and texts, that were considered unfit for Christian support. Student quotations were catalogued to prove the unsettling character of class-room discussions. The League's president prepared an impressive memorial for the Kansas City meeting.[34] But regular Methodists had full confidence in their schools and extension courses. To a memorial asking that the three bishops be omitted from the commission on Courses, the legislators gave non-concurrence. To another, that a two-thirds vote of approval on the part of the Episcopal Board (then a majority vote) be required of the books which the Commission recommended, a similar decision was made.

Apparently the Methodist League for Faith and Life has demonstrated its futility as an instrument of denominational control in shaping the fortunes of its church ministry. Whether in the seminary or in the surrogate work of extension studies, not a single ideal which the essentialists cherished was realized.

THE Methodist emphasis upon holy living has militated against the progress of the traditionalist movement in recent Christian controversy. Arminian-trained men have refused to make doctrinal questions the test of church loyalty. An article by Bishop A. W. Leonard in the *Northwestern Christian Advocate* [35] showed how this principle works in the church. The contributor had been hailed as a supporter of the League for Faith

[34] See p. 172.
[35] "Essentialist," April 21, 1927, p. 372.

and Life because he had given public approval of certain evangelical dogmas. The bishop granted that he was a conservative in theology, but denied that he shared any "ism" to make beliefs a measure of faithfulness in the Christian enterprise. The *essential* matter was Christlikeness of character.

Besides, the system of connectionalism in Methodism has tended to suppress partisan propaganda. According to the *Christian Century,* this church's superintendency is the most powerfully geared ecclesiastical machine which the Protestant world possesses. Be that as it may, the officials of the denomination do beget remarkable loyalty from their travelling ministry. The desire for parish and economic advances, which are largely in the keeping of district superintendents, partly explains the fact. Besides, the strong denominational press, which canvasses the church with its chain of weeklies and holds the standards of Wesleyanism foremost in policy, has proved a boon to administrative purposes.

It might be inferred from these two facts that Methodists were disturbed little by the contemporary conflict of Christian ideals. Philip L. Frick and Bishop F. J. McConnell have made such claims in the *Methodist Review* [36] and the *Homiletic Review,*[37] respectively. True, the theological phase of the controversy did not threaten the stability of this communion as it did certain other evangelical bodies. But the conflict has cut deeper than doctrinal debate. An orthodox religious culture asserted itself in contradistinction to a modern one. Traditional values pertaining to the Scriptures,

[36] May, 1924, pp. 421–26.
[37] Feb., 1924, pp. 94–96.

creeds, polity, offices, have been involved in the conservatives' appeal. Personalities were caught up in the conflict. Methodism shared with every other church the necessity of reinterpreting its historic testimony in terms of current idealism. In this struggle the essentialists have left an impress upon their communion.

In the orthodox reaction within Methodism there came forward no outstanding leaders who could command the loyalty of all conservative forces in the church. The League for Faith and Life represented the most enterprising group. And, because its founder was accused of entertaining personal ecclesiastical ambitions, his influence was curtailed. When the League altered its constitution in the latter part of 1928 to provide for a full division of activity in the Methodist Episcopal Church, South, and added a Lutheran to its editorial board, it manifested virtually its failure to survive as a vital determinant within the northern denomination.

Although organized conservatism has found it very difficult to survive in Methodism, there are correspondingly as many ultra-orthodox Wesleyans as there are traditionalists among Baptists, Disciples or Presbyterians. This is especially true among the clergy, of whom a large percentage are poorly equipped for educational leadership. The Methodist Church undertakes to remove its greatest source of arrested growth as it attempts to lead these professionally maladjusted men into harmony with the ideals of progressive Christianity.

CHAPTER NINE

TRADITIONALISM IN THE PROTESTANT EPISCOPAL CHURCH

WHEN the United States obtained its political independence the Protestant Episcopal Church was affected. The delicate task of gathering together the segregated Church of England and forming a disestablished faith fell chiefly upon William White (later a bishop) and certain founders of the nation. They patterned the church's constitution closely after that of the state. A balance of power rested between executive office and legislative and judicial functions. The English Prayer Book and the Thirty-Nine Articles of Religion were accommodated according to the exigencies of the American situation.

For nearly one hundred years this church cherished evangelical sentiments. The ideals of the Protestant Reformation remained the forces of paramount consideration. The "low church" party, as the evangelicals were called, emphasized personal piety through simple Prayer Book worship and the preaching of salvation through faith in the Saviour. It held ritualistic formularies and sacramental practices as strictly secondary values. The Oxford Movement entered America in the late eighties to challenge this Protestant ideal of worship. The "high church" party laid importance upon the historic continuity of "the Church," the official dignity of the sacraments, and meticulous regard for Prayer Book ceremonial. On the other hand, they remained uninterested in the appeals of higher criticism and inductive theology.

Low and high church ideals often conflicted in Episcopalianism.[1] Tract 90 had created almost as much ferment in the United States as in England. Bishops Griswold, Chase and Moore stressed the evangelical position as contrasted with Bishops Seabury, Hobart and Ravenscroft, who supported official churchism. The bipartisan situation was particularly marked in general convention proceedings and in separate theological schools, religious journals and missionary policies.

A third party arose within the communion during the last quarter of the nineteenth century. Signs of its presence were evident in the Church Congress in New York City in 1874. These "broad churchmen" were less dogmatic regarding ecclesiastical prerogative than either of the other groups, and more concerned for the humanistic implications of religion and for the findings of higher criticism.

Both high and low parties were shocked by Phillips Brooks and Richard Heber Newton, unconventional representatives of the new learning. The New Englander had emancipated himself from the orthodox trappings of the old evangel which struck fear into the common people. The humanity of Jesus was noted in his preaching, and ceremonialism was reduced to a minimum. Undermining treasured dogmas of both evangelical and Catholic persuasions, he was accused by his

[1] Consult, *American Church History Series,* VII, chap. XVI.

colleagues of being Unitarian and unchurchmanlike. A strong minority opposed his nomination to the bishopric in the General Convention of 1891. Phillips Brooks brought a new criterion into the episcopal office:[2] He was a vigorous Christian personality with a tolerant church-mind, and preached a Saviour of universal appeal to men.

During thirty years ministry in New York City, Newton developed a catholicity of human interest that denied for him reality to certain principles of orthodoxy. He preached a liberal conception of God, the Bible and religious experience. He invited clergy of other faiths to occupy his pulpit. Following Lent in 1890, a company of churchmen sent Bishop Henry C. Potter a remonstrance giving the alleged uncanonical practices of certain men in their diocese. Newton was the principal heretic. The Bishop refrained from intervention and was petitioned a second time. Newton then preached two sermons for the edification of his critics.[3]

The preacher claimed that the ethical and spiritual truths of the Scriptures were the Word of God. Creeds were to be understood historically and by means of the philosophy that characterized their structure. No church possessed an authoritative meaning of Christian doctrine. Newton wrote to the bishop expressing sympathy for him in attempting to meet diverse theological positions, but urged him to order a church trial. The bishop acted judiciously and dismissed the charges.

The Newton incident symbolized the presence of a

[2] Editorial, *Andover Review*, June, 1891, pp. 650–53.

[3] Richard Heber Newton, *Church and Creed.* (New York, 1891), chaps. II, III.

liberal leaven in the church, which precipitated a warning from the bishops in their Pastoral Letter in 1894. They announced that "fixedness of interpretation is of the essence of the creeds," and that the clergy were to abide by the historic pronouncements of the church.

No one can hope to understand the problems in culture conflicts within the Protestant Episcopal Church who does not take under closest observation the purposes and policies of the low, high and broad church parties.[4] For the divergent ideals of these groupings have given it its greatest trials in attempting to develop a denomination with imperialistic background, in harmony with democratic and scholarly interests in America.

[1.] The Traits of a Good Churchman

Episcopalianism has always been primarily interested in the creation of good and loyal churchmen. It tends to remain an ecclesiastical rather than a democratic cult. The chief responsibility for the perpetuation of this ideal has rested upon its priestly order. A clergyman promises to "minister the doctrines, and sacraments, and the discipline of Christ as the Lord has commanded and as this Church has received the same." The Bible, the offices, the Prayer Book and the Thirty-Nine Articles, constitute the rules of faith by which the loyalty of a Christian is attested. Within these prerogatives the three types of churchmen found principles to support their testimonies.

The quest for modern scholarship, that stirred Brooks and Newton, inspired other men. The outstanding rep-

[4] Note editorials, "Parties New and Old," *Living Church,* Oct. 13, 1928, pp. 779–80; "Definitions," *Churchman,* Jan. 8, 1927, p. 8.

resentative of this pursuit a decade later was Algernon S. Crapsey. He spiritualized the meaning of certain rubrics of the Apostles' Creed in order to retain them for personal use. This license in the face of Prayer Book instruction was considered sufficient heretical evidence to force his withdrawal from the priestly office. Crapsey explained the urge of conscience that many of his brethren felt, when (after his trial) he informed his bishop that, after years of painstaking study, he could not do otherwise than harmonize the meanings of creedal articles with the new learning.[5]

Ecclesiastical irregularity was no less satisfactory to orthodox churchmen than was strange doctrine. The high church group had become aggressive during the World War, and desired to make the sacrament of Holy Communion approach the Roman Catholic conception. This stigmatized the ideals of the Reformation church. Those who cherished the Protestant heritage organized the National Church League to conserve their values.[6] The Churchmen's Alliance sought to safeguard the interests of the Catholic party. The *Churchman* followed a policy of good-natured tolerance until the New York meeting of the Alliance. With its divisive announcements, the editor declared that the sacerdotal and Protestant views were opposed for each hailed contradictory essentials of Christianity. He observed that the Catholics were making an effort to subordinate the church to their religion and appealed to Protestants to release new convictions of faith.

5 Article, by Harris A. Corell, *Arena,* April, 1907, pp. 347–48.

6 Pamphlet, *The Church League; Its Necessity and Its Liberality,* Carl E. Grammer.

A third fellowship was organized in 1922 to consolidate the interests of strictly broad churchmen. Thirty leaders met and reproduced in name and purpose the Modern Churchmen's Union of England. They favored interpreting creeds in keeping with the viewpoint of science, co-operation between their denomination and other Protestant bodies, and the application of Jesus' ethics to social problems. Unlike Alliance and League, the Union refrained from engaging in ecclesiastical politics.

During the next two years, when controversy was acute within other denominations, the doctrinal test of Episcopalianism was applied against the utterances of Percy Stickney Grant, William Lawrence and Lee W. Heaton. The Virgin birth dogma was the main topic of controversy. Grant was accused of holding radical views and using his church for unconventional purposes.[7] The local bishop ordered him to abide by the historic teachings of the church, to leave the ministerial office, or to face a heresy trial.[8] In Lawrence's autobiography, *Fifty Years,* he gave direct support to men who practised doctrinal and ecclesiastical autonomy.[9] The *Living Church,* organ of the high church party, marked the New Englander as a heretic and unfit for holy office. Lee W. Heaton of Fort Worth insisted upon a place in his communion "for those who must reconcile theology with religion as well as for those whose religion is theology."[10] His bishop proceeded to institute

[7] See p. 206.

[8] The bishop's letter published in *Christian Work,* Feb. 3, 1923, pp. 133–34.

[9] See p. 207.

[10] See pp. 208–09.

a heresy trial. The whole Episcopal Church was restless due to conflicting ideals and personalities.

The Board of Bishops became so alarmed by liberal theologians that they attempted to arrest free thought by means of a Pastoral Letter issued November, 1923, from Dallas, Texas. The communication was an ultraconservative declaration of the doctrinal authority of the church's creeds. It inferred that the bishops possessed the divine right to put official interpretation upon them. The Letter [11] decreed that

> "It is not the fact of the Virgin Birth that makes us believe in our Lord as God; but our belief in Him as God makes reasonable and natural our acceptance of the fact of the Virgin Birth. . . . So far from imposing fetters on our thought, the Creeds . . . give us a point of departure for free thought and speculation on the meaning and consequence of the facts revealed by God."

This proclamation accounted for a rather serious reaction within the communion. The Modern Churchman's Union rejected the unwarranted officialism of the Episcopate. Percy Stickney Grant assailed the bishops for usurping rights delegated only to the General Convention. Professor Dickinson S. Miller of the General Theological Seminary protested against the Letter, and found his relations with colleagues so strained in a school of Catholic traditions that he resigned from his chair. The faculty of the Cambridge Theological School met the bishops' statement with a liberal appeal that men treasure the spirit of Christ rather than a legalistic mind in this time of crisis in the church. The theological

[11] The letter is published in Eldred C. Vanderlaan's *Fundamentalism Versus Modernism* (New York, 1925), pp. 366–69.

exchange brought forth some strongly partisan publications. In *Modernism and the Person of Christ,* W. J. Sparrow Simpson defended the traditional view of Christocentric beliefs. Frederick Palmer's *The Virgin Birth* and Leighton Parks' *What Is Modernism?* presented liberal views that were acclaimed widely. In a symposium by the theologians of the New England seminary, *Creeds and Loyalty,* ecclesiastical formularies were pictured symbolically as particular historic expressions of Christian idealism.

No man wrote more trenchantly for the preservation of the old faith than Father Shirley C. Hughson of the Order of the Holy Cross. Following the Grant and Heaton episodes, he circulated tracts to discredit modernism. More than three hundred thousand copies were distributed. He also travelled widely preaching his sectional gospel: modernism was "a congenial atmosphere in which any and all denials of faith might flourish"; Bishop Lawrence was a "loose thinker"; liberals had a "double standard of morality;" Leighton Parks and Percy Stickney Grant should be associated with the Roman apostate, Father George Tyrell.

Contradictory views of Christian doctrine were stressed in two national congresses early in 1924. The Catholic group exalted the doctrines that were emphasized in the Dallas Letter. Professor Francis J. Hall warned the church against Protestant liberals, for they embraced the doctrine of an expurgated Christ of the Gospels, which was without superhuman claims. Bishop Lawrence presided over a liberal congress at which the Catholic party was identified with fundamentalists as agents of doctrinal tests. A year later both parties shared in a congress in St. Louis to consider the subject of heresy. Theological differences were stated frankly and antipathies aroused by the Dallas Letter were absent in this face-to-face fellowship. The ultra-conservative Bishop Manning was willing to grant that "a new synthesis of the deep religious values represented by all Christian communions" was advisable to the church.

Notwithstanding a declination of local interest in creedal tests, Bishop T. D. Bratton asked for the retention of sound doctrines in his General Convention sermon.[12] But, under the influence of liberal sentiment, the Convention was moved to make more flexible the office of baptism by substituting a vow of loyalty to Christ for assent to the Apostles' Creed. High and low churchmen debated that the innovation would change the immemorial rule of Episcopalianism. A volume of "Noes" was registered to the question, and the doctrinal test of membership remained.

Following the convention Shirley C. Hughson supervised an impressive Catholic Congress in New Haven. The keynote was, "the necessity of the full Catholic faith for the solution of the world's problems." The Mass was presented as the chief act of Christian worship both in theory and practice. The *Churchman* noted the party's inflexible determination to control the whole communion, while the *Southern Churchman* granted the sincerity of the sacerdotalists but counted the congress one of supreme arrogance.[13]

[12] The sermon was printed in *Living Church,* Oct. 10, 1925, pp. 779–83.

[13] Editorial, "In the House of Re-Union," Dec. 5, 1925.

In an effort to dedicate all churchmen to a common spiritual mission, a Bishops' Crusade was started in the spring of 1926. Clergy and laity were invited to engage in ardent evangelistic appeals on behalf of the lost. Despite the good intention of the Episcopacy, Protestants and Catholics were divided in their witness to ecclesiology and basic Christian ethics,[14] and the purpose of the Crusade largely miscarried. Another Catholic Congress gathered seven hundred leaders at Milwaukee. An invitation had been extended to the presiding bishop of the church, John G. Murray, to grace the occasion with his presence. He accepted, much to the chagrin of those who cherished Protestant convictions. Father Hughson, as chairman, declared it was the purpose of the congress "to propagate and defend the religion of the Incarnation of God the Son, as that religion is made available to men through the seven Christ-ordained sacraments." Solemn Pontifical Mass in All Saints' Cathedral was the crowning event. Eleven bishops robed in cope and mitre, and guests from the Eastern Orthodox Church attended this event. The *Living Church* concluded that the future of the American Church lay with this party.

The Catholic demonstration of strength elicited sharp demands for a change of front in the Protestant Episcopal Church. The National Church League issued "A Call to Action" to the laity to prevent the "Romeward" trend of the Protestant Church. Bishop E. C. Seaman in a diocesan address characterized the Congress as

[14] Note editorials "Anti-Evolution Laws and the Church's Evangelism," *Living Church,* May 22, 1926, pp. 111–12; *Churchman,* Aug. 7, 1926, pp. 8–9; also article by Robert Johnson, "Protestant and Catholic: Can We Live in the Same House?", *Churchman,* June 12, 1926, pp. 11–12.

reactionary and anti-American, while Bishop Robert L. Harris told his people he feared that high churchmen intended to revive Mariolatry, intercessions to the saints, auricular confession, use of the rosary, and so on. The secretary of the Modern Churchmen's Union believed they were engaging their forces to control the next General Convention.

The Anglo-Catholics did desire to see the Thirty-Nine Articles removed from the Prayer Book proper to an appendix, at the Washington Convention. Though they considered them a distinctive of Protestant Christianity, and for that reason foreign to the continuity of Catholic faith, they argued for their deletion on non-controversial grounds; they said they desired to lighten the book of worship. The National Church League insisted upon a leave-it-alone policy. The *Chronicle* in the North and Judge C. S. Marsilliot in the South were instant in season and out to check the Catholic propaganda and to incite loyalty to the Reformation document.

The issue was accepted so seriously by prominent non-Catholics that a select number begged the whole church to memorialize the next Convention to retain the Articles of Religion in the Book of Common Prayer. Thirty-five thousand communicants responded. The *Living Church* interpreted the petition as a carefully prepared appeal to prejudice, and asked for a vote of ratification for their overture in terms of the merits of the case.

This Protestant communication had marked effect upon the church at large, and more particularly upon the judgment of the General Convention. The legislators feared for the security of their beloved church. Sentiment rather than logic controlled the decisions at Washington. Both houses voted to postpone indefinitely the subject of Article removal. In reference to theological dissension, the House of Bishops begged conciliation in their Pastoral Letter. The clergy should exhibit "honest loyalty" to the spirit of "the doctrine, discipline and worship of this Church." Above all, they should shun "subversive conduct" and cultivate confidence in an inclusive fellowship among the brethren; "If Catholic and Protestant cannot find a way to live together and to worship together the one Lord whom both adore, 'then is our faith vain. We are yet in our sins!' "

As good churchmen, the representatives of the various sectional groups acquiesced to the verdict of this authoritative body, although they continue to treasure their partisan ideals.[15]

In recognition of all forces making for the reconstruction of Protestant Episcopal idealism, it is necessary to mention a recent revival of old-fashioned orthodoxy in Virginia. In May, 1927, Langbourne M. Williams purchased the *Southern Churchman* and changed its policy.[16] He stood for the absolute and plenary inspiration of the Bible, and declared that he would wage war on modernists and evolutionists. He has fellowshipped with extreme fundamentalists of other churches and given a minimum of regard to the regular program of his own denomination. After two years of this type of editorship there is little evidence that the journal has

[15] For evidence of the perseverance of these ideals, see *Southern Churchman,* Nov. 17, 1928, pp. 11–12; *Living Church,* Oct. 27, 1928, pp. 859–60; *Chronicle,* Feb., 1928, p. 115; and of a different temper, "A New Spirit," *Churchman,* Nov. 3, 1928, p. 8.

[16] Op. cit., May 21, 1927, pp. 5–6.

revived any notable measure of interest in the former colonial faith.

[2.] The Distribution of Ecclesiastical Prerogatives

In the Protestant Episcopal Church the office of the bishop is an influential one administratively and legislatively. Of late that power has been used repeatedly with a view to regulating the theological thought of progressive men. Constitutionally men entertaining common interests within the church could organize for purposes of mutual enrichment. This policy resulted in the development of several fellowships whose partisan interests sometimes provoked misunderstandings. The treatment of denominational problems in terms of a homogeneous policy remained the work of the diocesan and general conventions. These three areas of churchmanship make clear the centers of structural conflict within Episcopalianism.

[a.] The Bishops and the "Heretics"

For a generation Algernon S. Crapsey had been the beloved minister of a workingmen's parish in Rochester.[17] In his publication, *Religion and Politics* (1905), conservative clergy noted that the author had put his private judgment above the official voice of the Church. They referred his position to Bishop William D. Walker. The investigating committee announced that a presentiment was unjustifiable; the bishop decided otherwise, instituted court proceedings, and wrote the accused that he had disturbed the peace of God's Church and taught

[17] See p. 197.

unofficial doctrine. The court, with one man dissenting, upheld the bishop's authority and suspended Crapsey from the ministry.[18] This decision of a theological court did not turn back the course of liberal learning. Other ministers accommodated traditions to current thought. This led the House of Bishops to attempt to curb the movement in 1913 by informing the church, "If one finds that he has lost hold upon the fundamental verities, in the name of common honesty let him be silent or withdraw."

Ten years later the Protestant Episcopal Church included many emancipated scholars. A few clashed with bishops. Percy Stickney Grant had been a source of disturbance to Bishop William T. Manning for years before he was reprimanded by his superior. Charges were made finally when the minister presented to his congregation (January, 1923) limited reasons for the consecration of churches, and questioned that Jesus possessed the power of God and that priests received unique power when ordained. Manning discussed the sermon with his priest and wrote him to reconsider his sacred vows. Grant replied requesting the privilege of interpreting the doctrines with the same freedom that Dean Inge and Canon Streeter enjoyed in England. As if to reinforce his independency, he preached a vigorous sermon the following Sunday on the theme, "A Religion of Reality."[19] Manning's earlier ultimatum was largely veiled in his later reply to the priest. He knew that the majority of his strongest clergy favored

[18] Note the correspondence passing between Crapsey and Edward Abbott in *Outlook,* Sept. 2, 1905, pp. 25–29; Sept. 30, 1905, pp. 284–86.

[19] Printed in *Christian Work,* Feb. 10, 1923, pp. 172–75.

liberty of thought. He knew also that leading bishops echoed the same ideal. The bishop dismissed legal proceedings against Grant, though he chastened him for his insubordination.

The church press revealed wide interest in the Grant case. The *Living Church* decided that he had received generous treatment from the bishop, considering his radical personality. This journal was impatient with the *Churchman* that it should have shown deference to Grant and discourtesy to Manning. While Bishop William Lawrence called upon Christians to open their prophetic minds to the truth,[20] Bishop Manning defended the miracles associated with Christ's person.[21] The *American Church Monthly* advocated the direct dismissal of men who denied the rubrics of the faith.

Fifty Years, by the Bishop of Massachusetts, contained the romantic story of how a brave soul, reared in the atmosphere of classical orthodoxy, had pioneered for half a century through an age earmarked with scientific quest and doctrinal criticism, and had emerged with a readjusted and refreshing faith. Belief in the Virgin birth and the Resurrection of Christ surrendered, he retained a rich loyalty to his Saviour. Faith, rather than an anchorage to the past, was an adventure of soul for enrichment in the present.

The publication increased anxiety among conservative men. The high church press failed to comprehend why the bishop disputed the doctrine of the Virgin birth: Had not the Nicene Creed said that Christ "came down from heaven," "was incarnate," "by the Holy

[20] Article, *Outlook,* Feb. 21, 1923.
[21] Article, *Living Church,* Apr. 7, 1923, p. 805.

Ghost," "of the virgin Mary," and "was made man?" A group of influential laymen (among whom was George Wharton Pepper) petitioned the House of Bishops (convening in Dallas) to warn such churchmen as disseminated unsettling beliefs to adhere more strictly to the creeds.

The occasion and some consequences of the Dallas Pastoral have been mentioned.[22] Karl Reiland of New York catalogued the bishops with fundamentalists. Professor George A. Barton of the Philadelphia Divinity School pointed out upon what flimsy grounds the group had attempted to justify faith in the Virgin birth. After his curate read the letter to St. Bartholomew's congregation, New York City, Leighton Parks as rector removed his vestments, donned his doctor's gown, and delivered an impassioned sermon on "Equal Rights of Fundamentalists and Modernists in a Comprehensive Church," the effect of which was felt throughout the denomination. His feelings were touched by the fact that the bishops had questioned the intellectual integrity of the clergy. Parks challenged the Episcopacy to bring him to trial, for he thought as Lawrence. Grant and others.

Hard upon the dictum of the Dallas Letter followed the Heaton heresy case in Texas. Bishop Henry T. Moore requested the diocesan standing committee to draw up a presentment against the preacher; he was determined that the Heaton case should be "the beginning of a concerted movement to cleanse the Episcopal Church of Modernism." Stuart L. Tyson, a representative of the Modern Churchman's Union, organized a

[22] See pp. 199–200.

defense committee and began to gather evidence and collect funds to support the accused liberal. "If one must go to trial, all (modernists) must go," became the slogan of the committee. Heaton submitted his modernist views in writing to the bishop;[23] there followed a prolonged silence on the part of the latter. A wave of disapproval of church trials influenced the bishop to change his mind (it was rumored that Bishop Manning urged him not to press his charges). Within two months Bishop Moore announced that the Fort Worth course of justice was postponed indefinitely.

Although the last notable heresy case was officially suppressed, the *Churchman* was unwilling to let the Heaton situation rest. The editor directed a careful study of southern conditions and reported that Bishop Moore, the Ku Klux Klan, Baptist fundamentalists, and the majority of the local urban people were consorting together to crush the Heaton parish. Whereupon he addressed himself to his fellow churchmen:[24]

> "It is time for the intelligent and progressive people in the Episcopal Church to recognize the fact that we have in this Church certain bishops that are thorough-going autocrats . . . who are attacking aggressive and intelligent clergymen by methods that would be scorned by the cheapest ward politicians."

Many bishops replied to the criticism that was turned upon them and their Pastoral Letter. Matthews of New Jersey called modernism "an old heresy exhumed" and made a veiled threat that he would bring Bishop Lawrence to trial for spreading Unitarian propaganda

[23] Letter published in *Christian Work,* Jan. 5, 1924, pp. 20–21.
[24] The first in the series of articles appeared May 3 issue, 1924.

in the church. Burgess testified to convention orthodoxy in his Long Island Diocese. The Dioceses of Tennessee and East Carolina, under the sovereignty of their bishops, resolved to uphold the official creeds. An illuminating comment on the New York situation was the almost-unanimous refusal of the Diocese to endorse the Dallas communication. Meanwhile Bishops Hall, Francis and Gravalt tried to render their orthodox cause further zealous service by presenting for trial the harmless socialist bishop, William Montgomery Brown.[25]

Certain New York clergymen finally agreed to bring to an end the bishops' public treatment of heresy cases. Broad, high and low representatives met in conference for weeks with a view to mediating a solution to the ecclesiastical disturbance. Early in 1924 they made public a report (acceptable to the bishops) "On the Creed and Scholarship," which was in reality a compromising armistice.[26] The irenic appeal had its desired effect; the Episcopacy has since employed its office for more constructive purposes.

[b.] THE INTER-RELATION OF SECTIONAL GROUPS

Naturally the three parties in the Episcopal Church became jealous for the preservation of their distinctive traits. When doctrinal problems arose, usually high and low churchmen sponsored orthodoxy in opposition to modernists. And when ecclesiastical issues were

[25] Editorial, "Bishop Brown's Case," *Churchman,* Feb. 23, 1924, p. 8.

[26] Printed in *Christian Work,* March 22, 1924, p. 373. While the signers recognized the unchangeable nature of the Church's creeds, they begged for charity toward those who held any "reverent and scholarly interpretation," as long as it did not overtly deny "the historic facts stated in the creeds."

pending, broad and low fellowships associated as a rule to suppress the aims of the Catholic order. The interaction of these groups represented an important phase of confused Episcopalian idealism.

In 1916 the Church League was instituted to safeguard the comprehensive purposes of the church. Certain liberals felt that Anglo-Catholics were hurting the cause by stressing sacerdotalism. They condemned the effort to make prayers for the dead an obligatory part of the Communion Service at the next General Convention. The League chose to support the Thirty-Nine Articles and thus keep the church Protestant. Despite the fact that certain bishops, clergy and editors disapproved of the League as a regrettable recrudescence of party spirit, the organization assumed national proportions and used the *Churchman* as its official voice.

Likewise the Churchmen's Alliance became a Catholic force to reckon with in America. Several hundred men gathered in New York in 1922 to consider its claims. Professor Chauncey B. Tinker of Yale, who presided, urged a more aggressive propagation of their ancient faith. Frank L. Vernon thought the Protestant "system," founded on negations, was weakening in their Church. The Alliance voted to be represented by a committee on faith and order at the Portland Convention.

This Catholic aggressiveness sharpened divisions in the Episcopal communion. The *Churchman* informed its constituency of the imperialistic motives of the high church party. Bishop Moore of Dallas defended the classical traditions of the Catholic faith; and the *American Church Monthly* made light of Protestants going to church to worship, an incident that its New York contemporary could not let pass without asking for a cessation of such bitterness.

Meanwhile the Modern Churchmen's Union[27] arose to help the church meet problems incident to heresy charges. Stuart L. Tyson became its publicity executive, while Shirley C. Hughson was the chief advocate of creedal subscription.[28] The latter taught the fitness of thrusting apostates out of the church. Tyson termed him a fundamentalist, and one with John Roach Straton. In a monograph, *The Eucharist in St. Paul,* this spokesman for the Union sought to discredit the Catholic view of transubstantiation and the necessity of fermented grape juice in the sacrament, and insisted that the apostle taught the finality of Christ's offering in the doctrine of the Cross. Tyson and Hughson by their traveling ministry heightened the distinctions of Protestant and Catholic bodies within the church.

Journalistic voices joined in the discussion.[29] The *Living Church* accused the Modern Churchmen's Union of misrepresenting its constitution by engaging in factional propaganda, and the *Churchman* of employing methods of sarcasm and ridicule in treating values of the Holy Cross Order. The Virginia journal (low church) considered the Milwaukee weekly subject to delusions of grandeur when it set forth the claims of Catholicism, while the *Witness* made a similar charge against the *Churchman* because it meddled in the doctrinal affairs of the Heaton parish. The latter paper pointed out

[27] See p. 198.
[28] See p. 200.
[29] For other phases of the discussion, see pp. 237–39.

that high churchmen practised the ideal of an exclusive church, modernists that of an inclusive church, and asked "Do all Anglo-Catholics feel that there must be an inevitable division?"

Catholics carried the factional spirit into their New Haven Congress.[30] Delegates were requested to wear cassock, surplice and biretta, to solemn mass. It was reported that the following auxiliary fellowships participated in the event: the Central Conference of Associated Catholic Priests, the Clerical Union for the Maintenance and Defense of Catholic Principles, the Priests' Fellowship of Albany, the Federation of Catholic Priests of Chicago, the Confraternity of the Blessed Sacrament of the Body and Blood of Christ, the Order of the Nail, the Society of St. John the Evangelist, and the Order of the Holy Cross.

Other congresses convened to evaluate liberal and evangelical ideals. The church's testimony was disintegrated to a noteworthy degree. It was to revive the corporate spirit that the Bishops' Crusade of soul-saving was launched.[31] This project gave the *Living Church* an opportunity to contrast the Protestant faith, which it claimed had collapsed in fundamentalism, with the Catholic evangel, which it was alleged substituted sacramental grace for hysteria and preached a gospel that was not in antagonism to the teachings of science. High churchmen illustrated this evangelism in their second annual Congress in Milwaukee.[32] Father Hughson interpreted his party's purpose, "to convert America to

[30] See p. 201.
[31] See p. 202.
[32] See p. 202.

the Catholic religion" by means of The Cycle of Prayer, the Bureau of Lectures, and periodic congresses; and to this end, he opened executive offices in Metropolitan Tower, New York City.

What further cleavage in churchmanship was occasioned by this exhibition of Catholicism has been noted.[33] The broad church press looked upon the Milwaukee Congress (1926) as a revival of superstition and magic, and the low party press described it as Romanism camouflaged under the Anglo-Catholic name. A handful of devout souls refused to be caught up in the wholesale controversy.[34] Stirred by the Bishops' Crusade, they organized the "Evangelical League" to preach traditional truths and to engage in old-fashioned revivalism. This small group has witnessed to primitive Christianity to the present time.

A clash of sectional interests preceded the 1928 General Convention. Each major party held a conference and chose an exclusive attitude in matters pertaining to creedal subscription and principles of worship. The final act of the Protestant campaign was the presentation of a petition to the General Convention to stay Anglo-Catholic domination of the Church and to retain the Thirty-Nine Articles in the Book of Common Prayer.[35] Two rather important events followed the Convention. Hughson, who had been the militant leader of the Anglo-Catholic party for several years, resigned

[33] See pp. 202–03.

[34] *Churchman,* Nov. 6, 1926, p. 5. Its leader was J. J. D. Hall in New York City.

[35] For Convention decisions, see p. 203 and the next section of this chapter.

his executive position in the late autumn. No reasons were given the public; nor was a successor chosen. This action has signalized a notable decline of ecclesiastical influence of the Catholic persuasion. The editorial confession of the *American Church Monthly* as to the outlook for Catholic Churchmen verified this. The following excerpt revealed a state of mind that suffers disappointment, though not a lack of confidence in the maintenance of its idealism:[36]

> "It is quite possible that we may be entering an era of persecution when the clergy of strong Catholic convictions will be discriminated against. . . . The Catholic Congress Movement has perhaps given us a false sense of security. . . . We must dig in and strengthen our position. The time for a general advance is not yet. . . . It is better that the world and worldly Churchmen should continue to be suspicious of us and even to hate us."

[c.] The Redefinition of Church Law

The General Convention of the Protestant Episcopal Church is a conservative legislative body. For one reason, it is the genius of the communion to safeguard its traditions and continuity as *the* Church of Christ. Because three types of Christians participate in its councils and yet preserve an orderly regard for affairs spiritual, another check is placed upon structural changes. Thirdly, any regulation affecting the church must receive the approval of three voting bodies: the diocesan conventions and the houses of deputies and bishops; the houses must vote favorably upon a constitutional question for two successive conventions

[36] Op. cit., Dec., 1928, pp. 275–77.

before the rule becomes operative. Although partisans resort to lobbying on occasion, the practice is thoroughly discountenanced.

For many years the Church has been engaged in revising the Book of Common Prayer. In 1913 a commission representing both houses was appointed to consider methods of ritual enrichment. Continued at the next two conventions, it published recommendations in advance of the Portland meeting in 1922. Controversial tracts presenting Protestant and Catholic estimates of suggested changes were circulated widely: the chief interest centered in the addition of the Benedictus, qui Venit to the eucharistic office. Anti-Catholics alleged that this ritual had been copied from the Roman Missal. When the theme was introduced to the legislators, the upper house declined to accept the addition.

Liberal churchmen regretted that the Convention did not recognize women as eligible for membership in the house of deputies; high churchmen were instrumental in keeping this prohibition. It was voted to strike the word "obey" out of the marriage ceremony. Bishop Lawrence labored with the upper house to have the vow to believe "all the articles of the Christian faith as contained in the Apostles' Creed" omitted from the baptismal office, but his motion was defeated by traditionalists. It was voted to omit from the ritual, "Have mercy on all Jews, Turks, infidels and heretics."

Not all diocesan conventions were free from conflicting interests, as witness that of Fond Du Lac in Wisconsin. In 1925 a liberal vestryman proposed a resolution to exclude the Order of the Holy Cross from the local convention, claiming that it was a source of discord.[37] Bishop Weller, whom Bishop Webb had characterized as a great defender of the faith, declared the resolution out of order. A lively discussion followed in which high churchmen were accused of using political methods to suppress latitudinarian sentiment. Contrary to thirty years' practice, some broad churchmen were elected to diocesan offices and the General Convention.

Continued Prayer Book revision engaged the New Orleans Convention in 1925. Though liberals desired a simplified confession of faith for baptismal candidates, traditionalists retained the doctrinal formula.[38] It was voted the second time to strike the word "obey" out of the marriage service, despite the undemocratic objections of certain churchmen. A Catholic spokesman considered that the Apostles' and Nicene Creeds made a sufficient statement of the church's faith, and moved that the Thirty-Nine Articles of Religion with their title page be removed from the Prayer Book. However strongly low and broad churchmen insisted that this landmark of Reformation theology be retained, the motion was voted. Other revisions favorable to the high church party included: provision for Holy Unction, for the transposition of the Prayer of Humble Access, and for the remembrance of the faithful departed. The lower house objected to the addition of the Reservation of the consecrated bread and wine at the holy communion.

The Pre-Convention (Washington, 1928) Protestant agitation to revoke the position taken three years previ-

[37] Reported in *Churchman*, Feb. 14, 1925, p. 21. *The Living Church* was published in this diocese, and its editor, Frederick C. Morehouse, was a leading figure in Catholic circles.

[38] See p. 201.

ously bore fruit in both houses moving to postpone indefinitely the omission of the Articles of Religion from the Prayer Book.[39] This decision was arrived at in advance of the convention session by representatives of the various parties, who consulted concerning the danger of open schism in their communion. Refusal to include in the Prayer Book the Benedictus qui Venit and the addition of a prayer for the departed, were disappointing features to Catholics and Protestants respectively. Notwithstanding the exercise of a give-and-take policy in ritual revision, there was evidence of a predominantly Protestant sentiment in the Convention.

This was especially true in the lower house. The majority of the laity are not in sympathy with Catholic ideals; on the other hand, an increasing number of bishops have become more kindly disposed to them. (The position of the clergy does not stand out as definitely.) The church's journals have begun to take account of these ecclesiastical trends. The Catholic press disapproves what it terms the unnatural intrusion of the laity, in accepting administrative positions in the church, whereas the *Chronicle* has lamented the increase in episcopal centralization of power in diocesan and general conventions.[40] It looked upon the election of a presiding bishop over the church at the 1925 Convention as an unhappy omen, for the spirit of America was anti-monarchical. Besides, the participation of the presiding bishop in Catholic congresses savored of a favoritism which evangelicals could not condone. The Protestant Episcopal Church is still involved in the

[39] See p. 204.
[40] Editorial, op. cit., Feb., 1926, p. 5

problem of accommodating an imperialistic cult to the demands of American democracy.[41]

[3.] The Church and Other Denominations

The administrative roots of the Protestant Episcopal Church reach back into the State-Church of England. As the parent institution experienced difficulty in defining its relations to disestablished churches, so has American Episcopalianism in associating with the evangelical denominations. The traditional attitude of insistence upon spiritual continuity and of separateness from what it conceived as the dissenting sects of Christianity, has not been subjected to notable change.

Richard Heber Newton had shown little sympathy with the sense of superiority which his church cultivated.[42] He attempted to bridge the gulf between his and other communions by inviting evangelical ministers to occupy his pulpit. This led his brethren to think that he was flouting the authority of the church, and retarding the restoration of the unity of Christendom. The Sunday following the delivery of the remonstrance to the bishop, the accused took for his text, "And other sheep I have which are not of this fold," and preached that, since the Lord had chosen no official church to represent his fold, for one fellowship to make that claim was evidence of "an arrogance which is excusable only on the ground of mental blindness." Quite naturally this viewpoint cost priests great discomfort nearly forty

[41] *e.g.,* Bishop W. T. Manning and Dean Howard C. Robbins have been unable to define each other's rights satisfactorily, "Episcopacy and Democracy," editorial, *Churchman,* Jan. 12, 1929, pp. 8–9.

[42] See p. 195.

years ago when traditionalism reigned almost exclusively within the church.

The problem of the "open pulpit" engaged the General Convention in 1907. High churchmen objected to liberals expressing a willingness to place other denominational men in their pulpits. They treated the irregularity as a factious measure; moreover, they could not concede that the preachers were sanctioned priests of Christ's Church.[43] The house of deputies ignored the Catholic criticism and declared for an open pulpit. The house of bishops compromised by adding a canon to permit ministers of other communions to preach in their church on special occasions, providing they have received episcopal license. This action did not bring comfort to the Catholic group; they circulated widely a pamphlet, *The Open Pulpit in the Episcopal Church,* which purported to answer the claims of the new canon.

The question of Episcopalian membership in the Federal Council of Churches of Christ in America was considered for the first time at this Convention and referred for further study to the commission on church unity. At the next triennial meeting the commissions on church unity and social service were instructed to cooperate with the Council. In 1913 the house of deputies voted to affiliate with the interdenominational agency, but the house of bishops declined. The subject was side-stepped during the World War.

The 1920 Lambeth Conference and the Bishops' "Appeal to All Christian People" presented the grounds on which Episcopalians considered the urgent need for

[43] The high churchmen considered that they were laymen. *Churchman,* Nov. 14, 1925, p. 16.

Christian unity. Their chief problem was the recognition of the validity of non-episcopal ordination of the clergy. Characteristic of the view of broad churchmen was that expressed by George Hodges in a series of articles in the *Churchman*. He took the position that the technique of ordination was not sacrosanct; it was only important that a man be acceptable to God. All forms of ecclesiastical ordination were experimental. The *Living Church*, conceiving the Catholic mind, made claims for the essentiality of apostolic succession in the Christian ministry: "We are fundamentally Catholic . . . and incidentally Protestant." [44]

The 1922 General Convention reconsidered its relation to the Federal Council of Churches. The upper house favored membership; the lower one disfavored it. They agreed that the two commissions should continue to co-operate with the Council, but refused to underwrite any share of its budget. The laymen feared to enter the inter-church fellowship because of the Council's firm declaration on social and industrial ethics. Bishop Charles H. Brent almost lost the office of presiding bishop because he was so energetic on behalf of the federated scheme.

Preceding the next Convention, the high church party renewed their opposition to what they considered was Pan-Protestantism. The *American Church Monthly* felt that were the Episcopal Church to become a member of the Council, people would conclude that it was simply a rather bizarre and eccentric Protestant sect using a liturgy. When the subject was introduced at the New Orleans meeting commissioners could not ap-

[44] Editorial, op. cit., June 24, 1922, pp. 259–60.

preciate each other's views. Due largely to the vigorous appeal that George W. Wickersham made on its behalf, the vote to join the Council carried in the house of deputies. In the other house the situation was tense; Bishop Irving P. Johnson of Colorado, who led the party opposed to membership in the Council, looked upon the proposal as a visionary experiment and objected to it temperamentally. Bishop Brent appealed tactfully for full endorsement of the plan. The house became deadlocked (the vote stood fifty to fifty); the former policy was continued.

Three years later the attitudes of Protestant and Catholic parties had not changed perceptibly. Bishop Brent at this time asked only that the additional commissions on evangelism and the Eastern Orthodox Church associate with similar departments within the Council. Liberal sentiment overcame Catholic criticism sufficiently to allow a majority vote on behalf of the first named commission; the second recommendation was defeated.

The recent recrudescence of traditionalism in the Protestant Episcopal Church reveals three types of ideals: a re-emphasis upon classical theology, a revival of interest in Catholic worship, and an effort on the part of certain bishops to regain imperialistic regulation of the church. Conservative movements have been called forth to check the demands of liberal churchmen for freedom to redefine their faith in terms of current thought, for the rights of all types of Episcopalians to cherish their particular values in a comprehensive church, and for increasing democratic government of the church in harmony with the social spirit of America.

These conflicting ideals have been shared by low, high and broad churchmen. The old-fashioned evangelicals are decreasing rapidly. A remnant pay their allegiance to the unyielding position of the *Southern Churchman;* more emancipated members are represented by the Virginia Theological Seminary; while the majority tend to become participants in the broad church fellowship. Evangelicals adhere to Reformation values as embodied in the New Testament gospel, the Prayer Book and the Articles of Religion. A majority of the laity and an increasing number of the clergy are finding their faith in the principles of broad churchmanship. This group regard the church's formularies as symbolic of creative occasions in an expanding Christianity, and subject to change as human knowledge increases. They cultivate Episcopal comity with other churches and desire the closest federation of Christians in order to rise to the requirements of this industrial age. They have not been as impatient with Catholic aims as have low churchmen.

The high church group believe that God gave the full deposit or revealed religion to "the Church" (their Episcopal Church) in the Scriptures and the priestly office of Christ. The Eucharist is conceived as the fundamental method of participation in God's saving grace. It is their bounden duty to preserve, unbroken in doctrine and practice, this faith, once for all delivered to the saints. They intend to maintain this ancient testimony in the face of apostasy within the church and godlessness without. Looking upon the Thirty-Nine Articles and other Protestant landmarks as schismatic, they disregard them, treasure the verities of the apostolic church and find them more or less concealed in the Church of Rome. The Catholic fraternity, recruited chiefly from the clergy and bishops, declare a strong positive witness, and to date have developed more coherence than either of the other parties.

The burden of assimilating within the church the diverse ideals for which Episcopalianism stands has led partisans to combine in various manners. Doctrinally, liberals have withstood evangelicals and Catholics in testimony to progressive views. When theological tests involved administrative readjustments, modernists shared fortunes with the "heretics," refusing to conform to the dictation of orthodox bishops. When Catholics pressed the superior rights of such ritual as cast reflection upon the validity of Protestant worship, broad and low churchmen joined to insist upon the fitness of Reformation values. On the contrary, when high churchmen desired to shift the Thirty-Nine Articles to an appendix in the Prayer Book, liberals approved theoretically, though for a different reason. The former looked upon the Articles as anti-Catholic in sentiment; the latter treated them simply as historic formulas.

Similar accommodative problems arose between parties in the determination of an administrative program for the church. For instance, the interests of Churchmen's Alliance and Church League clashed in convention policy. From time to time each company depended upon the traditional imperialistic authority in its church to enforce its sectional position. This attitude led to exclusive church actions. Fortunately this undemocratic procedure has not been asserted as forcibly at general conventions as in sectional congress, press, and theological schools, or the church would have been split into irreconcilable factions. Churchmen know how to moderate their judgment and re-establish their institutional fellowship when they meet to interpret the Protestant Episcopal Church to the world. The liberals' insistence upon the ideal of a comprehensive church and the necessity of each man respecting the other's sincerity have contributed much to the preservation of the church's peace in a period of considerable religious confusion.

At the same time, peace has been chosen more than once at the expense of Christian progress. Due to an officious group of bishops who cherish the authority of their office, the aggressiveness of Catholic claims for the restitution of an ancient church, the complicated methods of ecclesiastical legislation, and the sense of superiority to other Christians that many Episcopalians still entertain, the Protestant Episcopal Church faces heavy odds in this age of cultural revolution.

PART THREE

Current Conflict Beyond the Church

PART THREE

CURRENT CONFLICT BEYOND THE CHURCH

THE revival of modern orthodoxy began as an extra-denominational movement.[1] Soon, however, its leaders, as denominationalists, desired to bring their churches into conformity with the historic ideals that once had actuated them; but as independent Christians, they federated for the purpose of reinstating the principles of traditional faith in social institutions whose jurisdiction lay beyond the churches. In this secular parish conservatives precipitated a greater variety of activities (there were seventeen),[2] and discovered a field for the freer perpetuation of their reactionary testimony to modern culture.

[1] See chaps. III and IV.

[2] These various endeavors form the structural organization of the five chapters in this part of the study.

CHAPTER TEN

THE POST-WAR REVIVAL OF ORTHODOXY

THE challenge of *The Fundamentals* was instrumental in co-ordinating the diverse interests of conservative Christians into a corporate movement. The World War stimulated its momentum and contributed a spirit of militancy. In its earliest form the movement took a premillennial turn; men used the literal teachings of prophetic Scripture to support widespread social pessimism. Some Christians sought rest from the world's confusion by retreating to quiet camps and inciting experiences of mystical satisfaction. Other leaders chose in public and in print to dispute the soundness of liberally-conceived religion. The following enlistments represent these various ventures.

[1.] THE INCREASE OF PROPHETIC CONFERENCES

A half century of Bible conferences had developed a permanent type of social institution within Christianity.[1] Men of revivalistic temperament cultivated their faith by means of these periodic mass-meetings. The Bible schools became normal centers of appeal for this pattern of religion.

From nearly every state in the United States and Canada, two thousand men and women assembled at

[1] Chap. III, part one.

Moody Bible Institute in February, 1914, to study so-called neglected truths and their bearing on an apostate church.[2] It was pitiful, thought the company, that most Christians were as harlots flirting with the world, and substituting social service for the power of the blood. The Second Coming was considered to be the key to the philosophy of history and to the Holy Scriptures. Signs of the times gave ample proof that Christ's appearing was imminent.[3] When He arrived on earth He would crush the powers of time, and crown his own with joy unspeakable in an "Imperialism . . . infinite, eternal, unchangeable." The picture conception of adventism was impressionistic and stirred in delegates emotional excesses of visionary expectancy. This result was particularly marked as a result of the Bible expositions of C. I. Scofield.

On the closing day a conference testimony was adopted by a rising vote. "In view of the existing conditions in the professing church," these premillennarians restated their unswerving devotion to a set of dogmas and promised to contend for them, "so much rejected in our days." Complimentary copies of the proceedings were sent to theological students in America and to foreign missionaries. Leaders returned to their churches to repeat the Chicago program in St. Paul, St. Louis, Los Angeles, Minneapolis and other places.[4]

National conferences of a prophetic character were

[2] Proceedings reported by James M. Gray (editor), *The Coming and Kingdom of Christ*. (Chicago, 1914).

[3] "I do not know of anything revealed in the Word of God that has to come to pass before my Lord comes." Op. cit., p. 231.

[4] During the next summer, Moody Institute gave its moral support to twenty-two such conferences. A representative prophetic conference was held in Music Hall, Philadelphia, in May, 1917.

called in New York City and Philadelphia during 1918. The World War was exacting heavy burdens from religionists. It was comforting to contemplate that the end of the present cosmic dispensation was near. The first meeting was inspired by the same men who had supervised the Moody assembly. The second one owed its inception to a wealthy Philadelphia business man who had been traveling abroad, and had heard biblical prophecy explained in such a startling fashion that he hurried home and urged upon his ministerial friends the necessity of convening God's people to consider the challenge of the coming Messiah. The same speakers were used in both meetings.[5] These men possessed an utterly bankrupt confidence in modern culture. Republican and democratic forms of self-government were futile in handling a perverse humanity. The doctrine of evolution was made responsible for debasing secular and religious education in both lower and higher institutions of learning. The absolute sovereignty of the Word of God had been denied by higher critics, who were in league with Satan to destroy all faith from the world. A typical viewpoint was that of Courtland Myers who aroused patriotic passions of wartime people and then sublimated them in favor of militant orthodoxy:[6]

". . . But I also say to you that we ought to make war, and strenuous war, and fight to a finish, against foreign innovation into our religious world. . . . Go back to the fountain

[5] The New York Conference reported by A. C. Gabelein (editor), *Christ and Glory* (New York, 1918), and the Philadelphia one by W. L. Pettingill (editor), *Light on Prophecy* (New York, 1918). Besides the editors, other speakers included William B. Riley, R. A. Torrey, James M. Gray, W. H. Griffith-Thomas, and Courtland Myers.

[6] *Light on Prophecy* (New York, 1918), pp. 176–93.

head and you will find that your crimson stream has its source in the rank German theology that has been forcing its way into the veins and arteries of all our religious life. We ought to fight it to the finish. . . . I will fight German theology till the crack of doom, and if I go down, I'll go down with my colors flying and I'll go down singing,

> 'In the Cross of Christ I glory, Towering o'er the wrecks of time,
> All the light of sacred story, Gathers round its head sublime!' "

The Quaker City gathering memorialized their faith in eight theological formulas, six of which dealt with phases of premillennialism. How extreme leaders had become in their messianic faith, may be judged by the following recorded remarks:[7]

"I was preaching His truth (the second coming) and one night as I was going to my bed I heard my daughter . . . moving in her cot. I said, ' . . .why are you not asleep?' She said, 'Father, I was lying here wondering if Jesus might not come.' I thought, 'I have terrified this child.' She said, 'Father do you think he will come tonight?' and do you know what I found out, that while I couldn't say the hour nor the day when He will come, I could not tell the hour or the day that He wouldn't come. I did not dare say to that child, 'No, he will not be here tonight.' I said, '. . . , He might be here, what then?' I'll never forget her little face. It was aglow. She clapped her little hands and said, 'Oh, Daddy, wouldn't it be lovely?' I say, 'Come, Lord Jesus, come quickly.' When I think of my boys (his church had 400 communicants in the war), all those I love and those who are lying beneath the poppies of France, I say, 'Come, Lord Jesus, and take the scepter and reign. Come and cover the face of the earth with righteousness and peace. Come, Lord Jesus.' "

[7] Op. cit., p. 211.

In 1919 at the World's Bible Conference in Philadelphia, orthodox interest moved from the apocalyptic ideal to Christian fundamentals.[8] Over six thousand people rallied in response to a committee's publicity. Eighteen of the most widely known exponents of classical theology presented their ideals to the mass meeting. William B. Riley had arisen to command the interdenominational and international movement. At the opening session he predicted that this occasion marked the beginning of a new Protestantism, an event of more historic moment than the nailing up of Martin Luther's theses at the Wittenberg cathedral. Modernism ruled the regular churches; between them and his hearers was the great divide.[9] The hearty singing of revival hymns, the spirit of deep piety, the vigorous doctrinal conviction awakened by different types of preachers, and the development of suspicion and distrust toward progressive churchmen, empowered the company with a sense of Christian invincibility and with one of divine commission to champion the threatened faith. They spoke to the world the organized, militant mind of reactionary evangelicalism, for during this conference the World's

[8] Owing partially to the influence of English ultra-conservatives, who issued a creedal "Manifesto" in 1917 covering "The Significance of the Hour," American sympathizers announced "A Call" for a world-wide conference on doctrinal questions to be governed by representatives from both sides of the Atlantic. The Philadelphia addresses were preserved in the text, *God Hath Spoken.* (Philadelphia, 1919), William L. Pettingill, editor.

[9] Riley had already envisaged a great religious conflict in America between "the coming confederacy" of Christian liberals and the "great premillennial fraternity of the world." *School and Church,* Jan.–March, 1919, pp. 91–92.

Christian Fundamentals Association was conceived,[10] an Association that has endured longer and done more to flank the cause of cultural progressivism than any other agency that fundamentalism brought forth.

The organized will of the conference was expressed in the reports of commissions[11] to correlate Bible schools, colleges, religious periodicals, prophetic conferences, and faith missions, into a concerted movement. James M. Gray, presenting the first report, informed his brethren that the deans of Bible schools were taking counsel how best to deliver their leadership policy to the churches. President Charles A. Blanchard of Wheaton College asked Christians to beware of collegiate institutions which embraced scientific learning, and to cultivate the service of those which honored the gospel. C. G. Trumbull, editor of the *Sunday School Times,* stated that a chain of religious periodicals were co-operating to supply the people with official information about orthodoxy and means of arresting modernist propaganda. The chairman of the convention reported that a committee was at work to circumvent the continent with Bible conferences. The spokesman for missions lamented that regular denominational societies were employing leaders whom they considered were unregenerate or unsound in the faith, and asked church members to refuse financial aid to them. On the contrary, they should demand freedom to support such independent projects as the China Inland Mission and others like it. The resolutions' committee declared that liberals were forcing the denomina-

[10] For its history, see chap. XIV.
[11] *God Hath Spoken,* pp. 20–25.

tions into membership in the Federal Council of Churches of Christ in America. In the event of their adoption of the Council, the Philadelphia delegates decided that they would withdraw from the churches and form a non-sectarian fellowship.

William B. Riley lost no time in carrying out the projected program for regional meetings. He associated with him J. C. Massee, A. C. Dixon, W. L. Pettingill, W. Leon Tucker, Charles A. Blanchard and B. F. Fellman, who crossed the continent preaching factional ideals. After sessions in the Twin Cities in Minnesota, where seven thousand people waited upon their witness, they greeted like-minded Christians in Iowa and Colorado cities, later rallying militant parties in the chief centers of the Canadian West and on the Pacific Coast. Other coteries of evangelists traveled through Ontario and the East, and some penetrated the South. Such English spokesmen as Campbell Morgan, A. H. Carter, F. B. Meyer and Christobel Pankhurst, contributed to the crusade. Dean Gray in addressing a congress of leaders, characterized their mission as "an offensive and defensive alliance against the enemies of the Gospel within the professing church and secular and religious educational institutions." [12]

Since 1919 scores of Bible conferences have been conducted annually throughout America. The chief one has been that of the World's Christian Fundamentals Association. Bible schools supervise many every year, Moody Institute alone undertaking at least twenty. Pro-

[12] The various campaigns reported in *School and Church*, April–June, 1919, pp. 133–34; July–Sept., 1919, pp. 170–71; April–June, 1920, pp. 338–41.

fessional evangelist[13] promote their select assemblies. Some denominational groups gravitate at convenient retreats to press the claims of their sectarian dogmas. It is quite impossible to estimate how many tens of thousands of people pay their allegiance to this type of religious propaganda from year to year.

[2.] The Victorious Life Testimony

In 1914 a few Christian laymen gathered to a retreat near Princeton, New Jersey, to engage in inspirational reading of the Bible, and to share personal testimony as to the keeping power of Christ. They were mostly Philadelphians and Presbyterians, C. G. Trumbull being their guiding spirit. Having fortified themselves religiously, they returned to secular pursuits to demonstrate the reality of "the life that wins."[14] The experiment was rewarding and became an annual event. Within a few years growing interest led these men to promote activity of a similar nature at various places and times. A field secretary was appointed and an office equipped at 1114 Chestnut Street, Philadelphia. In 1920 the place of summer rally was changed to Stoney Brook, Long Island. Chapters of the Victorious Life Testimony, as the fellowship became known, have been established in Japan, Korea, China and Central America.

The Testimony teaches that personal holiness is a normal Christian experience. By abiding in Christ a

[13] These men are joined in a vigorous fellowship known as the Interdenominational Association of Evangelists, with headquarters at Winona Lake, Ind.

[14] Tract by C. G. Trumbull, *The Life That Wins.*

man may be saved from struggle against temptations. The condition is achieved by introspective exercises and other-worldly transactions. During the World War the laymen became involved in theological controversy and were constrained to publish their doctrinal position.[15] They clung to the whole Bible and the historic tenets of evangelicalism, including the approaching return of Christ. The missionary motive was given prominence, and members were asked to invest only in what they deemed were safe projects at home and abroad.

In 1926 the American group discovered their kinship with the English Keswick Conference, and affiliated. They opened a permanent six hundred acre retreat at Keswick Grove, in the pine region of New Jersey. One hundred youth from thirty colleges, universities and Bible schools were mustered to the first Student Conference.[16] Such laymen as Trumbull, Howard A. Kelly and Robert P. Wilder, undertook to steady their faith. War, race and industrial questions raised by the young men were resolved by their elders into the inclusive problem of sin and the conquest of the natural man. These difficulties were removed by a direct appeal to personal relation with Christ.

Similar emphasis governed the deliberations of adult conferences. Throughout its history the fraternity has feared the impact of modernism upon church and school, discouraged humanistic attitudes in religion, and met the current confused situation by inculcating pious principles in its members. The Sunday School Times

[15] Pamphlet, *The Victorious Life Testimony.*

[16] These students discovered a mutual interest with the orthodox Inter-Collegiate Christian Union of England, with which they exchanged greetings. *Sunday School Times,* July 24, 1926, p. 423.

Publishing Company is the literary and promotive agent of the Testimony.

[3.] The Christian Fundamentals League

Christian cultism thrived on the Pacific coast twenty years ago. Russellism, Christian Science, Bahaism and similar sects drew heavily upon the membership and financial rating of regular churches. The awakening threatened the historic dominance of the evangelical denominations. Certain Baptist, Presbyterian and Methodist leaders united in 1918 to ward off the common danger. As the Christian Truth Investigation Society, they promised to study these alleged pseudo-religions, and to present Christian polemics to suppress the error systems.

Within a year these clergy discovered that modernism within their churches was a greater menace to them than thriving competitors without. They became the Christian Fundamentals League.[17] Robert A. Haddon of Los Angeles has remained its president to date. At its inception the Advisory Board included such clergy as Mark A. Matthews, J. Whitcomb Brougher and Evangelist French E. Oliver. As the ideals of the League spread to similarly afflicted countries, representative conservatives from Canada, Great Britain, Australia and New Zealand were appointed to membership on the Board. International offices were located in the Columbia Building, Los Angeles.

The League set as its goal "the promotion of evangelical Bible conferences, scriptural evangelism, the distribution of the Holy Scriptures and biblical literature in

[17] Circular, *The Christian Fundamentals League.*

cities, towns and small communities." Aggressively its members began to combat every form of teaching that questioned the tenets of orthodoxy. They believed that modernism, as Christian Science, was disguising error under Christian titles and phraseology; that its spokesmen did not hesitate "to contradict and misinterpret the plain teachings of the Bible, striking subtly and diabolically at every truth within the pages of the Divine Book." In harmony with the times, the polemicists set forth their religious principles. The Articles of Incorporation forbade any person to serve as an officer who did not accept six familiar fundamentals.

The League began to print and disseminate tracts, charts and folders, which conveyed God's alleged indictment of man's cultist constructions. Literally millions of the tract entitled, "The Spirit of Truth and the Spirit of Error," were circulated in different languages throughout the world. The pamphlet introduced the reader in cross-hatch form to what the Bible, Christian Science, Spiritualism, Russellism, Mormonism, Seventh Day Adventism and the New Theology (i.e., modernism) taught in reference to sin, atonement, retribution and so on. Rebukeful letters in reply to this propaganda stimulated the authors to more zealous effort. They felt that God had laid it upon their hearts to perform this missionary ministry, as he had called upon Jonah to go to thankless Nineveh. By means of literature racks opportunely placed at railroad depots, boat landings, public garages, stores and church vestibules, the circulation of the materials has been facilitated. This medium, together with evangelistic and Bible conferences, has been used to bring thousands of people into the fold of these orthodox Christians.

[4.] The Publication of Reactionary Literature

In the bibliography that accompanies this study fifty-seven magazines are listed whose province it was to extend the interests of extra-denominational orthodoxy. Some represent a local church, a Bible school, or a faith mission; others that of a sectarian group which had run counter to the regular church program; and a few favor independent reactionary endeavor. Such foreign periodicals as influenced American conservatism noticeably, are mentioned.

An acquaintance with these magazines reveals significant information about the loci of conflicting cultures. Nearly one-half are denominational in name but sectional in spirit; as many express pronounced premillennial views. Thirty-two originated since the World War; at least a third of these have been discontinued. Sixteen sponsor separatist missions, and eight make anti-evolution their chief concern. Three of the papers are published in the South, ten on the Pacific coast, and eleven in New York City, Philadelphia and Chicago. One-quarter of the editors are laymen, while certain fundamentalist leaders serve on nine different editorial staffs. Not more than a score of men provide the major portion of the copy in all the journals. Reprinting and syndicating of materials are practised generally. A minority take strict care to quote liberal Christians accurately, and not infrequently the writers resort to questionable ethics of controversy.

The publicity policy of *The New Reformation* (formerly *The Minister's Monthly*) illustrates the principles which some editors found it advisable to adopt in view of shifting conditions. In a letter released by the editor on August 5, 1925, he informed the clergy that his journal "has never intended, and does not intend, to follow the policy of certain other 'fundamentalist' papers which are continually engaging in personalities, hollow denunciations, unloving and bitter controversies, etc. . . . *The New Reformation* is above that sort of thing. We believe in *speaking the truth,* but speaking the truth *in love.*" Two months after this statement of future policy, the editor circulated another letter among subscribers, in which he informed readers that his journal was merging with J. Frank Norris' paper, *The Searchlight*. He wrote, "*The Searchlight* is wont to speak in far from mild terms. . . . Do not let that upset anyone . . . the typical Modernist of our day is the Pharisee, Sadducee, Essene and money-changer of Jesus' time all in one. . . . Holy indignation has its place in the category of religious virtues." [18]

To treat of the editorial policy pursued by each type of orthodox periodical would involve too much space. An examination of the standards of the *Sunday School Times* will illustrate how one of the best known weeklies conducts its columns. The five factors which, the editor has claimed, contribute most to his religious experience govern the paper's purpose. They are beliefs in the inerrant Scriptures, in the imminence of Christ's second coming, in non-denominational orthodox causes, in the necessity of defending traditional dogma, and of warring upon the evolutionary philosophy of life. A glance at leading articles appearing from week to week shows a

[18] Copy first letter quoted, on author's files; second letter, published in *The Searchlight,* Oct. 9, 1925, p. 1.

preponderance of anti-modernist propaganda. Cartoons are common features in which the religious liberal is always pictured as the enemy of the Bible, faith and God. Such an eminent medical man as Howard A. Kelly of Johns Hopkins University is engaged by the magazine to give forceful sanction to the dogmas of mediaeval theology. His series of articles printed in 1925 and later published in book form under the title, *A Scientist's Belief in the Bible,* won nearly thirty thousand new subscriptions for the weekly. The power of suggestion makes a potent weapon in editorial policy. The high respect entertained for the anatomist was transferred immediately to his presumedly authoritative religious utterances. Whole churches in rural-minded Protestant communities are controlled by the Christian ideals of such magazines.

Tractarian publishers have done a large business on behalf of orthodox religion. The Testimony Publishing Company has won wide recognition by producing *The Fundamentals* and similar literature. The Great Commission Prayer League, organized by evangelists to prepare for a world-revival, early turned to speculative questions and to meet what it considered was growing apostasy. The titles of its "Winds of Doctrine" series of tracts indicated a sharp partisanship. The Gospel Missionary Union has disseminated a set of leaflets, each of which concluded with the slogan, "Sound the Alarm!" The Union Gospel Publishers of Cleveland prepare the Christian Life Series of Sunday school helps for premillennialists. The best known production of the Fundamental Truth Depot is John Horsch's *Modern Religious Liberalism.* It abounds in broken excerpts from the writings of liberal scholars with a view to proving how hopelessly shipwrecked the faith of denominational schools is. The book is used as a class-room text in most Bible schools,[19] while all such institutes are publishers and distributors of reactionary religious literature.

Of fundamentalist books there seems no end. Controversial publications followed a rather clear cycle of interest. First, biblical literalism was defended; during the War prophetism was revived; later the old dogmas were restated, and recently science has been caricatured. Every work harked back to supernaturalism, and, when necessary, forced the facts of history and science to fit into the old evangelical theory. The most representative volumes preceding the War were listed in the "standard" bibliographies published in *The Fundamentals*. The Moody Bible Institute Colportage Association has sold seventy-five thousand libraries of one hundred and twenty-five selected texts. A pamphlet, *Books that Stand for the Faith,* prepared by W. H. Griffith-Thomas, was used in Bible conferences for a decade. A similar one is printed annually by *The Sunday School Times*. A glance at the catalogue of publications of the Biola Book Concern (agent for the Los Angeles Bible Institute) indicates that this press gives primary consideration to anti-modernist tests of Christianity.

One book, Ernest B. Gordon's *The Leaven of the Sadducees* merits mention, because it is representative

[19] The American Institute of Sacred Literature has entered the tractarian field of adult education, and has sent forth thousands of pamphlets popularizing the cultural viewpoint of progressive Christians.

of this literature and has been hailed in all ultra-conservative circles. The author gathered encyclopaedic information from miscellaneous sources (mainly primary), to determine the length to which "Unitarianism" had advanced in evangelical churches, missions and theological seminaries. He has been especially severe in his treatment of seminaries. Andover was "looted" by the Presbyterian liberals; the vultures that "picked (it) white . . . are now gathering about Union (New York City)." The names of George B. Foster and Shirley J. Case are associated with Loeb and Leopold, as scholastic products of the University of Chicago. Garrett Biblical Institute harbored teachers who question the deity of Christ. The corrupt ideals of the Religious Education Association have "captured" the Young Men's and Young Women's Christian Associations, Sunday School Associations, the Chautauqua, and the Council of Church Boards of Education. A calamitous condition of official Christianity is pictured.

Secular publishing concerns have not hesitated to come to the aid of the reactionary movement. The Stewart Evangelistic Band, a business men's group, financed the monograph, *Jesus is Coming,* until over half a million copies were distributed. The Republic Syndicate used William J. Bryan's "Bible Talks" in one hundred and ten cosmopolitan newspapers. The Herring-Straton debates on theological issues received similar circulation in Saturday dailies. By 1923 schismatic religion had "superseded every other department of life in news value," asserted the owner of a leading New York paper. *World's Work* featured "The War in the Churches" in several numbers; Glenn Frank's editorials in the *Century,* John Dewey's in the *New Republic,* Harry Emerson Fosdick's in *Harper's,* and the lengthy discussions of fundamentalism in the *New York Times,* illustrate the striking part that this subject played in American thought. *The Manufacturer's Record,*[20] the *Wall Street Journal*[21] and the *National Republican,*[22] on occasion entering the ranks of religious reactionaries, and reprimanded liberal clergy or scholars for interfering with the peace and prosperity of the church.

[20] *The Churchman,* Oct. 31, 1925, p. 8.
[21] *The Presbyterian,* Jan. 17, 1924, p. 5.
[22] *Ibid.*

CHAPTER ELEVEN

THE PROFESSIONAL TRAINING OF ORTHODOX LEADERSHIP

As conservative Christians lost faith in the changing principles of theological education, they sought new training schools for their prospective clergy. Bible institutes and orthodox seminaries became their sources of hope. Such places of learning have developed a strong consciousness of kind since the World War. Traditionalists alleged that the reason for the prevailing scepticism of youth was the approach to secular education in the colleges of liberal arts and sciences. They therefore affiliated such institutions of higher learning as advocated historic Christian doctrine, in order to insure safe church leadership for the future. A third movement to regulate Christian education took form in an inter-seminary league of evangelical students. Each of these organizations pursued its course at the expense of regular denominational means of scholastic endeavor.

[1.] The Development of Bible School Learning

The Moody Bible Institute venture[1] has been repeated many times in American cities. The indoctrina-

[1] See chap. III, part three. Probably two score of these schools have been founded in the last two decades. Ultra-conservative seminaries were enumerated in chapters V to IX, inclusive. A partial list of Bible schools and orthodox colleges (fifty-one in all) is tabulated with fundamentalist criteria in *The Christian Fundamentalist*, July, 1930, pp. 26–28.

tion of youth in pre-scientific biblicism and in anti-modernist culture became popular. R. A. Torrey, recounting the reasons why he chose to be dean of the Los Angeles Institute,[2] mistook the rise of secular idealism in schools and colleges for the devil's cunning work; so-called 'intellectuality' had displaced spirituality in class-room and on campus. Under his deanship "education, special equipment, environment . . . play no part in the matter (of Christian training) . . . the business is simple. Get your message, go and deliver it!"

In 1914 C. I. Scofield founded the Philadelphia School of the Bible to advance scriptural, dispensational and premillennial truth.[3] The Northwestern Bible and Missionary Training School has flourished throughout a quarter of a century as an auxiliary of the First Baptist Church, Minneapolis. Its influence has permeated every denomination (in some of which it is the controlling spirit) in the North-West. At the nation's capital the Potomac Bible College offers a variety of study courses; "secular subjects are presented so that they do not destroy the faith of those who are answering the Call of God" to preach the gospel. The most important non-denominational school to be organized during the fundamentalist-modernist controversy was the Evangelical Theological College in Dallas, Texas. Its founders were W. H. Griffith-Thomas, A. B. Winchester (Canadian) and Lewis S. Chafer; the latter individual became its president. To date, Bible institutes have not been able to agree upon principles of educational standardization.

[2] *The King's Business,* Dec., 1926, pp. 701–02.

[3] The purpose reiterated in *Serving and Waiting,* May–June, 1927, p. 5.

Because the conviction that right belief is the touchstone of Christian piety is cherished, a doctrinal statement of faith governs the policy of every school. Moody Institute adopted the ten-point declaration put forth by the 1914 International Prophetic Conference. Seven years later it dropped the Second Coming article, for the reason that the dogma had become divisive. Dean Gray explained that though a teacher was not asked by the administration to subscribe to the doctrine, he was taught by the student body to embrace it. No more interesting commentary on the pragmatic tendency in such institutions can be found than in their accommodation of traditional courses of study to the newer values sponsored by liberal schools. The latest illustration is found in John M. MacInnis' book, *Peter, the Fisherman Philosopher, a Study in Higher Fundamentalism* (Los Angeles, 1928). Because he applied moderate views to fundamentalism, the author was dismissed from the faculty of the Los Angeles Bible Institute and his book publicly burned. Campbell Morgan as teacher, and four trustees, out of sympathy with MacInnis' position, resigned from their offices. The textbook, *An Elementary Christian Psychology* by O. M. Norlie, is used to meet the increasing demands of students for training in a popular theme. Religious education, a study frowned upon for twenty years by these schoolmen, has been added to the Moody curriculum. It is advertised as unique, however, for it is underwritten with the tenets of evangelism.[4]

[4] The Moody Bible Institute *Bulletin,* IV, 4, p. 2. Recently, the Bible Institutes have organized the International Bible Institute Council of Christian Education to neutralize the work of the International

The increase of religious scepticism in the world has enlarged the militant program of Bible schools. The Los Angeles institution has organized a Defenders of the Faith club to challenge unbelievers. Recently, members have been frustrating the teachings of the American Association for the Advancement of Atheism (formerly, The Damned Souls' Society). The Philadelphia School of the Bible considers that this tangent interest is due to a loss of the fear of God appeal among men, and is stressing that attitude in its educational policy. The Chicago Institute has extended its diploma course from two to three years to increase the fitness of leaders to meet growing heresy in the church and the world.

Bible schools have produced a variety of service agencies. They conduct missions among the foreign-born, in shops and factories and with seamen in the harbors. They publish journals and tracts, send out chapel cars with moving picture projectors, and promote extension schools in foreign lands. Such institutes as are located in downtown urban areas possess a tabernacle for revivalistic efforts, and broadcast over the air two to four hours of program daily. Seven thousand people elect correspondence courses with Moody Institute annually. This school draws conservative leaders from every denomination to its halls to preach and to lecture, which practice enhances its worth in the hearts of remote church people. Probably the Bible conference technique has been the most useful instrument for enlarging an orthodox constituency.

Council of Religious Education; William B. Riley and Louis Entzminger, president and field secretary, respectively. *The Christian Fundamentalist,* Dec., 1930, pp. 206–08.

Teachers from the Chicago institution travel to distant cities to conduct prophetic and preaching missions. At a 1926 meeting in Fifth Avenue Presbyterian Church, New York City, this Institute announced significantly that "so far as is known, none of these speakers (naming them) are connected with the fundamentals or any other movement, nor are they known as pre- or post-millennarians, both schools of teaching being represented among them." The precise purpose of the conference was to reaffirm the historic creeds of Christendom. During the past year or two orthodox educators have determined to suppress the terminology popularized in the fundamentalist movement, however slightly they have changed their philosophy of education.

The Bible school evinces a devout, though derisive, spirit in class-room, chapel and dormitory activities. The extreme loyalty that faculty and students invest in their work is a striking phenomenon. Their passion for saintliness often leads to near hysteria. The constant nervous strain due to exaggerated beliefs in the inner working of the Holy Spirit and the imminence of the Second Coming tend to provoke a psychopathic condition in the devotee. Lectures are inspirational rather than historical and interrogational. There is almost complete disregard of secondary cosmic and human forces in the interpretation of religious experience. On the other hand, neither instructor nor student deals kindly with liberal Christians. A frequent prayer to God is that they may be "saved from the Modernists." Seminaries are dubbed "cemeteries." They trade on the good names of Dwight L. Moody, Martin Luther and Paul. They resort to arbitrary use of the Scriptures to support their dogmatics. The Pythagorean superstition about the significance of numbers has its enthusiastic advocates. The Bible schoolman's feeling of inferiority in modern scholarship is compensated for in his sense of superiority in spiritual status, and this condition of mind permits him to engage ex animo in any diatribe he pleases against open-minded seekers for the truth that sets men free.[5]

[2.] The Association of Conservative Evangelical Colleges

For many years conservative administrators have been alarmed by trends in collegiate education. They considered that German rationalism, English deism, and Darwinianism were dominating the scholastic mind. They watched the spread of secularism and saw it crowd out the distinctive testimony of genuinely Christian colleges. Lowell H. Coate of California contributed an article to the Moody *Monthly* in 1923, entitled "A New Scholarship Needed." The "new" signified a disclaimer of modernist features and a retention of antiquated evangelical principles in higher education. The article appealed to disturbed men. William J. Bryan wrote Coate suggesting that each state affiliate its orthodox schools, looking forward to a national association of the same.

As a result, six schoolmen representing as many de-

[5] For illustrations, consult James M. Gray's address in the Founder's Week Conference at Moody Bible Institute, February, 1921, entitled, "The Need of Bible Institutes and Bible Conferences in the Light of What Some of the Theological Seminaries are Teaching in This Day"; also, reference to address same speaker made at Philadelphia conference, reported in *Philadelphia Inquirer,* Feb. 7, 1927, p. 2.

nominational institutions met and founded the Association of Orthodox Colleges of California. They forwarded a letter to seventy-five academic executives and invited an expression regarding a national convention to support their common educational ideals. Two-thirds of the schoolmen responded favorably and a meeting was called at Moody Bible Institute, November, 1924. Twenty schools denoting twelve denominations sent delegates, who organized themselves as the Conservative Protestant Colleges of America, later named the Association of Conservative Evangelical Colleges.[6] The convention combined the technical standards of the North Central Association of Colleges and an official statement of the Christian faith, to represent their platform. The third article in the latter document denied the hypothesis of evolution and claimed that God made man directly by holy fiat. Another article affirmed the doctrine of the Second Coming. President C. B. Widmeyer of Pasadena College was elected president, and L. Glenn Lewis of the Free Methodist Church, Chicago, secretary.

Wheaton College in Illinois became one of the strongest proponents of this Association. Its president, Charles A. Blanchard, supervised a strict school policy. Only men who professed a saving faith in Christ were eligible for trusteeship; they and the teachers signed a doctrinal statement annually to attest the vitality of their profession of faith. "In this manner," wrote the president to the *Sunday School Times*,[7] "we keep our knowledge of their faith up to date." To prospective

[6] Reported in *Sunday School Times*, Aug. 1, 1925.
[7] "A Christian College," op. cit., April 18, 1925, p. 265.

instructors a questionnaire is submitted bearing such interrogations as, "Are you a Christian? If so, how long have you been saved?", "Are you connected with any secret society?", "Do you use tobacco or other narcotic drugs in any form to any extent?", "Do you dance, play cards, attend theatres, attend movies, or associate with worldly people in other amusements such as are indicated above?" Students who actively oppose Christianity are expelled from the college.

Although President Blanchard did all in his power to inspire the Association with zeal, it proved to be a short-lived affair. At the second annual convention in the Spring of 1926 the delegates voted unanimously to merge their fellowship with the World's Christian Fundamentals Association, on the promise that the latter at its annual meeting would reserve an Orthodox College day.[8] The retiring group recommended to the more inclusive movement that it raise a Bryan Memorial Fund to establish a Christian university, and name it after the great Commoner.

A year later William B. Riley published the names of more than one hundred colleges and Bible schools that were presumably members of the continuing Association.[9] These schools were located in every sector of the continent. But many of the presidents did not wish to have their institutions labeled in this manner. Two months later he published a revised list. The group colleges. Their more recent testimony to traditional education is treated in chapter fourteen.

[8] William B. Riley, the president of the Fundamentals' Association, was present as a guest and undoubtedly had much to do with the convention's decision. He was anxious to unite all reactionary parties into a world-organization of fundamentalists.

[9] *The Christian Fundamentalist,* Sept., 1927, pp. 15–16.

[3.] The League of Evangelical Students

Theological seminaries have occupied a prominent place in the conflict of religious ideals. Students usually followed the inclination of their schools in doctrinal matters. Princeton Theological Seminary's stand for disciplinary Calvinism militated against its men entering into co-operation with the Students' Association of the Middle-Atlantic Theological Seminaries, a fellowship to deepen regard for the common ideals that guide young men in training for the Christian ministry. When this Association was formed at Drew Seminary late in 1924, some Princetonians disapproved of their delegates' affiliation. The Princeton student-body discussed the matter and by a vote of eighty-six to eighty-four decided to withdraw their membership in the organization, their president explaining in a letter to other seminaries that [10]

> "The Conference at Drew showed there was no common basis for work in recruiting men for the ministry. In fact, the majority of seminary student associations represented, if we are to judge them by declarations and opinions expressed by their representatives, have so far departed from the central message of evangelical Christianity as to make those purposes impossible of attainment and practically undesirable."

To safeguard their own position, the more conservative Calvinists proceeded to form a union of theological students based on fundamentalist principles. Delegates from six student bodies participated in a meeting at the

[10] Printed in *Christian Fundamentals in School and Church,* Jan.–March, 1925, pp. 9–10.

Reformed Presbyterian Seminary, Pittsburgh, in April, 1925, and organized the League of Evangelical Students. Qualifications for membership depended upon individual students pledging their belief in the infallible Bible and kindred doctrines, including Christ's Second Coming. The makers of the constitution implied that they did not desire to advance another creed nor erase the distinctives of the denominations, but rather to foster the common faith of supernaturalistic Christianity.

To an autumn meeting of national pretentions in Calvin Seminary, Grand Rapids, eleven theological schools and eight Bible institutes sent delegates.[11] They represented eight Protestant bodies. The League came under the paternal influence of the Association of Conservative Evangelical Colleges; its advisory board included J. G. Machen, Leander S. Keyser, Melvin Grover Kyle, and Harold Paul Sloan. The Grand Rapids program was provided by fundamentalist leaders in the churches; the business sessions were directed by youth. Machen addressed the men on the subject, "The Church's Historic Fight against Modernism from Within"; Keyser declared to the group that the world did not contain sufficiently well-informed men to question the accuracy of the Bible; Sloan claimed that liberals did not possess scholarship superior to that of conservatives, but that the former grounded their religion with different postulates; Kyle offered archeological evidence to defend the authenticity of the scriptural story of Sodom.

The League enjoyed an auspicious beginning. It chose E. Van Deusen as its general secretary and voted

[11] The names of the former were printed and of the latter omitted. *The Evangelical Student,* April, 1925, p. 2.

to encourage the formation of chapters in all types of schools, to conduct periodic retreats, to keep a bureau of genuinely evangelical speakers, and to recommend suggested orthodox reading matter. In April, 1926, the first issue of *The Evangelical Student,* the League's official quarterly organ, was published. Chapters had already been formed at Princeton Seminary[12] and Cornell University, while individual students in fifteen seminaries and as many Bible schools had joined the union. During the summer the interests of the seminarians were enlarged by the inclusion of their men in the Keswick Conference, under the supervision of the Victorious Life Testimony.[13]

This theological fellowship soon learned that their cause was unpopular on most college campuses. The academic atmosphere was not conducive to the approbation of a movement that questioned the validity of the scientific method of study. In the third issue of *The Evangelical Student* a member of the League tried to comfort his colleagues in their persecution: "If we who have banded together to witness for the Truth and against error, are on that account called narrow-minded, bigoted, intolerant, or even unchristian, let us call to mind the words of the Lord . . . 'Blessed are ye when men shall reproach you' . . . " The Princeton chapter itself suffered criticism. The commission appointed by the General Assembly of the Presbyterian Church to study conditions affecting the welfare of their New Jersey school, discovered that the local student chapter

[12] The more conservative students of Princeton overstepped the will of their president and abided by that of Professor Machen in organizing a chapter. The student body vote in its favor was 140:70.

[13] See chap. X, part two.

was a divisive force in the seminary.[14] The student body met to weigh the criticism and voted by a three to two ratio that their membership in the League was a happy means of expressing the religious sentiment of the men, and that they continue their unbounded confidence in Professor Machen, against whom the church had raised its official voice. The commission decided that the chapter had to be dealt with by patient elimination.

The second annual convention of the League brought together a score of men at Zenia Seminary St. Louis.[15] "Prayer and sound judgment pervaded every session," according to the published proceedings. Bible school influence was in much evidence. A few chapters were announced, principally among non-standardized educational institutions. New honorary members included men who had become militant leaders in orthodox schools and churches. The closing address by Lewis S. Chafer, president of Dallas Theological College, clarified "the divinely prescribed method of contending for the faith." A Northern Baptist Seminary student was chosen president of the fellowship.

Throughout the past three years the student organization has done little more than maintain its status quo. Its magazine and *The Sunday School Times,* previously ready informants, ceased to carry any important information of extension work. The third annual meeting was called at the Cleveland Bible Institute. The attendance was small and the interest so lagging that the group debated whether they should disband. The

[14] Dispatch in *Evening Public Ledger* (Philadelphia), Nov. 24, 1926.
[15] *The Evangelical Student,* Jan., 1927, p. 3.

appointment of a salaried secretary revived the League slightly. The only new feature in the next convention program was an exchange of greetings with the British Inter-Varsity Fellowship of Evangelical Unions. Because the inter-denominational fellowship is based upon secondary values of evangelicalism and has chosen the Bible school viewpoint in scholastic procedure, the League as an effective agent in theological education is collapsing.[16]

[16] In an article, "The League of Evangelical Students as an Expression of Student Interest in Historic Christianity" (*The Presbyterian*, Feb. 21, 1929, pp. 7–8), Paul Woolley as the secretary of the League offered no definite policy for the future.

CHAPTER TWELVE

THE ACCOMMODATION OF SCIENCE TO CLASSICAL ORTHODOXY

THE subject of anti-evolution first came into prominence in religious circles late in the World War. Probably William J. Bryan did more to universalize the social reaction to science than did any other individual. It was the "Scopes" trial that made the subject one of vital concern for all Christian traditionalists. Seven men felt divinely moved to initiate schemes with a view to eliminating the teaching of evolution from the schools of America. They justfied their action by the claim that scientific ideals had to be accommodated to those of classical orthodoxy.

[1.] THE ANTI-EVOLUTION LEAGUE OF AMERICA

In 1923 William B. Riley began to make open charges against the practice of the teaching of evolution in Minnesota schools. For him, this false science had displaced German theology as the devil's wedge by which the church was being split asunder. The modernist professor was the maul to hasten the cleavage. Riley had read A. W. McCann's book, *God or Gorilla,* and was convinced that the public school system was controlled by "unscientific, even flagrantly dishonest, methods of so-called science teachers." As a first step in his campaign of reform he called together a few Protestant ministers in Minneapolis and instituted the Anti-Evolution League of Minnesota.

These men informed the public that they were coming to the relief of parents and tax-payers.[1] They argued that, as religious teaching was prohibited in the public schools of the nation, so anti-religious instruction should be. Since for sixty years it had been demonstrated to their satisfaction that the evolutionary hypothesis was wholly unproven and a foe to the Christian faith, denying the veracity of the Scriptures, it was not right to allow this postulate to be propagated in civic education. Besides, was it not manifestly unfair to impose taxes upon Christian men to advance doctrine inimical to the Bible? The League claimed that it was moved in the interest of true science and fair dealing. Its leaders threatened school authorities that if action were not taken to remove text books favoring the theory of evolution and to suppress such teaching, the question would be carried to the law-courts.

The Minnesota organization provided for only two or three conferences in the next two years. Riley addressed a mass-meeting of local university men on the theme, "Is the Theory of Evolution Tenable?" In reporting the incident he remarked how distressed he was to meet professing Christians at that assembly who defended the affirmative side of the question. Although he repeated his ultimatum to the Minneapolis Board of Education to relieve the injustice in the public schools, and invited the university professors to debate with him

[1] Reported in *Christian Fundamentals in School and Church,* Jan.–March, 1923, pp. 16–17, 66–67.

the issue, neither party gave the subject any consideration. The preacher then delivered a challenge to any scholar in the United States or Canada to discuss with him the subject, "Resolved that evolution is unscientific, unscriptural, anti-Christian, and its teaching should no longer be tolerated in tax-supported or denominationally-sustained schools." One of the conditions was that a popular vote should determine the virtue of the question.

At the suggestion of the Minnesota crusader and in response to sympathetic sentiment in the South, the Anti-Evolution League of America was effected in April, 1924. J. W. Porter, a Kentucky minister, was elected president, and T. T. Martin of Mississippi, field secretary and editor of an official organ, *The Conflict*.[2] The secretary was commissioned to introduce a general campaign throughout the nation to prohibit the teaching of modern science. He was to enlist in the service certain English, Canadian and American evangelists, and the geologist, George McCready Price. The League executive advertised their program as a "Bible-Christ-and-Constitution Campaign against Evolution in Tax-Supported Schools." City, county and state wide demonstrations would be made. These apostles of educational democracy would carry their cause to legislatures and insist upon ridding the people of a philosophy that defied the nation's constitution and the Christian faith.

This pretentious undertaking never materialized. The League held very few meetings (and they were inspirational in character) and was extinct within a year. Its

[2] *The Baptist Beacon*, April, 1924, p. 14.

purpose was taken up by the Bible Crusaders of America, and Martin became a traveling secretary for this more vigorous agency of orthodox culture.[3]

[2.] The Bryan Bible League

Really, the Bryan Bible League was Paul W. Rood of Turlock, California. Rood is a Scandinavian evangelist. While ministering in a Seattle tabernacle, located near the university campus, he thought he learned of scientific heresies that were taught in America's higher institutions of learning. Chief of these he considered was "the damnable philosophy of life which logically results from Darwinism." It was responsible for present-day irreligion and lawlessness. Rood's dislike for evolution was only to be compared with his affection for William J. Bryan. The passing of the Commoner during the Scopes' trial left the passionate preacher temporarily distraught.

Soon he was visited with a vision: "In the year that Bryan died I saw also the Lord." The experience assured him that he was called to bear the prophetic mantle of his hero. He called a mass meeting at his Turlock church, delivered his eulogy, "Bryan the Modern Elijah," and organized the Bryan Bible League.[4] It had three aims: to honor the memory of Bryan, to continue the anti-evolution war, and to con-

[3] Martin also resorted to literary pursuits on behalf of the evolution issue. Among his published documents is, *Hell and the High School* (1923).

[4] Official organ, *Bryan Broadcaster.* In the November issue, 1925, Rood reported, "I am in this fight to the end. There is no retreat. . . . The fight must go on persistently, fearlessly, until the victory is won. . . . The League has come into being through a vision from God."

tend for the historic position of evangelical Christianity. Supporting the reformer, in the role of vice-presidents, were the medical men, Howard A. Kelly of Baltimore and Arthur I. Brown of Vancouver, and six clergymen. According to its founder, thousands joined the League. Rood needed a million citizens, for, he announced:

> "The issue is clear. . . . Shall Bible believers stand idly by while their children's faith is undermined in schools which they support with their taxes? The Bible is barred from the schools of California. We demand that infidelity shall be barred! . . . the moral and religious effects of evolution are too disastrous for us to be silent. We must present a united front. With a million members we can say: 'In the name of Almighty God, this modern Baal must go from the schools.' "

The president of the League wanted to build an institutional work of inter-denominational appeal for the far West. He courted the attention of W. B. Hinson, Mark A. Matthews, J. Frank Norris and William B. Riley. As an editor he complimented the *Sunday School Times* and *The Searchlight* for their orthodox stand. He fought "the dance." He published abroad his earlier defense of the faith against the clergy of Seattle. He believed that a universal revival of religion waited upon men who were willing to suffer persecution to abolish the evolutionary views of life fostered in the public school system.

As far as information is available, Rood's California campaign never reached beyond the environs of Turlock. His disciples' enthusiasm soon waned. In 1926 he became an active agent in the World's Christian Fundamentals Association; later, he was a leader in The

Defenders of the Christian Faith. Meanwhile, Rood established a small Bible college in his parish, and drew mainly Swedish youth to it. Besides preaching and teaching, he conducts periodic revivals, in which the ideals of anti-evolutionism and Christian orthodoxy are expounded in typical tabernacle fashion. But the Bryan Bible League remains only a name.

[3.] The Research Science Bureau

This organization has claimed that it is the only scientific association in existence whose charter specifically states that it is a corporation that is set for the scientific defense of the Word of God.[5] Harry Rimmer of Los Angeles, who had been a student of science for years, became a Christian in 1920, and forthwith heard a call to reconcile the facts of science with the teachings of traditional Christianity. During the next twelve months' inquiry for the purpose of establishing his claims in the country, he met fifty men of similar faith and interest; these formed the Research Science Bureau to act as a clearing-house for Christianized science.

Incorporated under the laws of the State of Colorado, it was the Bureau's intention to promote research expeditions in biology, paleontology and anthropology, to use the results of such inquiries to prove the harmony of true science and the Bible, and to disseminate their findings in periodic news-letters. Laymen who paid five dollars or more a year became associate members, and were to receive bulletins informing them about dis-

[5] *The Defender* (officially adopted organ), Feb., 1927, p. 6. See also pamphlet, *The Research Science Bureau.* The Bureau was organized in 1921.

coveries in the scientific world and the bearing of these upon the dogma of biblical authenticity. The Bureau's funds belonged to the active members (professional scientists), whose service in the cause was accepted in lieu of dues.

During the first five years the organization secured two hundred active members. In addition to their quest for truth (at the same time scientific and religious), they sermonized upon controverted themes in Bible conferences, chatauquas and men's clubs. Rimmer found that the most important sphere of anti-evolutionist lectureship was in the high schools. The Bureau's Advisory Board entertained hopes of sending him to Africa to study the gorilla; this investigation would greatly advance "the present growing conviction that man is not related in any way to this or any other animal. A careful and painstaking parallel dissection of the gorilla and human will complete this study, and the results will be given to each member." *The Defender* asked Christian people for ten thousand dollars to finance this project.

At the same time that this announcement was made, Rimmer joined the Flying Fundamentalists of the World's Christian Fundamentals Association,[6] and made William B. Riley's headquarters in Minneapolis the Bureau's alternate address. Under the Association's auspices, he and Arthur I. Brown, formerly a physician in western Canada, began to publish and circulate pamphlets, titles of which were, "Evolution and the Blood Precipitation Test," "Men, Monkeys and Missing Links," "Modern Science, Noah's Ark, and the Deluge," and so on.

[6] As to purpose, see chap. XIV.

An analysis of the position which Rimmer took in one tract, *A Scientist's Viewpoint of the Virgin Birth,* will illustrate the logical method of the Research Bureau. Two premises form the basis of this author's argument. One, that the truths of science are constantly shifting with the discovery of new evidence; the other, that of the absolute credibility of scriptural material ("I have searched it from beginning to end for scientific error, and have found none"). As a scientist he approached the Bible lost in wonder and amazement. The birth of Jesus was a biological miracle. The first prophecy of this was found in the third chapter of Genesis, verse fifteen. Isaiah taught it, and Gabriel witnessed to the truth; Mary made the confession when her son was crucified, and "Doctor" Luke had confirmed her belief in her son's divinity. Jesus' own testimony to the fact in the fourth gospel furnished added proof. Whoever denied the doctrine of the Virgin birth was either ignorant of the materials of revelation or hardened in heart: "If Jesus Christ was not the Virgin born Son of God, He was a blasphemous liar, who knew He was an illegitimate child and adopted this means of covering up this past shame. . . . " The author offered no scientific evidence whatever to support his convictions. He quoted proof-texts and submitted them to fanciful exegesis.

The ambitious task that the Research Science Bureau undertook was short-lived; apparently, on account of financial embarrassment. The founder's part in the World's Christian Fundamentals Association terminated after one year. He then joined the Defenders of the Christian Faith and published the first (Bureau) newsletter in the February number of *The Defender* (1927).

The material included nothing more than shibboleths of militant pseudo-science. Two months later Rimmer informed his friends that the African expedition had to be postponed indefinitely, owing to illness of members of the staff. No later bulletins were given the public. Presumably the Bureau had ceased to function.

[4.] The Defenders of the Christian Faith

During the most tense days of fundamentalist controversy in 1925, Gerald B. Winrod, a public lecturer, became perplexed over the harm that evolution in the schools and modernism in the pulpits were working. In his extremity he consulted with a small coterie of Kansas clergy and laymen. Later he wrote, "During that conference there were scenes, and words spoken, over which angels bent in silent benediction." The men shared their host's agitation and, at his suggestion, became "the Defenders of the Christian Faith."[7]

Article two of their constitution specified that, in view of the widespread scoffing at the Christian faith by school teachers who reckoned with the evolutionary tenet, it became their sacred duty as American citizens to "demand the elimination of such teaching from tax-supported schools." The group's personnel were mainly Methodist, Winrod being the secretarial power behind the organization. In his inauguration address as president, A. L. Carleton (a Beloit minister) praised the record that Kansas had made in rising to the support of

[7] Winrod was known as a reform agent when the prohibition question first became a national issue. A small publicity sheet, *The Winrod Bulletin,* was later enlarged and named *The Winrod Messenger,* which became the basis for *The Defender,* the ten-page, official organ of the Defenders; its initial edition, April, 1926.

great appeals of merit. He anticipated a similar response to this public challenge, for was not the faith of youth at stake? He could not imagine both pure Christianity and current scientific doctrine surviving. The latter must therefore be suppressed in order to preserve religion and culture. The orthodox cause won a strong following in the agrarian belt of Kansas.

Winrod was invited to speak for The Defenders at the 1926 convention of the World's Christian Fundamentals Association in Toronto. The delegates hailed him as a champion of the Christian faith and a dangerous adversary of all forms of modernist doctrine. Voted an extension secretary of the Association, he became leader of the Flying Fundamentalists. Previously *The Defender* had been published infrequently; beginning in February, 1927, it became a monthly periodical, for the editor had discovered urgent causes to engage him. In addition to carrying forward the ideals of the Kansas' agency, the paper maintained sections devoted to the World's Association and to the Research Science Bureau.[8] Arthur I. Brown, William B. Riley and Harry Rimmer were added to the editorial staff.

This new lease of public life for the midwest reformer was a welcome discovery. He vacated his Kansas office to share anti-evolution campaigns in Minnesota and elsewhere. Since Winrod was really The Defenders, it may be said that the Kansas organization also moved away. The February issue of the paper did not advise of any program bearing upon the local purpose for which the movement was founded. As a Flying Fundamentalist, he opened his trans-continental crusade in

[8] See p. 306.

Riley's church in Minneapolis. Winrod caricatured Harry Emerson Fosdick as one who looked for the genesis of man in a speck of jelly; he fraternized with Bryan as an opponent of teachers who (Bryan had declared) had strung millions of guesses together in the name of science. He ridiculed textbooks in biology and history used at the University of Minnesota, and pointed to bolshevist Russia as a sample of the harvest of naturalistic philosophy. The agitator closed his campaign speech thus—"With the prayers of devout Christians back of us everywhere, with the moral support of the great middle classes, we will say to the powerful minority (of evolutionists), 'You shall not pass!'" State legislators in the North-West did not take the campaign's purpose seriously, and the reactionaries' cause was dropped.[9]

Winrod led his squadron of fundamentalist speakers into California and succeeded in getting a proposed anti-evolution law before the state legislature. According to the editor of *The Defender,* the bill was killed by Jews, Catholics and infidel adversaries. He told his constituency that if the Lord continued to supply the funds with which to conduct the campaign, his party would remain in the state and force a referendum on the question at issue. The necessary funds were not forthcoming. In May, 1927, a rather desperate effort was expended to increase subscribers to the Kansas paper, but with slight reward. The June number renewed the campaign: "Careful students of world conditions realize more and more the need of a great and powerful magazine operated on the plan of this one, to counteract the

[9] For particulars, see chap. XIV.

destructive forces now rampant." Although the movement made its appeal to simple-minded and devout Christian people, the ambitious hopes of the field party dissolved.

The Defenders of the Christian Faith have made two further efforts to keep their organization before the American people. At a widely-advertised mass meeting at the Cadle Auditorium in Indianapolis late in 1928, Winrod and his associates tried to impress citizens with the imperative nature of their orthodox task. The official organ did not even publish a comment about the proceedings. The other scheme was the Defenders' (desired) Missionary Tour to Africa to evangelize the heathen. Winrod and Paul W. Rood, who would direct the revival, were waiting for funds.[10] The original plan, for which The Defenders were organized, has ceased to be a factor in the periodically shifting interests of its founder and sole exponent.

[5.] The Bible Crusaders of America

A local revival was in progress at Clearwater, Florida, in November, 1925. George F. Washburn, a Boston capitalist who owned a set of Florida hotels, lent his religious zeal to the endeavor. The Scopes' trial and related modernism had made many people panicky in the South. Washburn's disturbance was exaggerated by the sacrifice of his life-long confidential friend, William J. Bryan, in the campaign on behalf of Christian orthodoxy. Moved also by the revivalist's invitation to men

[10] Announced in *The Defender,* Dec., 1928, p. 1. In the February number of 1929, the editor asked readers to advance five dollars (or more) toward the tour, in return for which donors would receive a letter from Jerusalem enclosing an olive leaf from the Mount of Olives.

to fill in the ranks of faithful fundamentalists, the layman arose and addressed the assembly:

". . . to secure the triumphant success of this great movement, I hereby dedicate my fortune, my family and myself to its success, and I will also underwrite this movement to the extent of $100,000, and if our success justifies it, I will underwrite it for another $100,000, if necessary; so that we may not have a church without a Christ, a pagan country without a Bible, a humanity without God. If this movement only stops the invasion of the modernists, I would rather be known as the founder of it than be the President of the United States." [11]

With this decision Washburn became founder and Commander General of the Bible Crusaders of America. That he felt he was divinely commissioned to succeed Bryan and perpetuate his classical ideals, cannot be doubted.[12] He envisaged eighty million fundamentalists in America who would respond favorably to his syndicated challenge. After picturing what he considered was a deep and premeditated plot of liberal people to gain control of the machinations of the Christian faith, he called upon churchmen to compel legislators in each state to enact anti-evolution laws, or to displace them for men who would do so; to notify modernist missionaries that unless they conformed to old-fashioned dogma, their financial support would be cut off; to cancel their subscriptions to church literature that tolerated loose thinking on the fundamentals; to withhold legacies from colleges that were unsafe for youth; to agitate in local churches and in associations of churches to keep those

[11] *Crusaders' Champion,* Dec. 25, 1925, p. 6.

[12] See Clearwater *Morning Herald,* Nov. 21 and Dec. 6, 1925; *Crusaders' Champion,* Dec. 25, 1925; Apr. 30, 1926, p. 6. Not only did he confess this belief himself, but his friends assured him it was so.

he termed "the old guard" in the denominational ascendancy; and to organize Crusaders' companies and notify Clearwater of the action: "This is the greatest uprising of this century and will overthrow the blighting influence of German philosophy just as German imperialism was overthrown in the World War." The prospectus read much like a radical socialist's call to a revolution.

The first issue of *The Crusaders' Champion* was distributed through the country during Christmas week. Associated with the Commander General were I. R. Dean, Scientist, Arthur I. Brown, Scientist General; John R. Straton, Director General of Discussion; T. T. Martin, Director General of the Campaign; and an International Advisory Council including most of the well-known fundamentalist leaders in the North and many members of the House of Congress from the South. The copy contained Washburn's challenge to Clarence Darrow (recently made famous in the South through the Scopes' case) or "any other Agnostic, Modernist, Evolutionist or Atheist of equal prominence," to meet William B. Riley, John R. Straton or J. Frank Norris, to debate the subject of evolution. The defender of naturalistic philosophy was to receive five hundred dollars for a single debate, or two thousand dollars for a series of six debates. These were to be given in Florida, and the relative merits of speaker and subject were to be settled by a popular vote. Simultaneously, anti-evolution campaigns were announced in Florida and Tennessee.[13] The crusade in the latter state was a

[13] The Washburn plan was far-reaching: "We will make and unmake governors on this issue. We are going to make the subject a congressional issue, and one which may reach presidential proportions." Op. cit., Dec. 25, 1925, p. 2.

counter-movement to that of the Academy of Science, which demanded the repeal of the law that condemned Scopes. Judge John T. Raulston, presiding judge at the Dayton trial, had already delivered several campaign speeches in the former state in favor of the Crusaders' gospel.

Within three months the Bible Crusaders witnessed legislative victories for their cause in Florida and Mississippi.[14] The former state voted that "it is against the interests of the State to teach any theory that relates man in blood relationship with any lower animal." The Mississippi decision was similar. Washburn informed the nation through the Associated Press that the South was the saving cultural factor in the country. It would not only check the invasion of northern rationalism, but also purify the religion of America. How intimately interconnected the reactionary Christian organizations of the continent were, may be judged from the scores of congratulatory telegrams from every section of the continent that reached the Commander General as soon as the state laws favoring ultra-orthodoxy were made public. These were printed in the April number of the official organ in such a way as to infer that America was being converted to fundamentalism.

In the spring of 1926 Washburn accepted an invitation to present to the World's Christian Fundamentals Association, meeting in Toronto, the fortunes of the Crusaders. The following excerpts from his Canadian address illustrate the temper and method of this reformer:[15]

[14] Harbor Allen, "Anti-Evolution in America," *Current History*, Sept., 1926, p. 894.

[15] Reproduced in *The Crusaders' Champion*, April 30, 1926, p. 5.

"Ladies and Gentlemen! It is with great and unfeigned pleasure that I submit my message to this distinguished Assembly. . . . We are Soldiers of the Cross. . . . The hour is past when we should longer temporize with paganism. The church of God cannot exist half pagan, half Christian—one or the other must go down and, with the help of God, the Modernists will 'bite the dust.' . . . the great battle of the Ages is now on between Christianity and Evolution. . . . The Bible Crusaders are now on the firing line, in the heat of the battle and at short range withstanding the fire of a desperate foe. Therefore, we crave any sympathetic cooperation you may render to our valiant Crusaders, and thereby tell the world you are with us and will help us to put the fear of God into the hearts of our opponents. This would strengthen the heart of the church and give needed encouragement to our brave followers of the Fundamentalist flag."

At this meeting the Florida capitalist accepted the chairmanship of a national committee to raise five million dollars for the erection of a Bryan Memorial University at Dayton, Tennessee. His first act was to interrogate the executives of American colleges and seminaries to determine which ones were orthodox institutions. Many schools replied, chiefly conservative ones. In the May number of *The Crusaders' Champion,* he published the name, location, president's name and church affiliation of fifty-four approved schools. Five-sixths of the number were Southern, and one-half associated with the Baptist denomination. Those interested in an institution of learning, the name of which did not appear in this official list, were asked to report it to Clearwater for purposes of inquiry. True Christians were besought to take every precaution when investing youth or money in higher education.

By midsummer the Bible Crusaders of America were

impatient for something new to do and say. According to the magazine's confession, the cause suffered also from need of finances.[16] The periodical shrank first from twelve pages to eight, and then from a weekly to a monthly. Its columns were filled with copy borrowed from other journals; non-evolutionary subject-matter of a general character predominated. The section devoted to "jokes" was by no means the least interesting. In the September issue, the editor made overtures to other orthodox scientific societies to join forces with his party in a unified campaign. As a matter of fact, this Florida movement was trying to unload its obligations upon other shoulders. The October number was the final issue of the magazine, and the revivalistic scheme to change the course of American education collapsed on its first anniversary.

[6.] THE SUPREME KINGDOM

Edward Y. Clarke became known generally through the South as the administrator of financial drives for commercial and civic institutions. He won widest notoriety as the man who popularized the Ku Klux Klan. Because Clarke quarreled over a division of profits with the man who conceived the Klan idea, and thus put the organization in bad repute, he withdrew and instigated another secret society to rival Klan control.

At the Forsyth Theatre in Atlanta, January, 1926, Clarke invited former Klansmen from Indiana, Ohio, Georgia and Florida, to meet him with a view to estab-

[16] There was a simultaneous collapse of the real estate boom in Florida.

lishing a mystery cult to depose evolution and reinstate Christianity throughout the nation. After the group had talked informally about the need for drastic action to meet the people's emergency, an individual arose and said that he had searched the country for a man qualified to lead in such a critical enterprise and that only one individual was qualified, namely, E. Y. Clarke. Whereupon a comprehensive resolution was drawn, and The Supreme Kingdom was initiated.[17]

The resolution condemned organizations that inspired strife and created factions in the state (presumably such as the Klan), and provided that men and women of any religion, race or nation, were eligible for membership in the Supreme Kingdom. It also repudiated the policy of those who thought they could correct public abuses by resort to coercive legislative measures (presumably such as the Bible Crusaders), and adopted the educative method to convert men to their ideals. After pledging themselves to support Clarke in "relentless warfare" against evolutionary teachings, the charter members promised "to do everything possible to so live that our individual lives from this time forward shall exemplify the thought and fact that we are the reflection of God and His highest creation."

The Kingdom received a charter from the State of Georgia in February. The technique of promotion copied the Klan pattern closely. Fantastic titles decorated chapters and officers. Clarke was Grand Sovereign. By paying an initial fee of five dollars, and by swearing

[17] Editorial, "An Old Acquaintance Bobs Up Again," *Christian Century*, Feb. 4, 1926; *New York Times*, April 5, 1926, p. 2; circular, *The Supreme Kingdom*.

fidelity to the doctrines of the inerrant Scriptures, the creation of man by divine fiat, and to the ideals of the Supreme Kingdom, a person became a Pioneer in a local Fortress; state work centered in Castles; Georgia Castle, 1840 Peachtree Road, Atlanta, became national headquarters.

Clarke led himself to believe that this project was the greatest feat to which he had ever dedicated his skill. He informed the public that, "The three-headed dragon which challenges the swordsmen of the 'Kingdom' is Atheism, 'Redism' and Evolution, and the deadliest of these is Evolution . . . the theory of evolution (has) swept the country (and) is causing the very foundations of liberty, morals and Christianity to totter . . . we must rebuild in the minds of the children the religion of our fathers." He pledged one hundred thousand dollars on behalf of his organization toward the building of Bryan Memorial University. His program called for the prosecution of five objectives: the dissemination of official literature, the cross-examination of public educators in church and state to learn what leaders were sympathetic to 'Kingdom' principles,[18] a campaign against 'tainted' text books in public schools, the institution of court proceedings to unseat so-called Darwinian teachers, and the erection of a home in Florida for veterans grown old in the battle with the dragon of apostasy. The headquarters show-window exhibited a gorilla in chains. William J. Mahoney, Prime Minister of the Kingdom and formerly lecturer of the Imperial

[18] Note the questionnaire directed to Georgia ministers, and the threat of boycott unless they returned their answers to headquarters; editorial, "Promoters of 'Old-Time' Religion Think It's Worth Ten Dollars," *Christian Century*, Feb. 25, 1926.

Kloncilium of the Klan, was Clarke's closest ally in the movement. For some reason Mahoney vacated his office shortly, and one, W. E. Floding, succeeded him. His multigraph letters sent out to inquirers promised interested parties generous concessions providing they helped to promote the secret society in their home community.

The first public event to catch the attention of the press was the engagement of John R. Straton of New York City to lecture in the South on behalf of the Supreme Kingdom. The Macon *Telegraph* opened a counter agitation, and accused the preacher of accepting a promise of thirty thousand dollars from Clarke (for sixty addresses) to war on evolution. This damaging report led the preacher to retire from the field after delivering four lectures, for which he received the sum of seven hundred dollars.[19] At the same time, it was commonly reported in the press that the founder was receiving huge emoluments from the new venture. These accusations put a rather serious check upon the progress of the Supreme Kingdom.

What strength the Clarke enterprise actually achieved, no one outside the inner circle knows. Apparently the movement gained considerable numerical support in the South-East and the South-Middle-West, where Klan activity had flourished. That it met with serious reverses, Clarke himself confessed to a (Macon) *Telegraph* pressman.[20] He said that its promotion met insuperable barriers because it had been founded on

[19] "Dr. Straton Quits Supreme Kingdom, But Defends It," *New York Times*, Jan. 20, 1927.

[20] Op. cit., July 2, 1929, p. 13.

religious principles; therefore he abandoned the order in 1928 and proceeded to install a new organization, "The Esskaye," on fraternal grounds and of international character to accomplish entirely different ends.

[7.] The American Science Foundation

Fred Ellsworth Bennett, a member of a Chicago mercantile house, spends his spare time regarding the hardships which secular culture has imposed upon this generation of youth. Crime is increasing; communism is becoming more and more popular; capitalism endangers the rights of the poor, and the spirit of militarism is spreading. There is one reason for these and other terrible conditions, according to this reformer; that is, the false theory of evolution as an explanation of man's biological background.

Bennett is therefore engaged avocationally in propagating anti-evolutionary teachings with the support of the Christian Scriptures. He is the American Science Foundation, and began his public service in 1928. On the Foundation's Board of Governors are the names of a score of educators and evangelists, most of whom have taken an active part in the recent anti-liberal educational movement, and are used to give moral support to the founder's crusade. Bennett's main medium of publicity is a twelve-page magazine, *Fax,*[21] published periodically. The editor offers no apology for pitching his materials in simple or crude English, for he feels he must get to the heart of the common people. Each succeeding issue (there have been ten or twelve to date) has shown an increasingly militant attitude to scholarly ideals.

[21] The organization's slogan is, "Always Get the Facts."

The most attractive program of the apostle of reactionism is The People's Institute.[22] This "correspondence school" provides courses in geology, biology and theology, ranging in charges from ten to thirty-five dollars each. Fathers and mothers fearing for the future of their children are begged to take advantage of this adult educational opportunity. Among the rewards held out to prospective students is the promise that "regardless of location or training we will help you into a position that will increase your income." Aside from the fact that the editor has reported that "Greeks, Catholics, Protestants and Jews" have availed themselves of membership in his order, the influence of the American Science Foundation is inconsequential in the American educational field that it was organized to reform.

22 Described in *Fax*, II, p. 10.

CHAPTER THIRTEEN

TWO EXPERIMENTS IN SECTARIANISM

THROUGHOUT fundamentalist history there has been a constant threat of ecclesiastical schism on the part of the more radical exponents of orthodoxy. In view of the very few major divisions that have actually occurred within the denominations, it is fair to infer that these men used their threat to coerce churches into conformity with their wishes; they were unwilling to follow the logic of their testimony by withdrawing and forming de novo a new cult. Two clear examples of the latter policy stand out. In one case Baptist agitators in Canada and the United States joined their forces to constitute the Baptist Bible Union of North America. In the other, men who had resigned from any sense of denominational obligation, yet still feared for the safety of their faith when confronted with the challenge of liberal Christianity, shared their fortunes in the American Conference of Undenominational Churches. The first party attempted to develop a sect in keeping with the literal interpretation of certain denominational distinctives; the second has undertaken to produce one by appealing for loyalty to beliefs that cut across all sectarian distinctives.

[1.] THE BAPTIST BIBLE UNION OF NORTH AMERICA

The Baptists of North America are represented by three general Conventions: the Northern, the Southern and the Canadian. During the decades of theological disturbance which were associated with the spread of popular science and secular culture, maladjusted individuals in these Conventions found it very difficult to tolerate the changing ideals of the corporate communions. There was one man in each area that stood out pre-eminently in such restlessness: In the South, J. Frank Norris; in the North, William B. Riley; and in Canada, T. T. Shields. Each leader gathered a coterie of disciples about him. Following the post-bellum adoption of expanding missionary and financial programs by the Conventions, the three men with their followers openly rebelled against modernist control. The prevailing purposes of the Bible conference movement reinforced their partisan convictions.

At the 1921 pre-Convention (Northern Baptist) conference of fundamentalists in Des Moines, Norris and Shields shared with Riley a desire to force upon the approaching Convention a doctrinal test of church membership.[1] Despite their strongest persuasion the plan miscarried and a pan-American fellowship of Baptist reactionaries was brought about informally. A year later, at the Indianapolis conference, the Massee-Goodchild party chose such a compromising position on controverted themes that the Riley-Straton bloc decided to seek independent means of group expression. Heartened by a similar break in Great Britain,[2] Shields,

[1] The reader should associate the materials of this study with those in chap. V.

[2] John Thomas and James Mountain delivered to British Baptists the ultimatum of "Evangelical Biblical Christians" (in "A Manifesto," issued early in 1922). A. C. Dixon, "Some English Baptists and Modernism," *Christian Fundamentals in School and Church,* Jan.–March, 1922, p. 40.

Norris and Riley delivered to the twenty thousand Baptist clergy of Canada and the United States a "Call and Manifesto," the aims of which were almost identical (even the Anglo-Saxon spelling) with those enunciated by the British group. The "Call" asked all true devotees of the Baptist heritage to meet in Kansas City, May 10, 1923, to consider means of self-perpetuation.

The Kansas meeting "declared war on Modernism within the Baptist denomination." [3] The Shields-Riley-Norris triumvirate were elected presidential leaders of the Baptist Bible Union of North America. The adopted Confession of Faith of eighteen articles, with many sub-headings and proof-texts, borrowed copiously from the New Hampshire Confession of earlier Baptist history. The following statement from their bulletin defined the Union's inclusive purpose:

"The Union will endeavor to give the people the fullest information respecting the ravages of Modernism in all departments of our denominational life,—in schools, and churches, and mission fields, at home and abroad . . . (it) will give no aid or comfort to the enemy at any time . . . (yet) it is not a club or a whip of cords. It is not an instrument of an organized ecclesiastical power to be used for the coercion of dissentients.[4] It is merely a scriptural basis of understanding upon which believers in the supernaturalism of the Bible can voluntarily associate themselves for the purpose of co-operation in the work of preaching the everlasting gospel."

[3] Pamphlet, *Information and Confession of Faith;* also, *A Call to Arms!*

[4] Although the Union informed the public that its purpose was "in no wise to disturb existing Baptist affiliations," it commended to its constituency the loyal services of "the Bible Institutes and Bible Conferences conducted by Christian Fundamentalists."

The leaders of the Baptist Bible Union were astute organizers. Straton commanded the reactionary churches of the eastern metropolitan area through the channel of the Baptist Fundamentalist League of Greater New York and Vicinity. William B. Riley associated with J. C. Massee in directing heretical charges against the American Baptist Foreign Missionary Society, and compelling consequent changes in Northern Baptist policy. J. Frank Norris aggravated first his state Convention and then the Southern Baptist Convention, by registering heretical indictments against their theological seminaries. Shields led a bitter controversy with Canadian Baptists over the alleged claim that McMaster University was curtseying to the faith of modernism. As president of the Union, he circularized the whole church's ministry to vindicate the spiritual ideals of his party and to allay suspicion, aroused by liberal leaders, within the regular conventions.

The first inspirational meeting of the Union was called in Straton's church in December. The entertaining minister was so preoccupied with other matters that he failed to report the proceedings in his League organ. However, *The Churchman* [5] took account of what the *New York World* and *Tribune* had to say editorially about the sessions, and quoted from the former newspaper the following impression of the sect:

"When they come to deal with disagreement on an article of doctrine, they are filled with bitterness, and eaten with hate. No one note of the humility of Jesus is found in the speeches of these men. Not one note of charity. . . . No

[5] Requoted with comments in *The Fundamentalist,* Dec. 15, 1923, p. 24.

doubt they are sincere and believe they are seeking the truth. But how pitiable. . . ."

The first annual meeting of the Bible Union was called for the two days preceding the Northern Baptist Convention in Milwaukee. The members voted not to compromise on a doctrinal test of faith at the pending Convention, when their spokesman would move the adoption of the newly-conceived Milwaukee Confession of Faith.[6] T. T. Martin and J. W. Porter represented the South on the speaker's roster. William Fetler of the Russian Missionary Society received the endorsement of his work in Europe. It was voted to move the Union's headquarters from Toronto to Chicago, and to employ a permanent secretary. The officers were re-elected, and leaders of state and provincial Bible Unions[7] were added to the executive council.

During 1924 Norris, Riley and Shields attempted to break down the morale of Southern Baptist service agencies.[8] J. F. Love, general secretary of the Convention's missionary work, had accused the Unionists of being actuated by personal ambitions for office and of going into the foreign mission business. T. T. Shields retorted that Love must stand in dread of the Union since he made such uncharitable remarks about it. He inquired of the Southern official if his Convention intended to repudiate the Bible truths for which the Union stood, and to encourage by his silence the growing modernist control within his denomination. The Cana-

[6] The outcome of this action is noted in chap. V.

[7] The Iowa, Jersey, Oregon and Ontario Bible Unions were very active.

[8] Note *Baptist Beacon*, April, 1924, pp. 7–8; June, 1924, pp. 8, 12.

dian's trenchant accusations were printed in the Norris paper and sent broadcast through the South. Meanwhile, Riley was accusing President E. Y. Mullins of entertaining evolutionary views, and (his) Louisville Seminary of harboring skepticism. Every effort the educator made to explain his position was used by his opponent in published documents to "prove" the incongruity of the Baptist leader and the sad condition of affairs in the Southern Convention. Norris had kept up such a caustic criticism of Baylor University that he became a problem at the State Convention. Texas Baptists voted (2500 to 10) a resolution of confidence in their university, and unanimously to exclude the Fort Worth preacher from future sessions of the Convention. Even this Unionist reverse was employed by the sectional party to make further serious inroads into the financial and personal loyalties of Southern Baptists.

Although the executive of the Union called a Prayer Conference at Moody Bible Institute early in 1925, the devotional purpose did not forbid the introduction of militant plans for the sect; they voted to continue what they called the great war.[9] This spirited procedure led A. C. Dixon, one of the Union's founders, to resign from the organization and to state in print that he considered that the Union did not have occasion to continue longer. Meanwhile, the Union leaders convened in Memphis, following the World's Christian Fundamentals Association meeting and preceding that of the Southern Baptist Convention, to press forward their campaign within the latter body. Norris and Martin had paved the way by disseminating literature to the effect that the Convention should

[9] Reported in *Gospel Witness,* Feb. 5, 1925, pp. 9–14.

be divided.[10] The Riley and Shields papers also were used to further this end. As planned, the Convention was engaged in creedal and anti-evolution debates (the Scopes' case had made the evolution question a timely issue), which almost broke up the sessions. By a vote of two thousand and thirteen to nine hundred and fifty, the delegates accepted the Mullins recommendation that "Man was created by the special act of God, as recorded in Genesis," rather than the Norris suggestion that he came into this world "by direct creation of God and not by evolution."

The Unionists moved directly to the Northern Baptist Convention in Seattle and made a bold attempt to force a doctrinal control of foreign missions upon that body.[11] The Convention's arrest of their strategy proved so disheartening to them that they called a private session of their leaders and decided upon organizing an independent missionary society.[12] That action was consummated in Toronto in the autumn when the executive committee adopted the Russian Missionary Society as their vehicle for foreign service.[13] A thirty thousand dollar budget was approved to care for the needs of one hundred and forty-four field evangelists. The executive decided to discourage the use of regular Baptist Sunday

[10] Norris's paper, *The Searchlight,* was sent to sixty thousand people weekly. Red headlines, sensational titles and bitter personal accusations characterized the publicity organ.

[11] For circumstances, see chap. V.

[12] A one-thousand-word resolution was prepared claiming denominational irregularities in the Park Avenue Baptist Church, in the Fosdick heresy case, in the Convention's ruling to govern the seating of delegates, and in its refusal to keep its missionary cause orthodox. *Gospel Witness,* July 9, 1925, p. 15.

[13] Op. cit., Sept. 10, 1925, p. 4; Nov. 8, 1925, pp. 4–10.

school supplies in local churches, and to substitute a *whole* Bible lesson course, which the Union Gospel Press of Cleveland promised to publish at a comparatively low price. However self-contradictory the resolution was in the face of the secessionists' action, it was voted that "the Baptist Bible Union . . . is determined to do its work as an organization within the existing Baptist denominations of this continent. . . . The Union proposes the only possible basis of union and of co-operative action for true Baptists . . . "

The activity of the Bible Union as such should not appear to conceal the work of its state chapters. Prosperous fellowships were busy spreading their leaven of sectarian literalism throughout Oregon, Pennsylvania, Iowa, Ohio, New Jersey, New York, Michigan and other sections. *The Baptist Spokesman* and *The Messenger,* organs of the first two mentioned chapters respectively, kept up a constant criticism of men and institutions of good rating in their state conventions. The latter monthly carried a saying, "There is something funny about the modernists—sometimes they tell the truth," and recorded that several local congregations had divided out of loyalty to the Bible. O. W. Van Osdel occupied the "bishopric" of a regional Association of Bible Union churches in Michigan. Under the stimulus of W. B. Hinson, J. Frank Norris and T. T. Shields a British Columbia Baptist Missionary Council was formed in contradistinction to that of the provincial Convention. Riley, Norris, Pettingill and Shields conducted a session simultaneously with the annual meeting of Ontario Baptists, and developed a vituperative campaign against McMaster University, and more particularly against its ablest theological instructor, L. M. Marshall. Meanwhile, Shields proceeded to found the Toronto Baptist Pastors' College to train another leadership for the church.

Preparatory to the 1926 Southern Baptist Convention, Norris and Shields renewed their accusations against Mullins on the evolutionary question. Their intention bore fruit; for the delegates, fearing greatly for the preservation of their time-honored faith, accepted an anti-evolution formulary. The Bible Union members of the Conventon called a special meeting forthwith and requested all boards and schools to sign the creedal statement. The Fort Worth Seminary and several other agencies gave unequivocable affirmation. Norris wired the president of the Union (who had departed for Toronto), "Unprecedented victory in Southern Convention will tremendously help the Northern Baptist Convention." [14]

But the futility of the Union's work in the North began to show clearly in 1926. J. C. Massee and J. Whitcomb Brougher, as well as many less spectacular figures in the fundamentalist party, upon whom Riley had depended for moral support in former years, were completely out of harmony with his factional spirit.[15] At the Washington Convention, the Union failed to assemble a strong company as in former years. Though F. M. Goodchild loaned them his support, they commanded less than three hundred votes in opposition to (against over two thousand registrations in favor of)

[14] *Gospel Witness,* May 20, 1926, p. 19.

[15] Note the Union's "grievous disappointment" that these men signed the "Chicago" delivery defining a Baptist church (reported in chap. V); *Gospel Witness,* April 22, 1926, pp. 7–9.

the 'Chicago' resolution. The separatists suppressed a confession that they suffered a complete failure as a providential agent in controlling the Northern Convention.[16]

A series of events transpired during the summer and autumn that weakened the Bible Union to a shadow of its former strength. No sooner had Norris added Shields and Riley to the editorial force of *The Searchlight* with a view to duplicating its copy in Chicago, than he killed a Fort Worth business man,[17] the climax to a quarrel he was waging with Roman Catholics in Texas. The following Sunday he preached from his pulpit on the text, "And we know that all things work together for good to them that love God." In January Norris was acquitted in a state court; eighty thousand Texans cheered him as he re-entered his church the next Sunday. J. C. Massee wrote an article in the Moody Bible Institute *Monthly* in which he berated the Union's leaders as men who "entertain bitterness toward their brethren . . . seek contention for contention's sake . . . (and impute) motives unjustly, or seek to spread suspicion without a cause." Riley accepted the article as a personal hurt and replied through the same medium that he failed to understand how one could describe thus his best beloved brethren. Riley proceeded to explain that had Massee only provided fundamentalists with a real program when he was leader of the conservative party in the Northern Baptist Convention, the Bible

[16] *The Searchlight,* June 4, 1926, p. 1.

[17] O. W. Van Osdel virtually granted that the cause of the Union collapsed with the Norris act. "The Case of Our Brother," *Baptist Temple News,* Aug. 7, 1926, pp. 1–2.

Union would never have been founded. Shields tried to bolster up fidelity in the broken Union by printing the Riley communication in his weekly, and sending the copy to all members of the organization. Meanwhile, his name and Riley's were dropped from the editorial staff of the Fort Worth paper.

The pan-American party which had set out four years previously to reform Northern and Southern Baptists failed to call special sessions in conjunction with their 1927 conventions. In April the corresponding and field secretaries of the Union resigned their offices because of inadequate finances. T. T. Shields served notice that his church duties had become so burdensome that he must surrender the presidency and membership on the executive committee.[18] He urged that the new president be selected from Northern Baptist territory. This was a tacit confession that Southern Baptists were too conservative to make good timber for the Union's orthodox purposes. As for Canadian Baptists, Shields was helpless among them, for the Ontario Convention had read him and his church out of its membership. O. W. Van Osdel published the resignations and raised the critical question, "Shall the Baptist Bible Union Live?"[19] As a member of its executive he made a desperate effort to revive the devotion of his colleagues. Among other remarks, he said:

"It has been a matter of serious disappointment that so few of our Bible Union pastors and churches have been regu-

[18] *Gospel Witness,* May 26, 1927, p. 7.

[19] *Baptist Temple News,* May 7, 1927, p. 3; note also, May 14, 1927, pp. 2–3.

lar contributors toward the work of the Union for either its own expenses or its missionary undertakings. . . . It is folly for us to undertake to continue the work of the Bible Union unless the brethren and the churches who are claiming to be loyal to the Lord Jesus Christ are willing to commit themselves to the support of the work. The plea has been advanced that the membership of the Union is composed of men with meagre salaries and weak churches. This probably is true, and yet we are feeling like asking the question whether it may not have been that some have identified themselves with the Union for the purpose of getting help rather than with the expectation of supporting the Union for the purpose of advancing the whole work along every line. If the Bible Union is to be made a force, it must have liberal support, it can be nothing more than an assembly of weaklings if it is destitute of contributing friends."

When the Baptist Bible Union gathered in annual meeting at Chicago in May, only a modern miracle, as Shields called it, saved the fellowship from utter collapse. That event was the purchase of Des Moines University by the generosity of a Unionist who advanced funds to make an initial payment on the property. The executive felt that they would receive wide support for their educational project because they possessed "the only Baptist University north of the Mason-Dixon line, in the United States or Canada, committed to conform its teachings in all departments to the Bible as the Word of God."[20] This happy intervention led the corresponding secretary and the Canadian leader to reconsider their resignations. Both were reappointed to office, but for reasons unexplained by the parties involved, the names of Riley and Norris were dropped from the Union's

[20] Des Moines *Evening Tribune,* June 2, 1927, p. 9.

officiary.[21] Thus the genius of leadership in the Baptist Bible Union passed from the three founders to the Canadian, and its functional purpose from the care of three supposedly modernist conventions to an independent school of learning in the mid-western States.

After an interim in which Shields remained acting-president of Des Moines University, H. C. Wayman, formerly the chief executive of William Jewell College, was appointed to the president's office. The corresponding secretary of the Union became the secretary of the school. Disaffections arose early in Wayman's and Shields' official relations.[22] The schoolman said that the Canadian was trying to run the institution. A climax was reached when the students accused Shields and the secretary (a woman) of engaging in improper conduct, and initiated a riot upon the campus during a special session of the Board of Trustees. Summarily, the head of the Union demanded the resignation of Wayman, the faculty, and all other employees, and closed the doors of the school. At a later meeting of the trustees the two accused parties were exonerated and a more strict program of institutional surveillance effected.

In September, 1929, Shields as acting-president, announced in the Toronto *Globe* that Des Moines University had been discontinued through lack of confidence in his supervision. With its passing, the Baptist Bible

[21] It was reported in the church press that Riley, Norris and Shields suffered personal differences which they could not meet satisfactorily. There was no mention of Riley and Norris in connection with the 1928 and 1929 annual meetings of the Union. *Religious Herald,* June 16, 1927, p. 6.

[22] *Christian Fundamentalist,* Feb., 1929, p. 61.

Union had spent itself. Only a few scattered Baptist churches, which by their own folly had alienated themselves from the three regular conventions, continued to hail its purpose. When T. T. Shields resigned from the leadership of the Union at its annual meeting in 1930,[23] delegates voted to surrender their fundamentalist name and to function in the future as The Missionary Union of Baptist Churches of North America.

[2.] The American Conference of Undenominational Churches

The North-Middle-West has provided a social milieu in which the community church has thrived best in America. In 1921 the late R. Lee Kirkland invited all such churches to meet in faternal council with the Zion congregation in Winterset, Iowa. This meeting eventuated in the organization of the State Conference of Union, Federated and Community Churches of Iowa. Two years of trial led Kirkland to conclude that some churches allowed denominational interests to bulk too largely in the Conference, while other tolerated modernist views of religion. These conditions prevented the homogeneous development of the new sect.

In September, 1923, Kirkland called out certain orthodox churches to form "The American Conference of Undenominational Churches." Negatively, it was decided that this communion should never become a denomination nor include in its membership churches of

[23] A few months later an open break occurred between William Fetler of the Russian Missionary Society and the Missionary Union of Baptist Churches of North America. The executive of the latter organization published a lengthy statement in the nature of an exposure of Fetler's activities. *The Baptist,* Nov. 29, 1930, p. 1492.

a denominational name; also, it was to have no fellowship with progressive Christians. The founder described the positive purpose of the sect as one devoted to missionary and evangelistic activities, whose men were true to the Word of God.

The cult's constitution provided for the freest kind of self-government within the local church.[24] Any orthodox Christian or congregation could join the Conference, which was disposed to cultivate unity without controversy. A transfer of letter was unnecessary for this purpose. Any "acceptable minister" could enter the fellowship without severing relation with his denomination.[25] Article eleven of the by-laws reads: "This Conference shall have the right to ordain men to the full work of the ministry, to issue ministerial credentials to the ministry belonging to it, which shall be valid for one Conference year." Unbaptized persons seeking fellowship in the sect were advised to follow their Master's injunction and submit to some mode of baptism, although the practice could be omitted in case the applicant had serious scruples.

B. F. M. Fahl, minister of an independent tabernacle in Philadelphia, attended the 1925 annual assembly of the Conference and was so favorably impressed with the communion that he returned to repeat the experiment in the East. In June the following year the Eastern Conference of Fundamental Undenominational

[24] *Handbook* of the American Conference of Undenominational Churches, Oct., 1928.

[25] A minister is asked to subscribe to a creed, one article of which calls for "the acceptance of the Scriptural doctrines held in common by all evangelical Christians, with freedom of conscience in matters wherein they may differ." Op. cit., pp. 24–25.

Churches was consummated. There were twenty-five charter congregations. A year later the State of Pennsylvania granted them the right to ordain ministers and found new churches. Though administratively separate, the Eastern and Western Conferences are associated in the promotion of identical ideals. Recently, a Canadian Conference and a Central (New England) States Fellowship have affiliated with the inclusive communion. *The Pioneer of the New Era,* published in Conway, Arkansas, is their official organ.

This monthly magazine of thirty-two pages serves the purpose of a vehicle of suggestions to the widely-scattered churches. The editorials give popular interpretations of the cult's doctrines. Inspirational addresses and sermon outlines form a regular part of its contents. The editor, M. S. Kirkland, believes his people should support Bible colleges and faith missions. To date, the magazine has lacked adequate financial help from the constituency it serves.

Judging from its published literature, this Conference has attracted a small following of churches. Its main strength is centered in Kansas and Indiana. The Eastern Conference has fewer than one hundred communicants in all, half of whom are ordained ministers who live in Philadelphia and environs. They do their Christian work in gospel tabernacles and rescue missions. The officials in East and West have never occupied places of prominence in any of the major denominations.[26]

Two difficulties have interfered with the peaceable growth of this sect. It has attracted people who stressed

[26] Officiary published in *Pioneer of the New Era,* May, 1929, p. 3.

charismatic manifestations of the supernatural, and illiterate men who believed that they were called to preach the gospel and requested professional rating as bona fide clergymen. The dual problem, for they tended to become phases of one, was brought to a focus at the Garnett Conference in August, 1927. Kirkland allowed himself to be reappointed president of the American Conference on the promise that a small band of disturbers would retire from the fellowship.[27] They did. Theologically, the leader said that the way of peace for his people was to keep the middle of the road. The Conference's stress upon secondary Christian principles and the geographical separateness of the small congregations have made it difficult for the sect to mark progress.

[27] Op. cit., Aug.-Sept., 1927, p. 20.

CHAPTER FOURTEEN

AN AMERICAN FEDERATION OF ORTHODOX FORCES

THE history of the conflict of Christian cultures beyond the church is not the record of a homogeneous movement. Most of the agencies that arose to champion orthodoxy chose some particular phase of the faith as their select gospel. Besides, they made their appeal through the personality of a single-handed founder and to a local constituency. A glance at the agencies described in the last four chapters bears out this fact.

There sprang up only one fellowship that enjoined the loyalty of ultra-conservative Christians in every sector of the continent and in terms of every phase of current religious protest. That was the World's Christian Fundamentals Association. This agent was destined to become the foster-parent of nearly all the fundamentalist factions which had spent their day and were breaking to pieces for want of moral and financial support. The chief enterpriser in this Association has been its founder, William B. Riley.

[1.] THE WORLD'S CHRISTIAN FUNDAMENTALS ASSOCIATION

In 1918 Riley and A. C. Dixon asked six biblicists[1] to meet them at R. A. Torrey's summer home and to

[1] They were John Campbell, William Evans, W. H. Griffith-Thomas, Robert McW. Russell, H. Wyse Jones and Charles Alexander, ***Christian Fundamentals in School and Church,*** Oct.–Dec., 1922, pp. 4–5.

consider the expediency of organizing disturbed evangelicals into a world fellowship of conquest. They felt that they were called to reindoctrinate the apostate church in the historic faith and to foster militant Bible schools and conferences to hasten the work. After several days of consultation, the group was convinced of the necessity of its mission. "The hour has struck for the rise of a new Protestantism," Riley informed the public. A World's Christian Fundamentals Convention was called in Philadelphia for the following summer.[2]

Six thousand expectant Christians greeted the promoters of the first Association meeting. The five divisions of labor instituted there point to the diversification of interests that prompted the party's action. Subscription to a doctrinal statement became the basis of individual membership in the movement; a religious group could affiliate by accepting the articles of faith and contributing at least ten dollars a year. The quarterly magazine, *Christian Fundamentals in School and Church*[3] (editor, William B. Riley), was chosen to voice the Association's ideals.

A Roster of forty speakers from Europe, Asia and America, were drafted to address the second annual mass-meeting in the Moody Tabernacle, Chicago. Though fewer fundamentalists attended, the sense of prophetic timeliness of the crusade was more keenly felt. They must succor Christianity from unbelievers in that very hour. President Riley pictured their situation as a camp of evangelicals pitched on one promontory with the forces of modernism bivouacked on another, a gap-

[2] For details of this convention, see chap. X, part one.
[3] Later, *The Christian Fundamentalist.*

ing gulf between them. "The opinions that dominate these camps express savage alienation. On that rock of alienation the craft of the 'Interchurch' is going to pieces, and on the same rock every evangelical denomination is grounding. This remark may excite the cry 'Pessimism!' but the Prophet is more concerned with truth than with terms . . . we must choose between Christ and chaos; between the Word and the wreck of the world." [4]

The five committees on correlation of orthodox enterprises that reported in Philadelphia were silent in Chicago. This led the committee on resolutions to express sincere regret; it recommended concurrence with the objectives adopted a year previously. The convention voted, at the suggestion of the committee, to withhold all monies from regular mission boards until they reconsidered the Lord's will, and to use their benevolences for independent causes that had the sanction of genuinely orthodox people. This rather mild action of the Association hardly embodied the implications of the grave situation which the president pictured.

Dixon and Riley supervised a strenuous religious campaign throughout the next twelve months. They attempted to cover the continent with local, regional and state Bible conferences. They commanded the services of twenty strong spokesmen for orthodoxy. The president himself conducted meetings in twenty-four cities in sixteen different states; and Dixon, in eight widely scattered areas. Iowa was the first state to

[4] *Christian Fundamentals in School and Church,* July–Sept., 1920, p. 361. By the "Interchurch," the speaker meant "The Inter-church World Movement."

organize an Association branch; several others followed. By thorough groundwork the executive considered that the whole nation could be captured for the cause of traditional evangelical culture.

The theme of the third annual convention in Denver was "the Conflict of Christianity with its Counterfeit." [5] C. G. Trumbull had sent a galley proof announcement of the prospective program to one hundred and eighty-one religious periodicals. The Great Commission Prayer League assisted in advertising the event. Only the two addresses given by Riley were published in the official organ. He continued to conceive of the Association's main work as "war." Modernists resorted to "a conflict as unfair in method as it is foul in morals . . . to make peace with such fighters is practically impossible. . . . Unbelief will be beaten back to the pit from whence it emanated." The allies of Christianity were " 'the Christian Fundamentals Movement,' multiplied Bible conferences (and) Bible schools, outstanding pastors, remaining orthodox colleges and seminaries, the majority of laymen, (and) . . . the Lord of Hosts"; the counterfeit were represented by " 'the Federal Council of Churches,' 'The Religious Education Society,' 'The Board of Control,' and the increasing leadership of the schools, secular and denominational."

Three standing committees made important declarations. Trumbull recommended that, in addition to the Association's use of periodicals for publicity purposes, it proceed to establish courses on Christian essentials for lay people, and on teacher-training for Sunday school workers. Riley informed the convention that

[5] Op. cit., July–Sept., 1921, p. 13.

the circuit plan of conducting Bible conferences had permitted his committee to supervise a hundred such meetings during the past year, at which thousands of men had discovered the perils of contemporary evangelicalism. This restorative work would continue on a large scale. Charles A. Blanchard, speaking for the committee on schools and colleges, deplored the extreme secularization of every grade of public and religious school. He asked his associates to help him scrutinize institutions of learning so that their Association might come to the help of the deserving and "hasten the disruption of those which are actually atheistic, while professing to be Christian."

During three years of propaganda the World's Christian Fundamentals Association had shifted its gospel appeal from premillennialism to Christian essentials to anti-evolutionism, in order to keep abreast of popular themes. The last dogma was treated systematically in a number of reactionary magazines in 1922. The deliverances of George MacCready Price, advertised as one of the greatest living scientists, were syndicated in most of the fundamentalist papers. Riley issued challenge after challenge to scholars to meet him in debate and to settle by mass vote whether or not God was the direct Creator of the human species. William J. Bryan popularized pseudo-science by delivering at church assemblies and on college campuses his anti-evolution diatribe, "Tampering with the Mainspring." How prolific were the conventions used to convert the mind of America to their views, may be estimated by the fact that the Association, in addition to other agencies, sponsored twenty-two in Kentucky within sixty days, and as many more in Indiana in half the time. Besides, Ohio, Texas, North Carolina and Michigan entertained missions and set up branches of the orthodox fellowship.

The committee in charge of the 1922 annual conference charted a week's anti-evolution program.[6] The Los Angeles Bible Institute was host to two thousand delegates. The president traced in church and school the wonders that he thought God had wrought through their instrumentality and concluded,

"If Christ delay, the defeat of Modernism is certain. . . . In every way there are periods of lull and there are other times when every cannon is belching out its blast. Today the conflict for the faith is hotter, more intense, and more wide-spread than since apostles were pitted against Pharisees, and lay students against Scribes. We do not claim that the Christian Fundamentals Association is the cause of all this; our contention rather, is that it is the effect of it, its frank and formidable expression."

The Association ratified several recommendations bearing upon a policy which the resolutions' committee presented. Orthodox Christians would continue to canvass the school situation, until they silenced every evolutionist teacher and eliminated every false text-book.

[6] The subjects included, "The Relation of Darwinism to Modern Destructive Criticism," "The Theory of Evolution: Does It Tend to Anarchy," "The Obligation of the Benevolent to Believing versus Unbelieving Schools," and "The Bible School—The Spirit's Approved Institution for Theological Training." The speakers included, T. C. Horton, L. W. Munhall, Robert Dick Wilson, J. Frank Norris, R. A. Torrey, and William B. Riley. To the generous criticism abroad that these men were incompetent to interpret modern science, Riley replied that there was no "company of men in America who have given as much time and thought to the evolutionary hypothesis"; he said that they were "almost without exception, university men of the highest attainments." Op. cit., July–Sept., 1922, p. 4.

They repudiated all existing Sunday school supplies and voted to create their own courses of study.[7] The cult promised such shelter and advice as were possible to ministers who believed that they were deprived of their rights in modernist-controlled denominations. An overture was forwarded to the latter begging them to desist from sending out agnostic youth to the mission fields. Information is lacking to determine what interim progress the Association made during the subsequent year.

The Riley forces were determined to invade the South during 1923. It promised the most hopeful field of response to their militant ideals. The president made excursions into Tennessee, Kentucky, Texas and Virginia to encounter the advocates of "science falsely so-called." The next annual convention of the Association was called at Fort Worth. J. Frank Norris and William E. Hawkins prepared the stage among Baptists and Methodists respectively, who represented the vast majority of southern evangelicals, by instigating bitter attacks upon their schools of learning. They were accused of abetting evolution. It was generally believed among church people that their colleges accepted the Bible from cover to cover; the convention undertook to prove that the scientific hypothesis was being taught, and consequently was robbing southern youth of old-fashioned truth.

[7] C. G. Trumbull of the *Sunday School Times* refused to cooperate with his friends in this departure. His paper was wedded to the International Lessons. Riley regretted his inaptitude to change his loyalty, and supported Norris, as the new chairman of the committee on periodicals, in the decision to have an independent *whole* Bible course. Later, Trumbull was converted to the merits of the Association's act and added an exposition of the fundamentalist course to that of the International Lesson in his paper.

One whole evening was devoted to a mock-trial of three Methodist schools in Texas.[8] Hawkins made the accusations and called upon six students to give their testimony. They read excerpts from class-room note-books to prove the charges. The "prosecuting attorney" asked if anyone would come forward before the five thousand "jurymen" and attempt to deny the institutions' "guilt." No one took the stand. Hawkins closed "the case" by delivering a peroration in which he concluded that Southern Methodist University and affiliated schools were one with the University of Chicago (the most dreaded school of higher learning in America among southern Christians). The great crowd retired to spread the modern-science hysteria among their people.[9]

Although the executive of the World's Christian Fundamentals Association requested at Fort Worth that the delegates enlist a hundred thousand new members, the majority of participants chose to give the federation emotional rather than financial support. Another reason for their neglect was imminent in the American situation. The fundamentalist movement was rising to the peak of its power in the country, but not as an inclusive organization; a great number of independent and local agencies were springing up to cope with modernism. Even Riley scattered his interests and stimulated men to associate

[8] "Stenographic Report," op. cit., July–Sept., 1923, pp. 71–86.

[9] Charles G. Trumbull, who was an eye-witness of the proceedings, recorded in his paper that the effect on the audience was tremendous. The committee on resolutions, referring to the school situation in America, announced that "the foundation of our government is imperiled . . . this propaganda (evolution) . . . is producing a condition that will bring Christian nations to the low level of present-day Russia." Note the editorial in *Texas Christian Advocate,* May 10, 1923.

in a dozen different societies.[10] Undoubtedly, he sensed the hope as well as the danger of the cause he eschewed, when he appealed to a convention of the editors of ultra-conservative periodicals to merge forces "in the war in the churches . . . the year 1924 is to prove a crucial, if not a deciding year, in this world-wide conflict."

The day preceding the sixth annual meeting of this inclusive cult in Minneapolis, Riley suffered an accident that depleted his vigor and that of the Association for the next six months. William J. Bryan and Leander S. Keyser presented the delegates with phases of the good news of a Christianized science. Hugh White of China and W. R. Roberts, founder of the Bible League of India, pictured the inroads of infidelity on the mission fields. By drafting a uniform constitution for state branches of the Association, the convention hoped to increase its control of semi-independent regional movements. The committee on text-books informed the members that a pamphlet was available, in which were listed the names of all authors and books that fairly represented the principles of their faith. Its qualified reference was significant:[11]

"The Committee is aware that a few of these books must be used in a few places with discrimination, but feels these works are in the main safe and sound in their teaching. The greatest difficulty that the Committee met with was to find texts on certain subjects, such as biology, geology, psychology and philosophy, that were not permeated and obsessed with the theory of evolution. The great need of the academic world today is for real and competent Christian scholars to

[10] Note his part in the creation or encouragement of orthodox movements treated in chaps. X to XIII inclusive.

[11] Op. cit., July–Sept., 1924, pp. 8–17.

write text-books on these important disciplines that will be in agreement with the evangelical Christian viewpoint."

The convention's signal emphasis upon the Coming World Revival revealed an arrest of their post-haste civic campaign and a transfer of interest to what God was going to do shortly.[12] In an eighteen-hundred word document they expressed their conviction that the time was ripe for a Pentecost. Fresh interest in the Scriptures always followed "idolatry, distress, war and wickedness"; revivals terminated periods of "political chaos, corruption in priestcraft, worldliness in the church, grossest immorality . . . "; the twentieth century had received its baptism of belligerent fire: "If Christ longer tarries, we are on the eve of a great spiritual awakening." This restful news was published in over twenty religious journals and circulated widely in mimeograph form, with the request that the faithful join in prayer to hasten His visitation.

During Riley's enforced retirement there was no responsible person to hold together the Association's aggregate of unsettled Christians. The official journal informed its readers that the founder had superintended two hundred and fifty Bible conferences and had raised nearly two hundred thousand dollars for the cause, during the six years of the Association's history. This was accomplished by him notwithstanding the demands made upon him by a great church, a Bible training school, the Baptist Bible Union and editorial work. While con-

[12] This transfer indicated that this people were tiring in their "war," that had cost them such a high expenditure of physical strength and nervous exhaustion. Some leaders were beginning to suffer under the prolonged strain; within two years Bryan, Dixon, Hinson, Lotz and Blanchard had fallen in the crusade.

valescing in California he formed ties with Paul Rood that later promised to bring the Bryan Bible League into the federation of fundamentalists. He helped to initiate "the Defenders of Science versus Speculation" ("Fighting Bob" Shuler, the president) to counter the influence of "the Science League of America" (Maynard Shipley, president), a society whose business it was to encourage the public's confidence in evolutionary teachings and related themes. The League's activity was a contributing cause to the organization of the Association of Conservative Colleges.[13]

The evolution issue in the public schools of the nation concentrated the Association's strength in 1925. In March, Governor Peay had signed a bill in Tennessee by which it became a criminal offense to advocate in school or college "any theory that denies the story of the divine creation of man as taught by the Bible and teaches instead that man ascended from a lower form of animal."[14] A teacher, Scopes by name, broke the ordinance and went on trial in Dayton. William J. Bryan became the chief prosecutor. Riley believed that the enemies of the Christian faith had already used surreptitious means to capture Protestantism in the North; and that the Dayton episode was a symbol of their present strategy to enter the South. He called the spring meeting of the World's Association at Memphis to defend the southern stronghold of orthodoxy.

The sessions were sandwiched between those of the Baptist Bible Union and the Southern Baptist Conven-

[13] See chap. XI, part two.

[14] Harbor Allen, "Anti-Evolution in America," *Current History*, Sept., 1926, p. 894.

tion. Riley's introductory address was a stirring exposition of "Evolution: Unscientific, Unscriptural, Anti-Christian and Anarchistic." Dean Israel H. Noe of the local Cathedral challenged the orator's views in pulpit and press. This response which delegates considered as from a foe was a welcome event, for the convention capitalized it to lend intensity of drive to their fight for the historic faith. Bryan gave the closing address before ten thousand people on the theme, "They Have Taken Away my Lord and I Know not Where They Have Laid Him." He made the resurrection story a departure for his attack upon modern science and an explanation of the Scopes' case. The following declaration of the orator became the most plausible argument that was used in the whole anti-evolution campaign:

> "Out of one hundred and ten million people in the United States, about ten thousand scientists and school men are seeking to say what shall be taught in our public schools. While the Bible is excluded generally from being read, teachers are perfectly free to teach an evolution that claims we are descendants of brutes. It shall not be. *The hand of the tax-payers that write the pay checks shall determine who shall control in our schools.*" [15]

Two months later Bryan fell pleading the cause of militant orthodoxy at the Scopes' trial. No sooner had his co-laborers in the retrogressive movement delivered their eulogies than they began to speculate upon whom his mantle should fall. Riley commented editorially that the newspapers regarded either himself or Straton as the best qualified successor. The public press reported the New York minister as saying, "Everywhere I have

[15] *Sunday School Times,* June 6, 1925, p. 373.

been, I have been urged to take up Mr. Bryan's work. It was unique and should be carried on. I would be willing to attempt it." Paul Rood of California appointed himself to the enviable rôle;[16] and George F. Washburn, the Florida financier, claimed the honor by rallying the Bible Crusaders of America.

Rather than be drawn into futile argument, Riley increased his zeal for the Association. He challenged Clarence Darrow and Shailer Mathews, who had contributed evidence at the Dayton trial as supporters of the scientific ideal, to debate the evolutionary hypothesis. He did debate the question with Professor Edwin A. Burt of the University of Chicago, Edward A. Cantrell of the Science League of America and Professor Jos. B. McCabe of England (concerning whom Riley wrote—"the author of sixty books, the translator of forty more, and perhaps the most brilliant representative of Rationalism in England"). He also began an appeal for funds to finance the building of a national Christian university in Chicago that would honor the name of Bryan.

Washburn wanted the school located in Dayton. Blanchard desired Wheaton College to change its name and become the nucleus for the institution. Straton favored Washburn's proposal. Miami and Dallas gambled for the scholastic honors. Riley regretted that the confusing appeals were dissipating the loyalty of orthodox Christians and insisted upon the Chicago setting. Soon, however, Washburn became the chairman of the finance committee of "the Bryan Memorial University Association" and proceeded to raise funds for the

[16] See chap. XII, part two.

Dayton project. By midsummer, 1929, nearly a million dollars had been pledged and the first building was under construction. In 1927 J. G. Machen was offered the presidency of the school, but declined the position. Two years later, the four disaffected instructors in Princeton Seminary were invited to join the Dayton faculty; they chose to establish an independent theological school in the North.[17] In the autumn of 1930 when the first class entered the university, it was announced that George E. Guille, extension Bible teacher of Moody Bible Institute, had become its chief executive.

Two factors interfered with the homogeneous development of ultra-orthodoxy at the time when that religious emphasis was most keenly exhibited in America. Riley's enforced rest for six months allowed the former leaders in the federated organization to drift apart. Besides, Bryan's sudden departure became an inspiration to jealous contenders for his mantle to champion their own causes. The western coast produced the Bryan Bible League, the Science Research Bureau, the Christian Fundamentals League and other similar agencies; the South nurtured the Anti-Evolution League, the Bible Crusaders, the Supreme Kingdom and other factions; in the North several sectional fellowships sprang up; besides, a network of Bible and doctrinal conferences covered the country. Riley observed the social misfortune late in 1925, and informed the scattered leaders that the World's Association was the originator of organic fundamentalism, and that, therefore, each lesser unit should become a chapter of the parent institution. As

[17] Op. cit., Oct.–Dec., 1925, pp. 51–54; Jan.–Mar., 1926, pp. 15–25; *Philadelphia Public Ledger,* June 19, 1929, p. 6.

a happy step in that direction he invited the various regional groups to provide a speaker for the 1926 Association program in Toronto.

The Canadian meeting took the form of a symposium on mooted religious questions. It was Riley's intention to coagment the powers of militant traditionalism in order to crush out the last vestige of modernist appeal in the regular denominations. The purpose took on local color when speakers attempted to unstabilize the lately consummated United Church of Canada. The Baptist Bible Union convened at the same time and place, to increase the possibility of concerted reactionism. Rood, Munhall, Hadden, Washburn, Winrod, Rimmer, Shields, Lucky, Riley, came to Toronto, representing as many individual enterprises. Aside from the resolutions adopted,[18] the most important action was the merger of five agencies [19] (which were experiencing great difficulty to survive independently) with the Association. Other more flourishing cults delegated men to membership on the Board of Directors of the federated movement. By this means, practically every ultra-conservative evangelical leader on the continent was included in office, committee or field service. This rather formidable array of talent was united for the first time in the Association's work.

To maintain the group morale of this loosely coordinated company of individualistic personalities was a difficult task. The editor of the official magazine

[18] They dealt with the subjects of "an imperative call to importunate prayer," "worldliness," "modernism," "the foreign field," "neutrality," "literature," "evolution" and "schools." The first two were clothed in extremely picturesque and revolutionary terms. Op. cit., July–Sept., 1926, pp. 12–13.

[19] The individual mergers are recorded in preceding chapters.

praised unstintedly the various leaders in an effort to strengthen a consciousness-of-kind within the group. To provide a workable program was no less problematical. The anti-evolution theme was the only subject to capture the imagination of a gullible public, and a few states in the South were the sole centers of interest in it.[20] With great animation Riley recited in regional conference and printed page every legal victory for pseudo-science. Arthur I. Brown and Harry Rimmer, as field agents for the Association, conducted a long and arduous itinerary from Minneapolis to California seeking to disciple men in the legislative crusade. They reported some real conversions to their cause.[21]

Beginning the first week in 1927, Brown, Rimmer, Winrod and Riley, self-styled themselves "the Flying Fundamentalists" and turned their combined efforts upon Minnesota to urge the adoption of an anti-evolution bill similar to those advocated in southern states. They addressed seventy-five communities during the five weeks' campaign. The Lutheran Church was the only denomination to give the squadron encouragement; it

20 Anti-evolution laws were introduced into three of the nine sitting legislatures. Tennessee had already written the law into its statutes. The Mississippi house enacted the law in February, 1926; the Kentucky legislators defeated the measure the same month; the Texas Board of Education, at the word of its governor and the State Text-Book Board, erased evolutionary materials from its biological texts; in Arkansas the house defeated the bill in 1926, but two years later it was passed in a state referendum and by a substantial majority; early in 1929 Texas added the statute to its books; West Virginia, Missouri, Oklahoma, New Hampshire, Delaware and Minnesota, rejected the bill. This review is a digest of the legislative movement to date. Harbor Allen, "Anti-Evolution in America," *Current History*, Sept., 1926, pp. 893–97; *The Defenders*, Dec., 1928, p. 5; *The Baptist*, May 11, 1929.

21 "On the Firing Line," *Christian Fundamentals in School and Church*, Jan.–March, 1927, pp. 31–34.

feared that evolutionary instruction in the public school might mean a secular state-religion. Riley received the privilege of speaking before the combined state senate and legislature in March. He urged that the bill his party fostered be approved for five reasons: it was conceded to be constitutional; admittedly, it met a popular demand; it was most manifestly fair; it did not restrict scientific research, and it was the evangelicals' only means of redress for their grievances. The speaker informed the law-makers that he had debated the subject seventeen times with scientific experts and had won sixteen decisions with overwhelming majorities. He quoted O'Toole, Price, More and Keyser as outstanding university graduates, and as his allies in this national crusade, and concluded by saying, "Certainly the members of this great body must be profoundly impressed with the fact that this is *no Riley movement* (the speaker's emphasis), as the opponents have sought to make it appear." The measure was defeated in both houses.[22]

The ninth annual convention of the World's Christian Fundamentals Association in Atlanta failed completely to measure up to the desire of its promoters. Beyond a bare statement of the resolutions adopted [23] and the print-

[22] Riley explained that "Evolutionists (atheists, theists and anarchists)" had resorted to unfair lobbying and forced the issue. He felt compensated somewhat, however: "This battle has been won in the State. The parents and tax-payers in overwhelming majority do not desire their children to be steeped in this pseudo-science. If it were made a matter of referendum, five-sixths of the tax-payers would vote against it. . . ." Op. cit., Jan.–Mar., 1927, pp. 14–15.

[23] There were no new features stressed nor any context that suggested a forward-looking program. J. Frank Norris was conspicuous by his absence.

ing of Riley's opening address, the magazines published nothing. The founder of the movement gave a summary of its history in his address; evangelicalism had produced the Book of Acts, conquered the Roman Empire, encountered the corrupted Roman Catholic Church in the Reformation, met the heresy of Deism . . . ; and had found its providential succession in the ideals embraced by the Atlanta Association. The closing remarks of the speaker revealed the next advisable step which he considered his company should take in their social evolution;[24] Riley had become a sectarian *in principle* as well as in spirit, and committed his followers to the same reactionary position. He said:[25]

"The history of the rights of denominationalism might be an interesting study, but it would clearly demonstrate no divinity. There is nothing in the New Testament to advocate or even justify its existence . . . they have tried to find in its sacred pages the differences of inherited heresies, and denominationalism has been the result . . . the great truth is that in every evangelical denomination there are thousands . . . of men who are practically in faith and heart *One,* and who ought, perhaps without further delay, to surrender up to the modernist-marauders their institutions, now uniformly manned by unbelievers, as a liability and not an asset. As a new organization we could then go forth as brethren in the Lord . . . who are my brethren? Baptists? Not necessarily, and in thousands of instances, No! My brethren are those who believe in a personal God, in an inspired Book, and in a redeeming Christ."

[24] To the student of the movement it appears the only practicable step left for this people, providing they desired to continue their retrogressive position. The evolutionary issue was passing out of public interest; the appeal to sectarian independence had the virtue of novelty and radicalism.

[25] *The Christian Fundamentalist,* July, 1927, pp. 13–14.

The official magazine lacked informative material bearing on program or field work, following the Atlanta meeting. Brown had terminated his contract as a field agent of the Association at the convention. By midsummer Rimmer had resigned a similar office and turned to collegiate teaching. The only remaining traveling secretary, Gerald B. Winrod, who was appointed to the post at Atlanta, divided his time between the inclusive enterprise and the work of The Defenders in Kansas. Riley made a rather desperate appeal to the country for funds to help revive the falling structure of extreme orthodoxy. When the faithful gathered in Chicago, May, 1928, to the annual conference, there were few factors in the situation to cheer them. On the contrary, Campbell Morgan, who had been associated formerly with the movement, testified in print that he had lost interest in its aims. No addresses or proceedings were given in the official magazine. Only two of the resolutions carried pertinent value—the delegates decided that the Federal Council of Churches of Christ in America was their chiefest foe in organized Christianity; also, they approved of citizenship military training as a patriotic measure, for were not wars inevitable until the return to earth of the Prince of Peace?

During the past two years the World's Christian Fundamentals Association has failed to sponsor any significant issue. Its conventions have been scarcely mentioned in the fundamentalist press; *The Christian Fundamentalist* reported that William B. Riley had resigned from the office of president in 1930 and was succeeded by Paul W. Rood. Since the founder of this inclusive orthodox movement has resigned from the leadership, and since the Association has disregarded the only logical step to safeguard its individuality (*i.e.*, to withdraw its members from the denominations and become an independent sect), this spectacular and most vigorous and inclusive of all fundamentalist Christian causes seems to have run its full course.

PART FOUR

Conclusion

CHAPTER FIFTEEN

CONFLICT WITHIN CURRENT CHRISTIANITY

SCIENTIFIC and industrial developments in the nineteenth century occasioned marked changes in American culture. Secular ideals grew up beside historic Christian principles that formerly had commanded the loyalty of church and society, provoking a serious misunderstanding within and imposing heavy responsibilities upon religious leadership. Under this duress a clear distinction arose between those who chose to accommodate their inherited faith to the requirements of social progress and those who intensified their witness to Christian orthodoxy.[1] There was a large middle-of-the-road class in the denominations throughout the controversy that developed. Many were among the church laity. The controversy may be characterized mainly as a conflict between types of church leaders. How far-reaching early orthodox rapprochement was may be judged from the conclusions reached in part one of this study.

By the time *The Fundamentals* were published in

[1] In John Dewey's latest book, *Individualism Old and New* (New York, 1930), he indicates in principle the nature of basic forces in our inherited and contemporary secular cultures, and the social inadequacy of the intellectual and moral patterns of the former to preserve the potential values springing up in the latter. The present writer has attempted to do a similar service, but with more regard to related problems, in the interpretation of the conflict of religious cultures.

1910 the variances between conservatives and liberals had become so acute that a clash of Christian cultures was inevitable. The problem of orthodox leaders shifted from protecting Christianity against the impact of secular idealism to safeguard it from the progressive position which liberal men were pressing within the church. They insisted that they were defending the fundamentals of the Christian faith and that modernists were dictating secondary or pseudo-religion. The traditionalists made a resolute effort to reinstate the principles of inherited Christianity in control of the churches. Certain extremists became disheartened in their attempt to accomplish this end by regular methods of rebuke, and, as they felt social forces threatened the survival of religious authority in America, they championed radical Christian measures beyond the churches. These reactions to modernism are differentiated in Parts Two and Three of this study.

Contrasting fundamentalist ideals, however, as defined within the churches invite comment. The occasion of conflict in each communion was the question of the priority of the historic distinctives that had given individuality to the particular denomination. The Baptists had treasured one set; the Presbyterians another; and other communions still other sets. Yet in every denomination orthodox men considered that their church's distinctives were *the* essentials of supernaturally-prescribed Christianity! In general, their ideals related to the Bible, doctrine, ecclesiastical forms and ethical principles. Probably they reached closest agreement in their estimate of the Protestant's Book. Even so, Baptist and Disciple traditionalists took a different position from that of Methodists or Episcopalians.

In the case of doctrine and church administration, contrasts are even more distinguishable. Fundamental beliefs ranged from a five-point system to thirty-nine articles. Some conservatives stressed premillennialism; others repudiated the view. Neo-Calvinists put forth a closely articulated theological schema; Restorationists refused to be bound by a closed formulary. As widely differentiated methods of church government as congregational, republican and episcopalian, were claimed by their adherents to have undisputed theocratic sanction. As for ethical ideals, certain factions claimed the believer's first duty was to obey the literal Word of God; others, that he should give primary loyalty to apostolic traditions; and yet others, that the observance of the Mass represented the epitome of Christian devotion. Notwithstanding fundamentalists' claims to the contrary, it is impossible to select a statement of principles that denote a common faith "once for all delivered to the saints."

It is clear that conservatives attempted to employ authoritative beliefs *as such* by which to regulate the denominations. They trusted in Christian absolutes, whereas relative doctrines were the order of the day. These absolutes had become institutionalized by Christian usage, and now they were cultivated by the affected feeling that they remained the sovereign will of God. The fundamentalist made generous use of primary religious causes to justify his views, and of secondary causes to account for those of the liberal. When he did resort to primary forces to interpret the latter's position, usually he made reference to the powers of evil. In either case this type of interpreter appealed to the principles of magic rather than those of science or religion. This approach is particularly apparent in Part Three of this study.

It is just as clear that doctrinaires were unable to maintain their beliefs unconditioned. Psychologically, a fundamental became such for them, because it bore a vital relation to some desired outcome in a controversial situation. The nature of the outcome depended upon the exigencies in a given conflict of religious groups, and upon the ecclesiastical wishes of the conservative leadership. In other words, even *the* essentials were subject to change as the seasonal problems of discordant parties necessitated. The permanent factor in orthodoxy has not been a residuum of so-called revealed truth to which men gave unyielding and universal allegiance, but an insistence upon loyalty to such tangible forms of authority as would anchor a conventional believer in any clash of Christian interests, and the vigorous defense of such forms (as long as they gave promise of denominational control) in opposition to the more democratic ideals of religious liberals.

A glance at fundamentalist activity beyond the churches reveals other striking characteristics of contemporary Christianity. Of the seventeen fellowships (considered in Part Three) that arose to redeem society from men presumed to be the enemies of true religion, eleven are defunct now; three are surviving amid extenuating circumstances; the only agencies that carry forward their programs unimpaired are the Bible conference movement, the publishers of orthodox literature, and the Bible schools. Six of the seven leagues instituted to accommodate the principles of science to classical orthodoxy have become inoperative. Geographically, three of these tangent movements served the South, four the West and one the East; six were national in purpose and two international.

Probably the strongest disintegrating force in these radical forms of orthodoxy has been the unyielding individualism of its leaders. Such was the confession of William B. Riley, the ablest executive that fundamentalism produced. Eleven agencies (treated in Part Three) owed their inceptions to as many independent commanders, and were indebted to them for such success or failure as attended their fortunes. The only all-inclusive fellowship to spring up was the World's Christian Fundamentals Association, and not even its founder could retain the cooperation of the factious advisors within it. Either these men disagreed upon the subject of Christian essentials, or (and more often) personal incompatibilities arose in council that militated against the solidarity of their cause.

The present status of orthodox Christianity can be audited with a considerable degree of trustworthiness. As for doctrinal prescriptions, apparently there are as many conservative believers as there were two decades ago. In other words, the recent controversy changed few minds, though it drove some progressives from positions of trust in the church. The Bible schools win a fair proportion of ministerial youth and graduate them into the several communions. (It is advisable to note, however, that these schools are slowly broadening their aims and methods to include elements in the new learning.) Bible conference and orthodox literature continue to enlist the support of many laymen and clergy. As long as the American people treasure community conditions that nurture the phenomenon of social like-mindedness, there will be large aggregations of defenders of the Christian faith. It is not a matter of chance that conservative preachers are more popular in rural districts, and that they still minister to the largest congregations in urban centers. The priestly rôle remains more popular than the prophetic one.

Traditionalists are forced to discredit an autonomous culture. Within every denomination fundamentalists retained the right to propagate their views. In certain instances they have established their own theological seminaries, colleges of arts and sciences, and sectional press and literature, as an integral part of the church's structural equipment. They have required that the mission boards send a reasonable number of their men to the foreign field. Sometimes deprived of a majority vote to control administrative appointments at home, they have used the occasion to inhibit liberals from promoting a progressive religious program. It is doubtful if the denominations in America are witnessing as devoutly to their spiritual ideals as they were a decade or two ago.

On the other hand, the dissentient agitation that became so factional during the heat of the theological controversy has subsided. This change is due to several reasons. Those conservatives who learned to cooperate with liberals, in spite of divergent world-views, received denominational deferences such as have been suggested above. Extremists, denied the fulfillment of their ambitions in the regular church courts, withdrew to establish faith causes. Resulting inter-denominational camaraderie endowed these men with a feeling of victory for their views and thus minimized tension within the communions. The World War animosities and the aftermath of popular reactionism to social change that fortified the religious issue, have been retired noticeably in the last few years. Not a few of the irreconcilables who spent themselves for the cause of authoritarianism have finished their earthly crusade, or have withdrawn from active service.

Whether extremists will attempt further divisions within Protestantism is a matter of slight conjecture. There is only one apparent source whence this action might arise; that is, under the impetus of the World's Christian Fundamentals Association. Its inspiring organizer has expressed his willingness to retire from the historic communions, which he believes are so hopelessly involved in modernism, and to found a new order of Protestantism patterned after the rules of traditional evangelicalism.[2] Thus far he has excused himself from this action on the ground that it would cost many of his ministerial followers great economic hardship. Tem-

[2] *The Christian Fundamentalist,* Oct., 1928, pp. 6–7; April, 1929, pp. 123–24. In the May issue, 1930, Riley has claimed that it would be inexpedient for fundamentalists to separate from the denominations; rather, it remains their special function "to contend against error" within the churches.

porarily, some of them would be without the means of livelihood. The decline of popular interest in the Association adds weight to the probability that Riley has slight intention of forming a fundamentalist sect.

What has brought about such a serious clash of Christian cultures in our generation? All parties to the cause of religion welcome light on this question. Are not two basic facts patent as a result of this historical and psychological study: that orthodoxy demanded the preservation of antiquated Christian doctrines in a world situation which made the rethinking of religion imperative for free churchmen, and that the conflict was critical due to a type of personality that religious disputations always produce? On the one hand, liberals were neglecting beliefs which conservatives cherished as the indispensable vehicle of their deepest spiritual experience; and on the other progressive leaders were thwarting their personal ambitions by denying them adequate self-expression in church affairs. These truths are most important for, but least understood by, the Christian forces in America.

Briefly, what was the nature of the religious values of conservatism? They were professed as certain essential beliefs, presumably based on the Protestant understanding of the Word of God. The liberal examined these doctrinal deliverances in the light of current principles of biblical and scholarly procedure, indicated wherein they were contrary to genuinely modern beliefs and waived them aside, assuming that thus he had evaluated the faith of his orthodox brethren. Far from it.

Fallaciously, he resorted to the logical rather than the psychological method to account for the real meaning of such values.[3] Nearly all the literature bearing on the fundamentalist-modernist controversy short-circuited psychology, employed the method of the conventional theologian, and failed to explain the orthodox positions. To estimate the values advisedly, it is necessary to recognize a two-fold function of religious language, the experimental and the pietistic.[4] In the first instance word-symbols are used to represent verifiable events in human experience; in the second, symbols, though referring to objects, signify more particularly the strength of the user's loyalty to such objects, and hence become invested with special emotional content. Quite naturally, Christian language (doctrines) tends to exaggerate subjective tenets of personal faith, for the reason that it is the genius of religionists to entertain a devout regard for beliefs that matter. But a man's commitment to what he considers are "essentials" to salvation is not necessarily one with a statement of tested religious truth. Unless any Christian leader submits his doctrinal beliefs to frequent objective scrutiny, unconsciously he will annex to them an overgrowth of evocative tone on account of the precious purpose they fulfill.[5]

[3] A perusal of *The Will to Believe* by William James is a good corrective for those who have committed the "logic" fallacy.

[4] C. K. Ogden and I. A. Richards, *The Meaning of Meaning* (New York, 1923), is a classical treatment of these uses in terms of secular language.

[5] This contrast suggests one difference between Christian and scientific methodologies. The scientist uses words to indicate experimental meanings of a disciplined intelligence. The Christian employs symbols to express his whole personality in terms of certain commanding loyalties. Note, "An Overlooked Factor in the Adjustment of Religion and

This is precisely what happened in the case of the fundamentalists. "People may be set off to action by words although the words may be as little freighted with (objective) meaning as they are deeply weighed with (subjective) emotions."[6] Evangelical theology that dominated the mind of America for over two centuries was conceived as a sacred deposit of absolute truth. When the new learning in regard to the Bible, natural law and church history, became the property of open-minded Christians, a more disciplined vocabulary referring to demonstrable phenomena came into vogue.

Misunderstanding and confusion followed within the church. The orthodox learned that it was painful to doubt and inquire, but pleasing to accept articles "by faith." The liberals made progress in their thinking through the stages of honest doubt, inquiry, discovery and truth-testing; the conservatives substituted an attitude of certainty for one of doubt, and rested their case on the impregnable rocks of so-called first principles and revelation. Failing to appreciate the grounds of restated doctrines, they proceeded to defend their ideals tenaciously, and as a natural consequence accused liberal thinkers of betraying the truth and entertaining falsehood. They augmented their religious phrases with a high degree of positive emotional value, while they accorded to their opponents' teachings a similar degree

Science," Gerald Birney Smith, *Journal of Religion,* July, 1927, pp. 337–60.

For reasons why religious people are inclined towards the pietistic use of words, consult Henry Nelson Wieman, *Religious Experience and the Scientific Method* (New York, 1926), pp. 51–54.

[6] Irwin Edman, *Human Traits and Their Social Significance* (New York, 1920), p. 236.

of negative emotional value. They played the passions of trust, love, hate, jealousy, prejudice and fear, upon the situation until a hiatus arose between the sponsors of the two views. While conservatives and liberals usually adopted different premises of Protestantism and proceeded to define their positions by converse logical methods, the contradictory psychological attitudes towards beliefs became the more serious wedge separating the two factions. The debatable beliefs, which fundamentalists found necessary to reinforce sentimentally in the face of modernists' criticism, grew resistant to doubt (to use F. C. S. Schiller's words) and were toughened by the shock of dissent. The faith of modernism did not so much damage the dogmas of the orthodox; rather, it invigorated them.

Such an approach to religious belief throws important light upon the controverted doctrines. A proposition was credited with shifting complexities of pietistic content, according to the immediate function it fulfilled in a group's placement of loyalty. Independently of its objective reference in history, a doctrine might shade from full-belief to half-belief, to quarter-belief, to make-belief, as it diminished in intensity of purpose for the group; it might have seasonal or momentary significance; it might be entertained as a doubt or a certainty under different circumstances.[7] In a given social atmosphere and accompanied by certain gestures of address, it might thrill, charm, bewitch, grieve, shame or deceive, as the spokesman intended. When a controversialist

[7] For an analysis of social forces contributing to psychological types of beliefs, see F. C. S. Schiller, *Problems of Belief* (London, 1925), chaps. III to VII inclusive. Illustrations of these doctrinal purposes are plentiful in the main body of this study.

declared, "I honestly believe . . . !", he inferred that dishonest beliefs existed, even for the speaker, for they might be suppressed unconsciously as a form of intellectual cowardice. When he asserted "I know . . . !", conceivably he was not thinking at the moment, but desiring very strongly to think and to help himself believe that he did know. Auto-suggestion is common in a leader who is suffering from a sense of religious uncertainty. A polemicist was guilty of dishonesty when he pretended to use words to refer to verifiable objects in history or experience, but in reality was employing them only because of their sentimental associations.

The foregoing critique of dogma indicates that when a partisan group announced that they believed in the Virgin birth of Christ (to use but one illustration), the affirmation *as such* evinces little meaning. It can be understood only in its psychological setting. If this doctrine were taken to have designative reference in history, it would require that the believers possessed a thorough acquaintance with the laws of biogenesis, and with all the necessary circumstances involved in Mary's conception; or, if that direct information were denied, then the same data from authentic first-century investigators. Manifestly, the doctrine has been believed for its pietistic significance. And what content of sentiment did it convey? This can be answered only by a careful appraisal of conditions determining the immediate intent of the declarationists. It might stand for one of many conceivable meanings. For instance, it might mean that simply because one or two biblical documents contain reference to the Virgin birth, the belief was precious and therefore "true"; it might point to a flat refusal to consider the possibility of the natural conception of Mary and the consequent humanity of Jesus; it might signify unintelligible faith in a manner of birth of the Christian's Saviour rather than a willingness to consider an explanation of the facts that would temporarily unsettle the soul; it might be used as an appeal to a convention's credulity in order to arrest the denominational control of liberals and fortify faith in conservative leadership; and so on.

In any case, such a fundamentalist declaration was made to convey certain intrinsic Christian values, and to insure the ascendancy of their users in a given controverted situation in the church. Paraphrasing and applying the words of Edman,[8] for orthodox men dogmas provoked powerful feeling and action, determining in no small degree the allegiance of fundamentalist groups and the satisfaction or dissatisfaction which they experienced in their causes. A phrase remained the nucleus of all the helpful associations that had gathered around it in the course of the church's history, though the object for which it stood might have utterly changed or vanished. The security-fear-veneration principles of loyalty unlocked the doctrinal values which fundamentalists treasured.

Why did they cherish these antiquated beliefs to the extent of stubbornly resisting fellowship with modernists? An understanding of the other basic factor in funda-

[8] Op. cit., pp. 238–39.

mentalism points the answer. As long as traditional Christianity was universally in vogue in America, evangelicals were "one body in Christ." When scholars began to cultivate the historical approach to the Scriptures, courageous churchmen welcomed the findings and advanced a more fitting program for the Kingdom of God.[9] The same leadership became dominant in theological seminaries and church colleges of liberal arts and sciences. Conservative men took stock to discover that their testimony and personalities were being neglected in on-going Christianity. Consequently, they felt themselves slighted in God's work in the world.

Religiously disturbed, these Christians were free to choose one of two alternatives. They could attempt to revaluate their evangelical heritage in terms of the new cultural ideals and thus enter into fraternal relations with modernists, or they could reinforce their inherited faith with dogmatic loyalty and attack the validity of their fellow-Christians' experience. As has been amply illustrated, they selected the second course. In doing so, they not only intensified attachment to their beliefs, but they submitted themselves to undue emotional tension and change.[10] Conservatives *became* fundamentalists. They suffered a sense of personal defeat when their views were being superseded by those of changing religious scholarship and when their personalities encoun-

[9] Note the "forward" movements and programs enunciated in the churches during the World War peroid, and referred to in chapters five to nine inclusive.

[10] For a treatment of this type of tension, see any standard text in psychology; for instance, Floyd N. Allport, *Social Psychology* (New York, 1924), pp. 404–06.

tered liberals, who were assuming increasing charge of outposts in the Kingdom enterprise.

The distressing situation called out three instinctive drives in fundamentalists. Their Christian actions were controlled by the desire for an unshakable religious security, the desire for a like-minded Christian fellowship, and the desire for the administrative direction of the Church of Christ. These sovereign desires were enkindled by a fear for the preservation of "the truth," a veneration for "the faith once for all delivered," and an antipathy towards "modernists" who were blamed for this inevitable stage of conflict in Christian progress.

In the condition of acute personal instability, the conventionalists worked out their salvation differently from the progressives. The latter made adventurous quest for a higher synthesis of old and new Protestant values. They trusted growing knowledge, reconstructed the grounds of their faith, and established harmonious adjustment with their world. The former, entertaining a disquieting (though usually suppressed) anxiety for the survival of their theological position as challenged by more convincing scholarship, resigned themselves to the traditional formularies. It became their supreme duty to accept what God had revealed, and defend it. This decision elevated religion above the sphere of experimental test and gave the defenders an absolute sense of divine security.[11] However, they rested their religion on the foundation of an uncritical piety. To retain this

[11] See John Dewey, "Fundamentals," *New Republic,* Feb. 6, 1924, p. 275; and chap. I, part five, as compared with chap. II, part five, of this study.

position in the prevailing conflict, they were forced to assume the rôle of authoritarian agents of the supernatural. Thus they spoke as God's priests to insubordinate "modernists," and felt a sense of supreme mastery in His cause.

But the progressive forces continued to interrogate the foundation of the historic faith, and they refused to be mastered in the church. The only other reaction the disturbed Christians could enlist, having refused to fraternize with modernists, was to promote independent fundamentalist fellowship. In sectional meetings within and beyond the denominations, orthodox men sought intimate associations in exercises that heightened their sense of self-importance. For this reason primarily, revivals and Bible conferences became surprisingly popular, and the traditionalists attached deeply stirring loyalty to their convictions. Theologically, fundamentalists challenged modernists on the grounds of the validity of supernaturally authenticated articles of faith; psychologically, they challenged liberals on the grounds of paramount Christian loyalty.

No doubt the allegiance of the orthodox to what they thought was right and abiding in evangelicalism was a most praiseworthy trait in their personal testimony; but because liberals embraced other religious ideals in the same situation, conservatives reacted in an agitated manner and entertained a censorious spirit toward their brethren. It became the policy of liberals to encourage the spirit of personal tolerance and an inclusive fellowship within the church; by force of circumstances, the conservatives declared for an exclusive policy. But, owing to the increased consideration which they and their principles have won recently in the church, the negative personal factor has been retired somewhat and the positive enlistment of Christian loyalty has been more definitely reaffirmed.

The fundamentalist-modernist conflict of religious cultures has vouchsafed to this generation of churchmen an exceedingly heavy educational task. Leaders must bring their people abreast of the problems and ideals that characterize the age. This obligation can be borne only in so far as men understand intimately the quality of the maladjustments that recent history has bequeathed them.

Though the disagreeable features of the controversy have been restrained, there is no evidence that the church has recovered either spiritual poise or clarity of vision. A distracted faith is never cultivated by the repetition of harmless platitudes or by other worldly contemplation; its robustness depends upon all participants in the Christian cause facing fearlessly the social conditions of faith and sharing mutually their values in the divine adventure. Christianity will reassert its power in the humanly-distraught world as men nurture the fine sense of religious loyalty that inspired conservatives, as men pioneer with strong heart the unbeaten highways of truth which liberals seek, and as they wed this fervor and discipline into the harmony of Christlike leadership.

BIBLIOGRAPHY

BIBLIOGRAPHY

I. BOOKS AND PAMPHLETS

Baptist Fundamentals. Being addresses delivered at the Pre-Convention Conference at Buffalo, June 21 and 22, 1920, pp. xv, 202, Judson Press, Philadelphia, 1920.

Barnes, Harry Elmer. *The Twilight of Christianity,* pp. xi, 470, Vanguard, N. Y., 1929.

Blackstone, W. E. *Jesus is Coming,* pp. 64, Revell, N. Y., 1904.

Bridges, Horace J. *The God of Fundamentalism and Other Studies,* pp. xviii, 319, Covici, Chicago, 1925.

Bryan, William Jennings. *The Bible and Its Enemies,* pp. 46, Bible Institute Colportage Association, Chicago, 1921.

Bryan, William Jennings. *In His Image,* pp. 266, Revell, N. Y., 1922.

Case, Shirley J. *The Millennial Hope: A Phase of War Time Thinking,* pp. ix, 253, University of Chicago Press, Chicago, 1918.

Coming and Kingdom of Christ: Proceedings 1914 Bible and Prophetic Conference, Biblc Institute Colportage Association, Chicago, 1914.

Christ and Glory: Proceedings 1918 New York Prophetic Conference, Revell, New York, 1918.

Creeds and Loyalty. Seven Members of the Faculty of the Episcopal Theological School, Cambridge, Mass., pp. 170, Macmillan, N. Y., 1924.

Cutshall, Elmer Guy. *The Doctrinal Training of the Travelling Ministry of the Methodist Episcopal Church,* pp. 125, Ph. D., Thesis, University of Chicago, 1922.

Day, William H. and Eddy, Sherwood. *The Modernist-Fundamentalist Controversy,* pp. 38, Doran, N. Y., 1924.

Dieffenbach, A. C. *Religious Liberty: the Great American Illusion,* pp. xii, 205, Morrow, N. Y., 1927.

Elliott, Walter Scott. *The Christian Fundamentals Mission in China,* pp. 12, Long Beach, Cal., 1926.

Faulkner, J. A. *Modernism and the Christian Faith,* pp. 306, Methodist Book Concern, N. Y., 1921.

Forrest, William M. *Do Fundamentalists Play Fair?* pp. 125, Macmillan, N. Y., 1925.

FOSDICK, HARRY EMERSON. *Christianity and Progress,* pp. 247, Revell, N. Y., 1922.

FOUNTAIN, REV. CHARLES HILLMAN. *Charges of Teaching False Doctrine . . . brought against the Rev. Wm. H. P. Faunce . . . and the Rev. Gerald Birnie Smith . . .* pp. 23, Plainfield, N. J., 1922.

Fundamentals, The. 12 vols., Testimony Publishing Co., Chicago, 1910–12.

GLADDEN, WASHINGTON. *Applied Christianity,* pp. 320, Houghton Mifflin, N. Y., 1886.

God Has Spoken: Twenty-five addresses delivered at the World Conference on Christian Fundamentals, pp. 246, *Sunday School Times,* Philadelphia, 1919.

GORDON, ERNEST B. *The Leaven of the Sadducees,* pp. 263, The Bible Institute Colportage Association, Chicago, 1926.

GORDON, ERNEST B. *A. J. Gordon—A Biography,* pp. 386, Revell, N. Y., 1896.

GRAY, JAMES M. *Why We Believe in the Virgin Birth of Christ,* pp. 10, Bible Institute Colportage Association, Chicago, 1924.

HORSCH, JOHN. *Modern Religious Liberalism,* pp. 331, Fundamental Truth Depot, Scottdale, Pa., 1921.

HUGHSON, REV. SHIRLEY C. *The Apostles' Creed: a simple explanation of the Christian faith,* pp. 35, Holy Cross Press, West Park, N. Y., 1923.

HUGHSON, REV. SHIRLEY C. *Modernism and the Virgin Birth of Christ,* pp. 10, Holy Cross Press, West Park, N. Y., 1924.

JOHNSON, JAMES W. *Fundamentalism versus Modernism,* pp. 51, Century, N. Y., 1925.

KEYSER, LEANDER S. *The Conflict of Fundamentalism and Modernism,* pp. 36, Lutheran Literary Board, Burlington, Iowa, 1926.

LAKE, KIRSOPP. *The Religion of Yesterday and Today,* pp. 183, Houghton Mifflin, N. Y., 1925.

LAWRENCE, WILLIAM. *Fifty Years,* pp. iv, 97, Houghton Mifflin, N. Y., 1923.

Light on Prophecy. Proceedings and addresses of the Philadelphia Prophetic Conference, pp. 362, Christian Herald, N. Y., 1918.

LUCCOCK, H. E. and HUTCHINSON, PAUL. *The Story of Methodism,* pp. 508, Methodist Book Concern, Cincinnati, 1926.

MACHEN, J. GRESHAM. *Christianity and Liberalism,* pp. 180, Macmillan, N. Y., 1923.

MACHEN, J. GRESHAM. *What is Faith?,* pp. 263, Macmillan, N. Y., 1925.

MACHEN, J. GRESHAM. *The Virgin Birth of Christ,* pp. vii, 415, Harper, N. Y., 1930.

MACINNIS, J. M. *Peter, The Fisherman Philosopher: A Study in Higher Fundamentalism,* Biola Book Room, Los Angeles, 1928.

MATHEWS, SHAILER. *The Church and the Changing Order,* pp. viii, 255, Macmillan, N. Y., 1907.

MATHEWS, SHAILER. *The Faith of Modernism,* pp. vii, 182, Macmillan, N. Y., 1924.

MCPHERSON, G. W. *The Crisis in Church and College,* pp. 238, published by the author, Yonkers, N. Y., 1919.

MCPHERSON, G. W. *Modern Conflict over the Bible,* pp. 215, published by the author, Yonkers, N. Y., 1919.

MCCANN, ALFRED W. *God or Gorilla,* pp. xiv, 408, Devin-Adair, N. Y., 1922.

MECKLIN, JOHN M. *The Survival Value of Christianity,* pp. viii, 260, Harcourt, Brace, N. Y., 1926.

MERRILL, WILLIAM P. *Liberal Christianity,* pp. 170, Macmillan, N. Y., 1925.

MITCHELL, HINCKLEY G. T. *For the Benefit of My Creditors,* Beacon, Boston, 1922.

MODE, PETER G. *Source Book of American Church History,* pp. xxiv, 735, Banta, Menasha, Wis., 1921.

MODE, PETER G. *The Frontier Spirit of American Christianity,* pp. x, 196, Macmillan, N. Y., 1923.

MUNHALL, L. W. *The Highest Critic versus Higher Critics,* pp. 249, Munhall, Philadelphia, 1896.

MUNHALL, L. W. *Breakers! Methodism Adrift,* pp. 215, Munhall, Philadelphia, 1914.

NEWMAN, A. H. *A Century of Baptist Achievement,* pp. xix, 460, American Baptist Publication Society, Philadelphia, 1901.

NEWTON, R. HEBER. *Church and Creed,* pp. xx, 212, Putnam, N. Y., 1891.

PANKHURST, CHRISTOBEL. *The Lord Cometh!,* pp. 115, The Book Stall, N. Y., 1923.

PANKHURST, CHRISTOBEL. *Some Modern Problems in the Light of Bible Prophecy,* pp. 192, Revell, N. Y., 1924.

PARKS, LEIGHTON. *What is Modernism?,* pp. xix, 154, Scribners, N. Y., 1924.

PATTON, FRANCIS L. *Fundamental Christianity,* pp. xi, 334, Macmillan, N. Y., 1926.

PIERCE, EARLE V. *Why I Am a Fundamentalist; Is the Whole Bible*

Trustworthy? Pamphlets published by the author, Brookings, South Dakota, 1924.

POTTER, CHARLES FRANCIS and STRATON, JOHN ROACH. *Debates,* vols. 1–5, Doran, N. Y., 1924. 1. *The Battle over the Bible.* 2. *Evolution vs. Creation.* 3. *The Virgin Birth—Fact or Fiction?* 4. *Was Christ Both God and Man?* 5. *Utopia—By Man's Effort or Christ's Return?*

Premillennial Essays: Proceedings of 1879 Prophetic Conference, pp. 528, Revell, Chicago, 1879.

Prophetic Studies: Proceedings of 1886 Prophetic Conference, Revell, Chicago, 1886.

RILEY, WILLIAM B. *The Menace of Modernism,* pp. 181, Christian Alliance Publishing Company, N. Y., 1917.

RILEY, WILLIAM B. *Addresses Delivered by W. B. Riley in debates between Maynard Shipley and W. B. Riley.* Pamphlet. Published by W. B. Riley, 1925.

ROBERTS, WATKIN R. *The Ravages of Higher Criticism in the Indian Mission Field,* pp. 28, Protestant Truth Society, London, England, 1922.

SCHILLER, F. C. S. *Problems of Belief,* pp. vii, 194, Hodder Stoughton, London, 1925.

SHIPLEY, MAYNARD. *The War on Modern Science,* pp. xiv, 415, Knopf, N. Y., 1927.

SIMPSON, W. J. SPARROW. *Modernism and the Person of Christ,* pp. 104, Morehouse Publishing Company, Milwaukee, 1923.

SMITH, GERALD BIRNEY. *Social Idealism and the Changing Theology,* pp. xxiii, 251, Macmillan, N. Y., 1913.

SMITH, GERALD BIRNEY. *Current Christian Thinking,* pp. ix, 209, University of Chicago Press, Chicago, 1928.

SMITH, HENRY PRESERVED. *The Heretic's Defense,* Scribners, N. Y., 1926.

SMITH, WILLIAM H. *Modernism, Fundamentalism and Catholicism,* pp. x, 152, Morehouse Publishing Co., Milwaukee, 1925.

SNEATH, E. HERSHEY. *Shall We Have a Creed?,* pp. vii, 69, Century, N. Y., 1925.

STRONG, A. H. *A Tour of Missions,* pp. xxii, 223, Griffith, Boston, 1918.

SWEET, WILLIAM W. *The Story of Religions in America,* pp. 571, Harper, N. Y., 1930.

THOMAS, W. H. GRIFFITH-. *What About Evolution?,* pp. 24, Bible Institute Colportage Association, Chicago, 1918.

TORREY, R. A. *The Fundamental Doctrines of the Christian Faith,* pp. 328, Doran, N. Y., 1918.

TROELTSCH, ERNST. *Protestantism and Progress, Translated by W. Montgomery,* pp. xi, 210, Putnam, N. Y., 1912.

TYSON, REV. STUART L. *Truth and Tradition,* pp. 22, published by author, no date.

VANDERLAAN, ELDRED C. *Fundamentalism versus Modernism,* pp. xxxvii, 452, Wilson, N. Y., 1925.

WARD, DUREN J. H. *Fundamentalism and Modernism,* pp. 32, Up the Divide Publishing Co., Denver, Col., 1925.

WIGHT, FRANCIS ASA. *The Beast, Modernism and the Evangelical Faith,* pp. iv, 311, Stratford, Boston, 1926.

WILLIAMS, JAMES M. *Principles of Social Psychology,* pp. xii, 459, Knopf, N. Y., 1922.

WILSON, ROBERT DICK. *Is the Higher Criticism Scholarly?,* pp. 62, Sunday School Times Co., Philadelphia, 1922.

II. MAGAZINES

American Church Monthly, New York City.

American Fundamentalist, John R. Straton, editor, New York City, merging with the *Crusaders' Champion.*

Annual, of the Northern Baptist Convention.

Baptist, The, weekly, John Earl, editor, Chicago, Ill.

Baptist Beacon, William B. Riley, editor, Minneapolis, Minn. Later merged with *The Searchlight.*

Baptist Fundamentalist and Bible Student, J. Lewis Smith, editor, Sacramento, Cal.

Baptist Spokesman, Harley L. Hallgren, editor, Portland, Ore.
Organ of the Portland Baptist Laymen's League.

Baptist Temple News, Oliver W. Van Osdel, editor, Grand Rapids, Mich.

Bible Baptist, W. S. Cole, editor, Santa Cruz, Cal.

Bible Call and Fundamentalist Advocate, J. Mountain, editor, London, England.
Organ of the Believers' Bible Union, including the Baptist Bible Union of England.

Bible Champion, Reading, Pa.
Organ of the Bible League of North America.

Bible Today, New York City.
Organ of the National Bible Institute.

Bibliotheca Sacra, William Grove Kyle, editor, St. Louis, Mo.
British Columbia Baptist, F. W. Anvache, editor, New Westminster, B. C.
Brookes Quarterly, St. Louis, Mo.
Organ of Brookes Bible Institute.
Bryan Broadcaster, Paul Rood, editor, Turlock, Cal.
Organ of the Bryan Bible League.
Bulletin of the Bible Union of China.
Organ of the Bible Union of China.
Call to the Colors, Harold Paul Sloan, editor, Haddonfield, N. J.
Later, *The Essentialist,* organ of the Methodist League for Faith and Life.
China's Millions.
Organ of China Inland Mission, Toronto, Canada.
Christian, The, Burris Jenkins, editor, Kansas City, Mo.
Succeeding *The Scroll,* organ of the Campbell Institute.
Christian Advocate, official organ of the Methodist Episcopal Church.
Christian Century, C. C. Morrison, editor, Chicago, Ill.
Christian Fundamentalist, William B. Riley, editor, Minneapolis, Minn.
Organ of the World's Christian Fundamentals Association and Northwestern Bible and Missionary Training School. Continuing *Christian Fundamentals in School and Church.*
Christian Fundamentals in School and Church, William B. Riley, editor, Minneapolis, Minn.
Organ for the World's Christian Fundamentals Association and Northwestern Bible and Missionary Training School, later becoming *The Christian Fundamentalist.*
Christian Register, A. C. Dieffenbach, editor, Boston, Mass.
Christian Standard, Cincinnati.
Organ of the Christian Restoration Association.
Christian Work, Frederick Lynch, editor, New York City.
Christian Workers' Magazine, Chicago, Ill.
Organ, Moody Bible Institute, continuing the *Institute Tie.*
Chronicle, The, monthly, Poughkeepsie, N. Y.
Churchman, The, weekly, New York City.
Citadel of Truth, Bangalore, India.
Organ of the Bible League of India, Burma and Ceylon.
Conflict, The, T. T. Martin, editor, Blue Mountain, Miss.
Later merging with the *Crusaders' Champion.*
Continent, The, Nolan R. Best, editor, Chicago.
Crusaders' Champion, Coleman Craig, editor, Clearwater, Fla.

Organ of the Bible Crusaders of America, continuing the *American Fundamentalist* and *The Conflict.*

Daily Christian Advocate, Proceedings of the General Conference, Methodist Episcopal Church.

Defender, The, Wichita, Kansas.
Organ of the Defenders of the Christian Faith.

Eastern Methodist, L. W. Munhall, editor, Germantown, Pa.
Later *The Methodist.*

Echoes, Binghamton, N. Y.
Organ of the Binghamton Bible School.

Essentialist, The, Harold Paul Sloan, editor, Haddonfield, N. J.
Continuing *The Call to the Colors.* Organ of the Methodist League for Faith and Life.

Evangelical Christian, R. V. Bingham, editor, Toronto, Canada.
Organ of the Interior Soudan Mission.

Evangelical Student, Princeton, N. J.
Organ of the Evangelical Student League.

Faith, The, John R. Straton, editor, New York City.
Formerly, *The Fundamentalist,* later the *American Fundamentalist,* later merging with *The Crusaders' Champion.*

Fax, Fred E. Bennett, editor, Forest Park, Ill.
Organ of the Christian Science Foundation.

Fundamentalist, The, John R. Straton, editor, New York City.
Later *The Faith,* later *The American Fundamentalist,* later merging with *The Crusaders' Champion.*

Gospel Message, George F. Fisher, editor, Kansas City, Mo.

Gospel Witness, W. G. Hawks, editor, Kansas City, Mo.
Organ of the Gospel Missionary Union.

Gospel Witness, T. T. Shields, editor, Toronto, Canada.
Organ of the Baptist Bible Union of North America.

Grace and Truth, Clifton L. Fowler, editor, Denver, Colo.
Organ of the Denver Bible Institute.

Herald of the Times, Oswald J. Smith, editor, Los Angeles, Cal.

Institute Tie, Chicago, Ill.
Organ of Moody Bible Institute. Later the *Christian Workers' Magazine.*

Kingdom Truth, Washington, D. C.
Organ of the Potomac Bible College.

King's Business, T. C. Horton, editor, Los Angeles, Cal.
Organ of the Los Angeles Bible Institute.

Last Hour, Philip Mauro, editor, Boston, Mass.

Living Church, weekly, Milwaukee, Wis.
Living Oracles, Chicago, Ill.
Organ of the Illinois Christian Fundamentals Association.
Methodist, The, L. W. Munhall, editor, Germantown, Pa.
Previously *The Eastern Methodist.*
Methodist Review, Quarterly, Louisville, Ky.
Ministers' Monthly, John C. Monsma, editor, Chicago, Ill.
Later the *New Reformation,* later joining with *The Searchlight.*
Minutes of the Presbyterian General Assembly.
Moody Bible Institute Bulletin, Chicago, Ill.
Issued by the Institute for Bible Study.
New Reformation, John C. Monsma, editor, Chicago, Ill.
Formerly the *Ministers' Monthly.*
Our Hope, A. C. Gaebelein, editor, New York City.
Pilgrim, The, Pasadena, Cal.
Organ of the Pilgrim Bible College.
Pioneer of a New Era, R. Lee Kirkland, editor, Sulphur Springs, Arkansas.
Organ of American Conference of Undenominational Churches.
Presbyterian, The, Samuel G. Craig, editor, Philadelphia, Pa.
Later becoming *The Presbyterian* and *Herald* and *Presbyter.*
Princeton Theological Review, Princeton, N. J.
Organ of Princeton Theological Seminary.
Prophet, The, W. G. Brown, editor, Toronto, Canada.
Recorder, The, Toronto, Canada.
Organ of the Toronto Bible College.
Religious Searchlight, John R. Straton, editor, New York City.
Later becoming *The Fundamentalist,* later *The Faith,* later *The American Fundamentalist,* later merging with *The Crusaders' Champion.*
School and Church, Wm. B. Riley, editor, Minneapolis.
Later *Christian Fundamentals in School and Church.*
Searchlight, The, J. Frank Norris, editor, Fort Worth, Texas.
Serving and Waiting, Wm. Pettingill, editor, Philadelphia, Pa.
Organ of the Philadelphia School of the Bible.
Signs of the Times, A. L. Baker, editor, Mountain View, Cal.
Southern Churchman, weekly, Richmond, Va.
Spotlight, The, Cincinnati, Ohio.
Later *The Touchstone.* Published by the Christian Standard Publishing Company.
Sunday School Times, C. C. Trumbull, editor, Philadelphia, Pa.

Sword of the Lord, J. R. L. Haslam, editor, Wilder, Idaho.
Organ of the Idaho Baptist Bible Union.
Touchstone, The, Cincinnati, Ohio.
Formerly *The Spotlight.*
Watchman-Examiner, Curtis Lee Laws, editor, New York City.
Wonderful Word, Leon W. Tucker, editor, New York City.
Word and Way, R. K. Maiden, editor, Kansas City, Mo.
Zion's Herald, L. O. Hartman, editor, Boston, Mass.

III. MAGAZINE ARTICLES

American Review, 2:1–9, Jan.–Feb., 1924. "Fundamentalism and Modernism: An Interpretation," Shailer Mathews.

American Review, 2:478–485, Sept.–Oct., 1924. "The Challenge of Fundamentalism," John M. Mecklin.

American Journal of Religious Psychology and Education, 3:165–209, 1908–09. "Four Types of Protestants: A Comparative Study," Jean du Buy.

Christian Century. Editorials and articles during 1920–25.

Christian Work. Editorials and articles during 1920–24.

Current History, 24:893–97, Sept., 1926. "Anti-Evolution in America," Harbor Allen.

Forum, 70:1665–80, July, 1923. "The Fundamentals," William J. Bryan.

Forum, 73:796–803, June, 1925. "The Earth Speaks to Bryan," Henry F. Osborn.

Forum, 74:101–07, July, 1925. "Mr. Bryan Speaks to Darwin," William J. Bryan.

Forum, 74:258–65, August, 1925. "Behind the Scenes in Tennessee," John P. Fort.

Forum, 75:245–51, Feb., 1926. "The Fancies of the Evolutionists," J. R. Straton.

International Journal of Ethics, 33:202–09. "The Rôle of the Fundamental," Norman Boardman.

Journal of Religion, 2:190–96, 1922. "The Reconstruction of Religious Loyalty," Gerald Birney Smith.

Journal of Religion, 2:245–62, 1922. "Can Christianity Welcome Freedom of Teaching?" Gerald Birney Smith.

Journal of Religion, 4:611–631, 1924. "The Fundamentalist Movement Among the Baptists," Robert A. Ashworth.

Journal of Religion, 5:14–36, 1925. "Fundamentalism in the Presbyterian Church," Robert Hastings Nichols.

Journal of Religion, 5:225–238, 1925. "Modernism and Historic Christianity," Eldred C. Vanderlaan.

Methodist Quarterly Review, 74:387–412, 1925. "Modernism—A Calm Survey," O. E. Brown.

Nation, 118:53–4, Jan. 16, 1924. "The Shame of the Churches," Algerton S. Crapsey.

New Republic, 37:161–62, Jan. 9, 1924. Editorial, "The Parsons' Battle."

New Republic, 37:275–76, Feb. 6, 1924. "Fundamentals," John Dewey.

New Republic, 38:35–9, March 5, 1924. "Conscience and the Bishops: a Historic Step," Prof. Dickinson S. Miller.

New Republic, 38:230–37, July 23, 1924. "Christianity as a Way of Life," Herbert Croly.

New York Times, Sunday, Feb. 26, 1922, Section 7:1, 11. "God and Evolution," William J. Bryan.

New York Times, Sunday, March 5, 1922, Section 7:2. "Reply to Mr. Bryan," Henry F. Osborn.

New York Times, Sunday, March 5, 1922, Section 7:14. "Reply to Mr. Bryan," E. G. Conklin.

New York Times, Sunday, March 12, 1922, Sec. 7:2, 13. "Reply to Mr. Bryan," Harry Emerson Fosdick.

North American Review, 211:577–92, May, 1923. "Ten Years of American Protestantism," Shailer Mathews.

Outlook, 136:10–11, Jan. 2, 1924. "An Exclusive Gospel," Ernest H. Abbott.

Outlook, 136:13–14, Jan. 2, 1924. "The Bishops' Pastoral Letter," E. P. V. Wheeler.

Princeton Theological Review. Several articles during 1922–28.

Publications of the American Sociological Society, 18:116–120, 1924. The Sociology of Authority, Ludwig Stein.

Survey, 50:518–19, Aug. 15, 1923. "Youth and Fundamentals," Robert E. Lewis.

World's Work, 45:509–13, March, 1923. "Freedom in School and Church," W. H. P. Faunce.

World's Work, 46:605–14, Oct., 1923. "Down With Evolution," R. L. Hartt; 47:48–56, Nov., 1923, "Fighting for Infallibility," R. L. Hartt; 47:161–70, Dec., 1923, "Is the Church Dividing?", R. L. Hartt.

World's Work, 47:418–24, Feb., 1924. "Protestantism at the Crossroads," William Pierson Merrill.

INDEX

INDEX

E

F

G